THE REDCAPS

A History of the Military Police
and its Antecedents
from the Middle Ages to the Gulf War

This book is dedicated to to the memory of my grandfather,
J R (Jim) Plumstead, (1907–91), Sergeant,
56th (County of London) Battalion, Home Guard, 1940–44.
Also to all members of the RMP, Past, Present and Future.

THE REDCAPS

A History of the Royal Military Police
and its Antecedents
from the Middle Ages to the Gulf War

G D Sheffield

Department of War Studies,
Royal Military Academy, Sandhurst

BRASSEY'S (UK)
LONDON · NEW YORK

First English edition 1994

UK editorial offices: 33 John Street, London WC1N 2AT
orders: Marston Book Services, PO Box 87, Oxford OX2 0DT

USA orders: Macmillan Publishing Company, 100 Front Street,
Riverside, NJ 08075–7500

Distributed in North America to booksellers and wholesalers by the
Macmillan Publishing Company, NY 10022

Library of Congress Cataloging in Publication Data
available

British Library Cataloging in Publication Data
A catalogue record for this book is
available from the British Library

ISBN 1–85753–029–2 Hardcover

Typeset by
The Word Shop, Bury, Lancashire.

Printed and bound in Great Britain by
Bookcraft (Bath) Limited

Contents

Part Four: The Postwar Era – From 1945 to the Gulf War

Foreword

Field Marshal Sir Peter Inge GCB ADC Gen
Chief of the Defence Staff

The Redcaps, the authorised history of the Royal Military Police, is a comprehensive work of reference which highlights the great diversity of activities in which The Royal Military Police have been engaged during their history. More importantly, it brings to life the dedication, loyalty, bravery and self sacrifice of a very special group of men and women. I expect that the full scope of their roles and capabilities will be a surprise to many and, in particular, the courage with which these roles have been undertaken in many operational theatres throughout the world is exemplary.

It is right that the Redcaps' gallant, unusual and diverse history should be depicted in such a readable and detailed form. As a past Colonel Commandant, I have been privileged to have been associated closely with them. I congratulate Dr Gary Sheffield on this excellent book which I commend to anyone with an interest in military history or police work; it will be a revelation.

Preface

BY

Brian Bond

Professor of Military History
King's College London (KQC)

Provost Marshals, military police, Redcaps, however designated are rarely
likely, due to the nature of their duties, to be 'stars' in the military
firmament. Yet nor have they been, during the long span covered by this
new corps history, the martinets, sadists and enemies of the ordinary
soldier depicted in legend. On the contrary, without trying to blot out
occasional examples of brutality, injustice or mismanagement, Gary Sheffield's aim has been to demonstrate the great variety of essential, albeit
mostly unglamorous, tasks performed by the military police. These duties
have included the apprehension and custody of prisoners, detection of
military crimes such as looting and the theft of weapons and stores,
manning vehicle check points, protecting civil and military VIPs, controlling ports in both successful advances and disastrous evacuations and,
most important in modern operations, the control of civil and military
traffic.

One of the many revelations in this volume is the method by which
the military police have maintained discipline and morale just behind the
battle lines. In the First World War, on which the author writes with
particular authority, the military police ran a cordon of Straggler Posts
which rounded up, sorted and re-directed the various types of exhausted
and confused soldiers who came their way – by no means all of them
would-be deserters. The Redcaps seemed to have behaved more huma-
nely in this difficult role than is popularly imagined, sometimes for
example dispensing hot tea as well as new equipment and weapons.
Though some offenders would doubtless consider this interpretation to
be over generous, the Corps' practical philosophy in both world wars
was encapsulated in the slogan; 'guide the responsible, check the
irresponsible and incarcerate the incorrigible'.

Policing duties frequently involved their personnel in active combat; at

El Alamein, for example, Divisional Provost Companies were responsible for illuminating gaps in the British minefield to direct advancing troops and, during the bombardment they went ahead to mark the route. They then helped clear the enemy minefield and, after the breakthrough, took over the vital task of traffic control. According to one desert veteran, 'It was the Sappers, Signals and Military Police who led the armour into battle'.

This account devotes a whole book (out of four) to just 1945 activities and covers the retreat from Empire in considerable detail. The Royal Military Police, as the Corps became in 1946, suffered proportionately high casualties in these operations losing, for example, eight men killed in Palestine and ten in Cyprus, thus disposing of another myth that the Redcaps kept well clear of combat.

Gary Sheffield brings his history right up to date by describing military policing duties in the Gulf War where the RMP was a small but vital cog in the huge machine of logistic support. This conflict served to underline the lesson brought out in the numerous wars described here; namely that 'effective military police are an essential element in modern offensive (and defensive) operations'.

By his admirable arrangements of periods and topics the author has achieved a balanced coverage of a vast subject; he has made splendid use of a variety of sources, including official papers, diaries and interviews; and he writes with the crisp authority to be expected from a senior lecturer at the Royal Military Academy Sandhurst. In sum, Gary Sheffield has succeeded in transforming what could so easily have become an introverted and rather dull Corps chronicle into a genuine work of military history with a considerably wider appeal.

Brian Bond
Professor of Military History
King's College London (KQC)

ERRATUM: The Publishers wish to draw the reader's attention to the fact that Brigadier L F Richards is still very much alive although he has been cited in the Acknowledgements as 'the late Brigadier L F Richards'. The Publishers regret this mistake and are happy to set the record straight.

Acknowledgements

I am most grateful to the Provost Marshal (Army) who commissioned me to write this book, Brigadier Norman Allen, and his successors, Brigadiers Ray Bell and Iain Cameron. All three offered an enormous amount of encouragement and have shown an equal degree of patience during what must have seemed a never-ending project. Similar thanks are due to successive regimental secretaries, Lieutenant Colonel (Retd) R A Costain, and especially to Lieutenant Colonel (Retd) Maurice Squier, who saw this project through to the bitter end. At the RMP Museum, Sergeant Alan Wells and Mrs Sue Lines have proved towers of strength.

Many members of the Redcap family have given freely of their time, memories and historical material. I hope my benefactors will forgive me if I refer to only the most senior by their rank, and omit all honours and awards. I would like to thank Colonel J R Archer-Burton, D A Ashley-Hall, Captain J C Atkinson, Colonel P E Barton, R A L Belben, Captain F Bell, Major D J A Bergin, Major R T M Bishop and the Warrant Officers and Non Commissioned Officers of 174 Provost Company, G Brennan, Major H Burden, the late Colonel A V Burge, W S Calvert, E L Collins, A Conn, Major M Cuthbert-Brown, A C Dart, the late M Dale, H Dibbens, D Dyson, the late Colonel L and Mrs J East, T H Eaton, Brigadier A R Forbes, Lieutenant J Geden, Captain M Hawkins, Colonel P B Hewlett-Smith, F S R Higgins, R D Holland, R G Hopkins, Captain P C House, D G James, R Jones, J Kempton, Lieutenant Colonel S C McLean, G Moore, M W Morris, G Nimse, Lieutenant Colonel N W Poulsom, R P Ratcliffe, Lieutenant Colonel B A Rawlings, the late Brigadier L F Richards, Lieutenant Colonel G Ripley, S Robbins, R F Rogers, F J B Smith, Major W H Stabback, R Wilkins. My apologies to those who I may have inadvertantly omitted.

I owe a special debt to Major (Retd) Pepi Simpson, and her husband Mr Keith Simpson, who introduced me to the Corps in the first place.

I would like to acknowledge the generosity of the following for allowing me to quote from material for which they hold the copyright: the Trustees of the Royal Military Police Museum; the Trustees of the Liddell Hart Centre for Military Archives (E J Paton-Walsh papers); the National Army Museum (Mounted Staff Corps and W H Davies papers). Crown copyright material in the Public Record Office appears by permission of the Controller of Her Majesty's Stationery Office. I would also like to thank the Trustees of the Imperial War Museum and the copyright holders of the following collections held in the Museum: Mr M J Durham (G W Durham papers); Mr M J Dible (J H Dible papers). It has, unfortunately, proved impossible to trace the holders of copyright in the C H Butt papers and A W Bradbury papers, both held in the Imperial War Museum. To anyone whose copyright I have unwittingly infringed I offer my sincere apologies.

Many of my Sandhurst colleagues, past and present, gave me helpful references, read through portions of the manuscript and generally steered me through some of the less familiar periods of history. I am especially grateful to Dr Duncan Anderson, Dr Ian Beckett, Matthew Bennett, Dr David Chandler, Dr Anthony Clayton, Dr Christopher Duffy, Dr Tony Heathcote, Dr Andrew Lambert, Mrs Martine de Lee, Mr Nigel de Lee, Dr John Pimlott, Dr John Sweetman, and members of the RMAS War Discussion Group. An enormous debt of thanks is due to Mr Andrew Orgill and his staff at RMAS library, and Mrs Pam Bendell and her staff at Staff College library. At Brassey's, thanks are due to Jenny Shaw and Bryan Watkins.

Outside Sandhurst, thanks are due to Mike Hibberd, Mrs Sarah Patterson, Simon Robbins, Peter Simkins, Nigel Steel, and Rod Suddaby at the Imperial War Museum; Professor Brian Bond and the Military History seminar at the Institute of Historical Research; Dr Edward M Spiers; Peter H Liddle of the Liddle Collection, University of Leeds; John Maclaren; the late Brian Lyndon; Tim Moreman; Dr Alf Peacock; Julian Putkowski; Mrs Judith Blacklaw of the MOD library; Steve Spear; Jan Simpson; and members of the various Western Front Association branches to whom I have spoken on the subject of military police.

My Sandhurst colleague Dr Stephen Badsey, Lieutenant Colonel (Retd) Bob Wyatt, Major (Retd) R A J Tyler, and Brigadier (Retd) D B Rendell all read through the manuscript before it went to press. All made many helpful suggestions and saved me from numerous errors. Any that remain are, however, my responsibility.

My final thanks are to my wife Vivienne, who has given me steadfast support throughout, not least in keeping our children, Jennie and James, away from the word processor.

GDS
RMA Sandhurst
March, 1994

List of Plates

Abbreviations

2/Lt.	– Second Lieutenant	DAPM	– Deputy Assistant Provost Marshal
21 AG	– 21st Army Group file		
		DCM	– Distinguished Conduct Medal
AA	– Automobile Association	DH	– Draft History
A & Q	– Adjutant-General's and Quartermaster-General's Branches	Div	– Division
		DJAG	– Deputy Judge Advocate General
Acc	– Accession Number	DMC	– Desert Mounted Corps
ALFSEA	– Allied Land Forces South East Asia	DP	– Displaced Person
		DPM	– Deputy Provost Marshal
Armd	– Armoured	DZ	– Drop Zone
AB	– Airborne	DSO	– Distinguished Service Order
AG	– Adjutant-General	DMSU	– Divisional Mobile Support Units
APM	– Assistant Provost Marshal		
Appx	– Appendix		
ATS	– Auxiliary Territorial Service	ed, eds	– editor, editors
AQ	– Army Quarterly	edn	– edition
Aus	– Australian	EAR	– E Area Report
		EHR	– English Historical Review
BAOR	– British Army of the Rhine		
Bde	– Brigade		
BEF	– British Expeditionary Force	FARELF	– Far Eastern Land Forces
BFME	– British Forces Middle East	FMA	– Force Maintenance Area
BM	– Beach Maintenance	FFMA	– Forward Force Maintenance Area
BOR	– British Other Rank		
Brig	– Brigadier	FP	– Field Punishment
		FPM	– Force Provost Marshal
c	– circa	FWW	– First World War
Can	– Canadian		
Capt	– Captain	Gen	– General
CMG	– Corps of Mounted Guides	GHQ	– General Headquarters
CMP	– Corps of Military Police	GMP	– Garrison Military Police
CMP (I)	– Corps of Military Police (India)	GO	– General Orders
		GOC	– General Officer Commanding
COB	– Corps Order Book	Govt	– Government
CO	– Commanding Officer	GS	– General Staff
Col	– Colonel		
Coy	– Company		
CP	– Close Protection	HJ	– Historical Journal
Cpl	– Corporal	HMSO	– Her/His Majesty's Stationery Office
CSM	– Company Sergeant Major		
CUP	– Cambridge University Press		
CVHQ	– Central Volunteer Headquarters	IEME	– Indian Electrical and Mechanical Engineers

Ind	– Indian	OC	– Officer Commanding
IOL	– India Office Library	Op	– Operation
IOR	– Indian Other Rank	OUP	– Oxford University Press
IP	– Intelligence Police; Information Post	PC	– Provost Company
IRA	– Irish Republican Army	PM	– Provost Marshal
IWM	– Imperial War Museum	POW	– Prisoner(s) of War
JNCOs	– Junior Non-Commissioned Officer	PRO	– Public Record Office
		Pte	– Private
		PU	– Provost Unit
JSAHR	– Journal of the Society for Army Historical Research	PVCP	– Permanent Vehicle Check Point
KOSB	– King's Own Scottish Borders	QMAAC	– Queen Mary's Auxiliary Army Corps
KOYLI	– King's Own Yorkshire Light Infantry	RDBG	– Route Development Battle Group
L-Cpl	– Lance Corporal	RE	– Royal Engineers
LHCMA	– Liddell Hart Centre for Military Archives, Kings College London	RMASL	– Royal Military Academy Sandhurst Library
L of C	– Lines of Communication	RMP	– Royal Military Police
Lt	– Lieutenant	RMPA	– Royal Military Police Archives
Lt Col	– Lieutenant-Colonel	RMPJ	– Royal Military Police Journal
LULLC	– Leeds University Library, Liddle Collection	RMPTA	– Royal Military Police Territorial Army
LZ	– Landing Zone	RP	– Regimental Police
		RSM	– Regimental Sergeant Major
MA	– Military Affairs	RUC	– Royal Ulster Constabulary
Maj	– Major		
Maj Gen	– Major-General	SCC	– Staff Corps of Cavalry
MCR	– Midland Command Report	SCL	– Staff College Library
MEF	– Mediterranean Expeditionary Force or Middle East Forces	SIB	– Special Investigation Branch
		SMG	– Sub-machine gun
MFP	– Military Foot Police	SMPS	– Special Mobile Provost Section
m.i.d	– Mention in Despatches	SP	– 'Straggler Post' file
MMP	– Military Mounted Police	Ssgt	– Staff Sergeant
MP	– Military Police, Military Policeman	Sgt Maj	– Sergeant-Major
MPSC	– Military Provost Staff Corps	TC	– Traffic Control
MRLA	– Malayan Races Liberation Army	ts	– typescript
		TP	– Traffic Post
Ms	– Manuscript	Univ	– University
MSC	– Mounted Staff Corps	USMC	– United States Marine Corps
MSR	– Main Supply Route		
MUP	– Manchester University Press	VCP	– Vehicle Check Point
		VIP	– Very Important Person
NAM	– National Army Museum	VP	– Vulnerable Points
NATO	– North Atlantic Treaty Organisation	VPP	– Vulnerable Points Protection
NCO	– Non-Commissioned Officer	WD	– War Diary; War Department
NCR	– Northern Command Report	WDK	– War Diary, Korea
nd	– not dated	WO	– Warrant Officer; War Office
		WPV	– Women Police Volunteers
OB	– Mounted Staff Corps Order Book	WRAC	– Women's Royal Army Corps

Introduction

Before the Corps of Royal Military Police commissioned me to write this book, I knew just enough about the subject to suspect that the popular view of the Redcap as a fire breathing martinet, whose role was limited to harassing 'real' soldiers going about their lawful business, was unfair and wrong. Before my research had progressed very far, two things had become clear: that in addition to its disciplinary duties (and most people will admit, however grudgingly, that an army needs a police force) provost had a vital operational role in time of war. Moreover, this role was little understood outside the RMP. I also soon became aware that popular and scholarly interest in the question of the discipline of the British Army, which in the last 10 years has generated a TV documentary on the Salerno Mutiny of 1943, a TV 'docu-drama' on the Etaples mutiny of 1917, and public debate on military executions of the First World War, has been accompanied by the haziest of knowledge about British military police in the two world wars.

In this book I have attempted to combine a conventional regimental history with an analysis of the development of the various roles of Britain's military police. It is a work of both synthesis and original research. My debts to other historians will be clear from the footnotes. In particular, I am very conscious of standing on the distinguished shoulders of previous historians of the RMP, in particular Major L V Lovell-Knight, Major R A J Tyler, Major S F Crozier and Captain H Bullock. Without their pioneering work this present book could not have been written. I have not infrequently used that work as a foundation on which to build, using material which was not available to my predecessors. My indebtedness to them, and particularly to Majors Lovell-Knight and Tyler, who gave freely of their expertise, cannot be underestimated.

I have been fortunate to have had access to a great deal of archival material which will enrich our understanding of provost history. The chapters on the Crimean and Boer wars are a case in point. Particular attention has been paid to the role of provost in the First World War. That war was a watershed in the history of the Corps, but it has tended to be neglected; even by military policemen. I hope that this book will go some way to rehabilitating the reputation of the Corps during this crucial

1

period. Other campaigns for which archival material has been used for the first time include the First Army's operations in North Africa and Tunisia in 1942–43, and some operations in Burma in 1942–45.

When examining the history of the Corps over the last 50 years, the problem has been to decide what material to leave out. Two substantial volumes could be devoted to the work of the Corps during the World Wars alone. Some readers will feel that some episodes in the history of the Corps, and some units, could have received more attention. I can only plead guilty but ask that the reader bear in mind two facts. First, historical evidence for some periods and units is scanty or non-existent. Secondly, I was commissioned to produce a balanced work which reflected the history of the Corps and its antecedents over 500 years, and this inevitably involved making some hard decisions about the selection of material. Those wishing for more detail on particular periods may well find my predecessors' works helpful.

Bitter experience has taught me that no amount of research or proof-reading can eliminate the odd misdated event, transposed numbers or even a field marshal wrongly described as a lance corporal. I would welcome comments or corrections that could be incorporated in a future edition. Please send them through the Curator of the Regimental Museum of the Royal Military Police.

Although this book has the status of an authorised history, all opinions expressed are my own and not those of the RMP, the Ministry of Defence, or the Royal Military Academy Sandhurst. It is a pleasure to be able to state that the RMP has allowed me maximum discretion in my interpretation of events; at no stage has anyone connected with the Corps attempted to influence my writing, beyond offering advice and correcting factual errors.

Prologue

The most ancient military officer under the Crown?

The first recorded Provost Marshal in English history was one Henry Guylford, who was active in the early 16th century. While the office may then have been a recent innovation, the duties attached to it were not. English armies had been growing steadily more 'disciplined' and 'professional' (in every sense) over the previous three centuries, and the emergence of an officer charged with the maintenance of discipline was the natural culmination of that process.

Military discipline was the biggest single difference between the armies of Republican and Imperial Rome and their successors in medieval western Europe. However, medieval soldiers never lost sight of the importance of 'discipline' in its wider sense.

When in 1066 William the Bastard gathered an army in Normandy prior to his invasion of England, he prohibited plundering. Wisely, William did not rely solely upon his word to keep the peace. Instead, the future Conqueror recognised that one of the simplest and most effective ways of maintaining discipline is to ensure that troops are regularly paid and fed.

On the battlefield, the concept of '*disciplina militaris*' continued to be of importance, but in contrast to the discipline of the Roman legions, which gave Roman commanders great tactical flexibility, the medieval version was limited in practical terms to a recognition of some basic 'rules' for the conduct of war. Twelfth century crusader armies recognised the need to restrain the enthusiasm of the soldiery by keeping them in formation until the climax of the battle arrived, when the army charged forward to defeat the enemy: in 1115 a foretaste of the role of provost marshal was given by one Crusader leader, Prince Roger of Antioch, when he rode through his camp threatening to kill any man who went out to attack the enemy. March discipline was also recognised as being vitally important when campaigning against an enemy who used lightly armed cavalry to harass Crusader columns. Orders, backed up by punishments, were issued not only against straggling, but also against rising to the enemy's bait and breaking formation to attack the assailants, thus exposing themselves to defeat in detail. On one occasion, a force of disciplined Knights Templar acted in effect as 'military policemen' for a

Frankish army on the march, preventing straggling. However, the fact that penalties existed demonstrates the difficulties experienced by medieval commanders in enforcing disciplinary rules.[1]

The emergence of the professional soldier, who gradually replaced the ill-trained and often unwilling feudal levy, was an important step on the road to the return to a disciplined army. Improved discipline undoubtedly played a role in the success of the English forces in the Hundred Years War (1337–1453). Indeed, a concept of discipline lay at the very heart of the code of chivalry with which a knight was required to conform. Thus the discipline of chivalry was seen as the natural successor to the discipline of the Roman legion. In addition, the Church attempted to place some restraints on war. The knight saw himself both as a member of a Christian calling and also of a 'hereditary noble class', both of which went beyond national boundaries. Transnational military courts were established, which were presided over by the Constable and Marshal, the principal law officers of the army. Discipline – as expressed by increasing codification of the laws of war – was also the product of the growing commercialisation of war. Men could expect to make a good living out of soldiering, not by plundering on an individual basis, but by serving in a larger body which distributed, in an orderly fashion, the proceeds of war such as ransoms and loot. The threat to disallow a soldier's title to a ransom was used as a means of maintaining discipline.[2]

By the time Henry V took the field in France in the early 15th century, the English Army was a professional force, fighting for pay, operating under laws of war which governed its soldiers' conduct and ensured an orderly distribution of booty and ransom. The discipline of English armies of the period was noted by contemporaries.[3] They were governed by a series of 'standing orders' intended to prevent indiscipline and with which the men were familiarised. The idea was not new. As early as 1190, the army of Richard I had also possessed such a code. Various 'Statutes and Ordenances' (sic) have survived from Henry V's reign. Soldiers were forbidden to rob churches or molest priests or nuns, and were also forbidden to rob merchants or 'vittlers' who provided the army with supplies. Other parts of these codes were concerned with ensuring that good order was maintained on the battlefield, in camp, and on the march (the army even had a rudimentary form of traffic control). 'Every souldeour' was ordered to 'obey his capitaine in all lefulle things, kepe wacche and warde'. Significantly, soldiers were forbidden to 'make assault' without permission; commanders were determined to keep tactical matters in their own hands. Likewise, desertion was forbidden. The mercenary nature of warfare in this period is emphasised by the numerous clauses on the taking and ransoming of prisoners.[4]

How was discipline maintained in late medieval English armies? Much depended on the personality of the commander and the regular payment of the men. However, then as now, disciplinary matters could not be dealt with purely at the level of the unit. As we have seen, medieval armies were provided with two principal law officers, the Constable and the Marshal, part of whose duties would later be carried out by the Adjutant and Quartermaster-General respectively. In 1296, the Deputy Marshal in Edward I's army, John Lovel, fined men for brawling and others for insubordination. The punishments laid down in Henry V's Statutes ranged from fines, including the forfeiture of money gained as a result of battle, to death.

It should not be forgotten that, in medieval terms, 'discipline' was a relative concept. On campaign it was difficult to inflict any effective punishment short of death. Despite the advances in the maintenance of discipline, late medieval English armies still lacked effective military police, that is, soldiers whose role was to enforce discipline by deterring crime and arresting offenders. Some form of camp police probably did exist. It has been said that Richard I's Household Sergeants at Arms were 'the first actual Military Police', and references to an existing provost organisation occur in documents of the early part of the 16th century.[5] However, these 'tipstaves' were probably few in number and had only limited powers. English, and later British armies were not to recognise the importance of having an effective standing body of military police for another 450 years.

Who then actually carried out the orders of the Marshal and Constable? Perhaps the Battle of Agincourt in 1415 provides us with a clue. At one point, the rear of the English army was threatened by French forces. Henry V ordered that the French prisoners who were kept with the baggage train should be killed. A number of English soldiers were reluctant to carry out this order so Henry ordered a squad of 200 archers under the command of an esquire to carry out the massacre. Henry's archers were not part of the chivalric system. They were professional soldiers, many of whom had a background of crime, and were accustomed to carrying out the dirty work of the army. It is likely that similar, *ad hoc* bodies of troops were used by the Marshal and the Constable to carry out sentences and to arrest offenders. Certainly, the system of 'Hue and Cry' – using informal 'posses' to pursue villains – was used by Henry V in France, and in July 1428, a troop was commissioned for the suppression of a band of 200 freebooters who were terrorising the countryside.[6]

At least some of the duties later associated with the Provost Marshal were carried out by the Marshal, in addition to his other responsibilities, as far back as 1296. Possibly an officer was carrying out the duties of the

Provost Marshal as early as 1415, even if the title was not yet in use, but a claim that a Provost Marshal was appointed as early as the 13th or 14th centuries is rather over-optimistic.

A more likely conjecture is that at the turn of the 16th century, the office of the Deputy Marshal of the Household (a deputy of the Earl Marshal) was divided between two officers who ranked as Deputy to the Earl Marshal. These two new posts were those of the Knight Marshal, and Provost Marshal, 'provost'* being a title which had long been applied to those in authority. If this is the case, it can be seen that the status of Provost Marshal has sunk a little from its original exalted position. Whatever the precise status of the office, the medieval origins of what A V Lovell-Knight has described as 'the most ancient military office[r] under the Crown' are indisputable, and there is some truth in the assertion of another historian of the Corps that 'it is probable that Provost could trace a reasonable claim to numbering "Crécy" and "Agincourt" among its earlier battle honours!'[7]

---

*The word 'provost' comes from the Latin *Praeponere* (placed before, to superintend) via the old English word Prafost or alternatively from *proepositus*, a chief or governor. R A J Tyler, *Bloody Provost* (Chichester, Phillimore, 1980) p.1.

Part One:
The Antecedents, 1511–1902

The Emergence of the Provost Marshal, *1511 – 1660*

On 1 June 1511, a force of English soldiers arrived at Cadiz to co-operate with the Spaniards in an expedition against the Moors. The commander of the force, Lord Darcy, allowed some of his men to go ashore, where they:

> fell to drinking of hote wynes and were scace (sic) masters of them selfes, some ranne to the stewes [brothers], some brake hegges, and spoyled orchardes and wyneyardes, and orynges before they were ripe, and did many other outragious dedes; wherfore the chefe of the toune of Caleys [Cadiz] came to complaine to the lorde Darcie in hys shippe, whiche sent forth his Prouost Marshal which scarcelie with payne refrayned the yomen archers, they were so hote and wilfull, yet by commaundement and policie, they were all brought on borde their shippes.[1]

These troops, let it be noted, were those which Darcy had judged to be sick and feeble.

This passage contains the first recorded mention of a Provost Marshal. His name, as we have already stated, was Henry Guylford, who was later knighted. The passage also reveals some of the disciplinary problems which faced commanders in this period. The military system which had provided Henry V with such an effective army had decayed by the early 16th century. The English Army now consisted of a small body of regular troops, supplemented by the militia, foreign mercenaries and auxiliaries. There were also more-or-less unwilling conscripts. In the second half of the century, a soldier complained: 'We disburden the prison of thieves, we rob the taverns and alehouses of toss-pots and ruffians; we scour both town and country of rogues and vagabonds'.[2] Yet others were enticed into the army by the most potent recruiting sergeant of them all, poverty. Governments found it difficult to pay their soldiers and, on occasions, to keep them adequately supplied; in any case, the colonel of the regiment might be deliberately keeping his men short in order to line his own pocket, as was very often the case. The consequences of this were threefold; men plundered, mutinied, and deserted. Boredom and idle-ness, a constant feature of army life, seems to have been at the root of the problem in Cadiz, for once the English had arrived in Spain, King Ferdinand informed Darcy that the campaign against the Moors had been called off. It is against the background of these problems, which to some extent also held true for another two centuries or so, that the importance of the Provost Marshal should be considered. It is perhaps no coincidence that as discipline in English armies improved, his status declined.

For England, the 16th century was a century of war. In addition to conflicts with the French and Spanish, campaigns were fought in Ireland, and a number of internal revolts needed to be supressed. A study of the 1513 campaign in France reveals much about the role of the Provost Marshal in the reign of Henry VIII.[3] He was a man of considerable importance who rode, in the advance guard, with the Knight Marshal, the High Marshal's second-in-command. It was the Provost Marshal who decided where and when merchants could assemble to sell their wares, and who fixed the price at which food could be sold. He and his men had powers of arrest to enforce the articles of war, although malefactors were tried by the High Marshal's court rather than by the Provost Marshal himself. The Provost Marshal, did, however, have responsibility for prisoners. When on campaign, he was required to confine prisoners in his tent (or marshalsea). The Provost Marshal's other responsibilities were manifold. They included informing the officers of the watch of the watchword for the night; the prevention of gambling; and the enforce-ment of basic standards of hygiene. He was also responsible for the banishment of prostitutes from the camp. An English broadsheet of 1513 threatened that any 'common woman' found within the camp would be branded on the face.

Another document, which dates from c.1515, sheds further light on the Provost Marshal's duties. He was intimately concerned with the encampment of the army. Among other things, he was to lay out the camp and allocate the various units to their places, to order the captain of the pioneers to entrench the camp, and to post and visit the watches during the night. At night, it was the Provost Marshal's responsibility to ensure that the night gun was fired to warn that silence was to be kept in the camp. In battle, he was to serve 'in his owne person with the footment'. The Provost Marshal was assisted in his duties by a number of subordin-ates. He had a deputy or lieutenant, and there was also a separate 'provoste of the artillerie' who had his own rights and duties; he also had his own military police, which were on occasion referred to by the modern title of 'provost company'. However these tipstaves were few in number, and any serious large scale indiscipline was dealt with by the use of an *ad hoc* force. In July 1513, a group of German mercenaries ignored Henry VIII's strict instructions and began to pillage the town of Ardes. Henry had to lead a party of troops against them and eventually hanged three of the rioters.[4]

The hanging of prisoners was a frequent part of the Provost Marshal's job. Just one of many such examples concerns Sir Anthony Kingston, who was Provost Marshal with the army sent to put down the rebellion in the West Country in 1549. Kingston gained a reputation as a ferocious disciplinarian. On one occasion Kingston was said to have asked a man whether he was a certain miller who was believed to be a rebel. Upon the man admitting that he was, Kingston ordered his men to hang him. His intended victim protested (quite truthfully) that he was not the miller, but a servant whom the real miller had persuaded to take his place. 'Thou art a false knave then,' the Provost Marshal replied, 'to be false in two tales: therfore hang him'. And hanged he was.[5]

Thomas Audley, who served as Provost Marshal c. 1543–44, wrote 'A Treatise on the Art of Warre' in which the duties of the Provost Marshal appear to have been roughly similar to those of his predecessors. The Provost Marshal was to have 'A sufficient number of Tipstaves or Sergauntes for the apprehension of offenders and the safe keping of theme' in addition to two clerks, of 'the Watche' and of 'the Market', and an executioner.[6]

The Provost Marshals of Elizabeth's armies served much the same purpose as in Henry VIII's day, as can be judged by comparing the disciplinary code issued by Robert, Earl of Leicester for the campaign in the Low Countries in 1585 with earlier codes. The force of military police available to Leicester's Provost Marshal was still small. It consisted of about 30 men, armed with firearms. In theory these numbers could be augmented in a crisis, for men were ordered to 'ayde and assist' the Provost Marshal if called upon to do so. As in earlier times, codes were issued at the beginning of new campaigns, and slight variations can be detected from campaign to campaign. The Provost Marshal remained the second most important officer concerned with discipline, under the general supervision of the High Marshal, who ranked as second-in-command of the army, below the commanding general. The Provost Marshal was concerned with the day-to-day administration of discipline, although the High Marshal would become involved in the gravest military misdemeanours.

The disciplinary machinery of Elizabeth's army, founded upon disciplinary codes and articles of war and administered by the High Marshal, Provost Marshal and the tipstaves, was essentially sound. The roots of the poor discipline of late 16th century armies lay in other causes, notably the lack of enthusiasm of the soldier for fighting for the state rather than out of loyalty to an overlord. Indiscipline not only threatened the efficiency of the army but also on occasion made the life of the Provost Marshal a hazardous one. In 1585, the Provost Marshal of the army in the Low Countries arrested a representative of the rank and file who had demanded arrears of pay from no less a person than Leicester himself. To prevent their representative being hanged, other soldiers liberated him from the Provost Marshal and threatened to shoot the Provost Marshal and his subordinates. Order was only restored by the timely arrival of loyal troops.[7]

In the mid-16th century, Provost Marshals of a rather different type to those discussed so far began to make an appearance.[8] These were 'civil' Provost Marshals, who had authority over civilians other than rebels. From Mary's reign (1553–58) onwards, Provost Marshals were appointed to carry out a policing role within England itself. In 1589, for instance, the arrival of a fleet which disgorged a large number of sick and destitute soldiers onto the streets of London and other ports was swiftly followed by the return of Lord Willoughby's army from France. Elizabeth's government was sufficiently unnerved by the threat to law and order posed by these men to appoint Provost Marshals in every county. Soldiers had two days to obtain a passport, which would allow them to proceed home. If they failed to obtain documentation, Provost Marshals were empowered to execute them under the provision of martial law. However, a number of other 'vagrant and ill-disposed persons' were also covered by the Provost Marshal's sweeping powers; those who posed as soldiers, for example, were also liable to summary execution.

1589 was an exceptional year. The Spanish threat, despite the defeat of the Armada in the previous year, had still not entirely receded; the fear of internal unrest was also a strong one. More usually, the Provost Marshal's 'internal security' role was directed against the poor, especially those regarded as rogues and vagabonds. Thus the role of the 'civil' Provost Marshal developed at something of a tangent from that of his military counterpart, becoming in part a civilian policeman, and in part poor law official; 'civil' Provost Marshals continued to operate, although with reduced powers, as late as the 18th century.

Francis Markham's *Five Decades of Epistles of Warre*, published in 1622, states that the Provost Marshal's 'office . . . is both worthy, necessary, and good, a calling fit for a Gentleman of Blood and Quality'. The fact that Markham found it necessary to stress the social acceptability of the office of Provost Marshal is perhaps a reflection of the extent to which the position had slid from its pre-eminence of a century earlier. Markham suggests, in words that reflect the fact that the Provost Marshal's responsibilities went beyond the mere enforcement of discipline, that the ideal Provost Marshal:

would be a man of great Judgement and Experience in all Martial-Discipline, well seen in the laws and ordinances of the Camp, and such a one as knew well the use, benefit and necessity of all things belonging either unto Food or Raiment, he should be a Lover of Justice, impartial in his dealings, and free from the transportation of Passions: he should have an ear that contemptuously could beat back, not furiously drink in, Slander and railing language: he should have an eye that could gaze on all objects without winking, and an heart full of discreet compassion, but not touched with foolish or melting pity. In brief, he ought to be only the Law's servant, and indeed to challenge no more in himself, than so much as expressed to her his obedience.

In Markham's words, the paragon of virtue that was the Provost Marshal 'is the first and greatest Gaoler of the Army, having power to detain and keep prisoner whosoever shall be committed unto him by lawful authority'. Although some sneeringly referred to the Provost Marshal as 'the Hangman, or executioner of the Army' (and thus a dishonourable, low fellow), Markham pointed out that just as civilian law officers deputed underlings to carry out unpleasant tasks, so did the Provost Marshal, 'and to that end it is not lawful for the Under-Provosts to go at any time without Halters, Withs, or strangling cords of Match, ever about them'. Furthermore:

> The Provost Marshal hath charge of all manner of tortures, as Gyves, Shackles, Bolts, Chaines, Bilbowes, Manacles, Whips and the like, and may by his Ministers use them, either in the case of Judgment [sic] or Commandment from a Marshall-Court, or otherwise upon unruliness at his own discretion: he is by his officers to see all places of Execution prepared and furnished with Engines fitting to the Judgment, [sic] whether it be the Gallows, Gibets, Scaffolds, Pillories, Stocks, or Strappadoes, or any other engine which is set up for terror and afright to such as behold it.

Other duties of the Provost Marshal, as we have seen, included overseeing camp sanitation and cleanliness, guarding of prisoners of war, supervision of 'Victuallers, Viandors, Merchants and other which bring any provisions to the camp', and the general maintenance of discipline in the camp.[8]

Markham's list of instruments of execution and torture indicates the lengths to which 17th century armies were prepared to go to maintain discipline. Men were executed mainly by shooting or the rope, occasionally by beheading, and sometimes even by burning to death. In 1691, a French incendiary who had attempted to set fire to a powder wagon of William III's army was executed in the latter fashion. The execution began with the lopping off and burning of the condemned man's right hand by a provost's man; the victim was then tied to a stake and burned alive, in front of detachments from every regiment in camp. The Provost Marshal also played a major role in executions by firing squad. He commanded the firing party, and was responsible for dispatching the victim if he survived both the initial volley and that of the reserve party. Flogging, riding the wooden horse (forcing a prisoner to sit astride the ridge formed by nailing planks joined together, sometimes with the legs weighted by muskets) and running the gauntlet (more properly, gatloup) were other punishments available to the Provost Marshal.[9]

Twenty years after Markham's work was published, civil war broke out in England. When Charles I raised his standard in Nottingham in August 1642, he signalled the beginning of a military revolution as well as a political one. Before the Civil War, Charles could call upon the services of probably fewer than 1,000 soldiers. By late 1643, the rival armies could field perhaps 110,000 men between them. Such a massive and rapid expansion had important implications. With the exception of some units, such as the London Trained Bands and members of the militia, most of these 110,000 men were amateurs without military experience. Inevitably, their discipline was poor. Since the experienced officers and NCOs needed to instill that discipline were few and far between, the role of the Provost Marshal assumed a new importance. Civil war opened up the terrifying prospect of England becoming exposed to the same fate that had befallen Germany, which since 1618 had been ravaged by war. Ultimately, England was spared Germany's fate: and, by enforcing discipline, the Provost Marshal played a part in shielding the English population from the worst excesses of war. By helping to create and enforce the discipline that was the salient feature of the Parliamentarian New Model Army, Provost Marshals can also be said to have had a hand in deciding the outcome of the war and thus radically reshaping the history of England.

Both the Royalist and Parliamentarian armies followed standard practice in appointing and promulgating military codes and in appointing provost marshals. From the very beginning of the war, the ill-disciplined behaviour of some troops of both sides demonstrated the need for such a disciplinary structure. Despite the promulgation of a military code on 6 September 1642, Essex's Parliamentarians pillaged and looted during their march from London to Northampton in the few weeks of the very first campaign of the war. Essex's code followed that of the Earl of Arundel, issued for the King's army in 1639, in reducing an unwieldy body of law to a manageable format by introducing 12 subheadings, thus making the code easier to remember. Future Parliamentarian codes were largely based on that of Essex's army, which therefore laid the foundations for modern British military law.

Civil War articles followed those of previous years in many respects, in attempting to give substance to the unwritten but well understood 'laws of war' and, once again, the Provost Marshal's duties were carefully defined. There were several varieties of Provost Marshal. The senior provost officer was the Provost Marshal General. Later, Parliamentarian armies had separate Provost Marshal Generals for horse, foot, artillery and dragoons. Below this level, there were regimental Provost Marshals. The Provost Marshal General was a person of some consequence, even if he was not quite as exalted as the Provost Marshal of the early 16th century.

The role of the Provost Marshal had changed little since Markham's day, 20 years before. Arundel's code of 1639 had recognised the Provost Marshal as the executioner of the Army and that he was also responsible for carrying out lesser punishments. The 'Lawes and Ordinances' of the New Model Army declare that 'No man shall resist the Provost-Marshall (*sic*), or any other Officer, in the execution of his Office, or breake prison, upon pain of death'. The Provost Marshal's role as 'the greatest and principal gaoler of the Army' is also stressed: he was forbidden to take charge of prisoners sent by other officers unless he is given 'the cause and reason for imprisonment', and the Provost Marshal was to convey this information within 48 hours to the 'Advocate of the Army' (who oversaw the legal side of trials). If this was not done, without good reason, the prisoner was to be released. The Provost Marshal was also to receive captured deserters. Should he release a prisoner without authority, or be lax enough to allow him to escape, he was liable to receive the same punishment [as was] 'due unto the dismissed or escaped offender'. As in the days of Henry VIII, the Provost Marshal was also responsible for keeping the camp clean and for overseeing the sale of food by camp followers. Royalist articles of war, and duties of Provost Marshals, seem to have followed along broadly similar lines.

Provost Marshals proliferated during the Civil War. In 1642, Captain James Seinger was appointed Provost Marshal General of Essex's army and Sir William Smith became the Royalist Provost Marshal General at Oxford in early 1643. Smith was notorious for his ill-treatment of prisoners. He was also unprincipled and allowed himself to be bribed by a prominent Parliamentarian prisoner, John Lilburne, who was allowed to escape. In January 1644, Charles removed him at the request of his (Royalist) Parliament, which was sitting in Oxford. The New Model Army had a Provost Marshal General of Foot (Captain Wykes), who was apparently the senior Provost Marshal General, and a Provost Marshal General of Horse (Captain Richard Lawrence). In 1647, the New Model Army's Provost Marshals General of Foot and Horse were paid 4s 5d and 3s 4d per day respectively. As in the previous century, Provost Marshals were appointed to serve away from the main armies. On July 8

1643, the Provost Marshal at Stafford, Thomas Richards, was ordered to 'take a party of musquettiers' and seize goods to the value of £15 if a local man failed to pay a fine. Provost Marshals also played a role in the military government of England under the Commonwealth.

Each Parliamentarian regiment of horse and foot also had its Regimental Provost Marshal. These officers, the forerunners of the modern provost sergeant, were first provided for in the 1625 Articles of War.

According to a contemporary, they had local powers similar to those of the Provost Marshal General. A Provost Marshal 'had power to apprehend any Soldiers whom he sees transgressing the Laws and Articles of War' and no officer was allowed to hinder him in this duty; he had to take offenders into custody, deliver prisoners for trial, 'and be present at the execution of every sentence' (and to land the first blow when a prisoner ran the gauntlet). He also had duties similar to those of the Provost Marshal General concerning 'sutlers' and 'vittlers'. The increased numbers of Provost Marshals was accompanied by a growth in the number of military police. The 1625 Articles of War stated that 'the Provost must have a horse allowed him, and some soldiers to attend him'. In fact the Provost Marshal General of the New Model Army had a troop of 20 mounted men to assist him. In 1647 it was recorded that the Provost Marshal General of Horse had eight men, and regimental Provost Marshals of Horse had two men, although no men were provided for their counterparts in the regiments of foot. These men received two shillings per day, the normal pay of a trooper in a regiment of horse, and this is possibly significant, in that troopers in regiments of horse tended to be a superior type of person to the common infantryman.[10]

This growth in the number of Provost Marshals and military police reflects an increasing concern with discipline, and, as important, an increasing willingness to instill it into armies. The discipline of Civil War armies appears savage by modern standards, although it was comparable with civilian justice of the period. It has been suggested that the Provost Marshal had the power to inflict summary punishment, including death, although generally the formalities of a court martial – either a general court martial or a regimental one – were observed. Some 45 offences were punishable by death, and other offences could result in lesser punishments. Such punishments were intended to act as a deterrent; a not untypical incident occurred in 1644 when two Royalist infantrymen were hanged, and the entire army marched past the corpses.[11]

Yet despite the numbers of Provost Marshals, and the severity of the punishments they were able to inflict, civil war armies – including the New Model Army – were capable of bouts of savage ill-discipline. Concepts of discipline and responsibility were somewhat alien to the 17th century mind, and the efforts of Non-Commissioned Officers and Provost Marshals in attempting to instill discipline into men who might well be unwilling conscripts, or alternatively ne'er-do-wells, met with only limited success. Added to this fundamental problem were the usual ones of armies of the period – irregular pay, poor examples being set by amateurish officers, drunkenness, and the like. Provost Marshals and military police were too few in number to deal with widespread indiscipline, and handicapped in their attempts by numerous factors ranging from the need for tact when handling mutinous troops to the lack of military prisons. Much of the success of the New Model Army, which was created early in 1645, can be explained by the fact that it was a truly professional army, inspired by the promise (and sometimes the reality) of regular pay. The hard school of campaigning had produced effective discipline and effective officers.

The importance of discipline to the New Model Army, and the disastrous consequences for armies which lacked it, is demonstrated by the campaigns in the west of England. The poor discipline of the Royalist army was a vital factor in the King's failure in the West Country in 1643 when soldiers alienated the local population by pillaging Bristol and the surrounding countryside. By contrast, the people of the Royalist county of Somerset were pleasantly surprised by the behaviour of the well-disciplined New Model Army when it marched into the area in July 1645, and civilians proved willing to co-operate with the Parliamentarian forces. The discipline of the New Model Army did not merely enable it to win battles; it also enabled it to win the 'hearts and minds' of a people weary of war, with decisive results.[12]

2

A Standing Army, 1660–1800

The restoration of the monarchy was followed by the creation of a tiny standing army. Within 50 years, this army had been moulded into a formidable fighting force. Its growth paralleled the emergence of Britain as a great power. By the end of the 18th century, the Army was firmly established as an essential, if domestically unpopular, instrument of British foreign policy which regularly saw service not only in Europe but also in Asia, Africa and the Americas.

The Army of the Restoration period inherited a provost organisation from its forebears, but this organisation was to undergo considerable evolution in the next century-and-a-half. With the exception of the troops of Horse Guards and Horse Grenadier Guards (later the Life Guards), who shared a 'Marshal to the Horse', each regiment of Charles II's army had a Provost Marshal. In 1678 Thomas Sherbourne was appointed as Provost Marshal General, and all the Provost Marshals of the recently expanded army were placed under his aegis. From about 1680 onwards, and as early as 1665 in the case of some regiments, the post of Provost Marshal was combined with that of Quartermaster. During the 18th century, the post of Regimental Provost Marshal vanished altogether and his functions were taken over by the drummers who administered corporal punishment, and by the Adjutant, who supervised the execution of punishments awarded by regimental courts martial. The powers of these courts martial were very broad. Only death sentences (only awarded by a general court martial) fell outside their authority. Throughout the century, there were complaints that cases which should have been tried by the latter were being dealt with at regimental level.

Official instructions issued to commanders of British forces serving in Germany in the Seven Years War (1756–63) reveal that by this period Provost Marshals were appointed on an *ad hoc* basis for field armies, while 'permanent' Provost Marshals were appointed for garrisons. The three Foot Guard regiments, who unlike the 'marching' regiments of foot had a permanent station, shared a Provost Marshal. The position of Provost Marshal to the Foot Guards was sometimes given to a senior NCO, such as Sergeant-Major Harpar of the First Guards, appointed in 1759. Such an appointment served two purposes. It rewarded a long serving soldier, and it filled a post which 'gentlemen' would have regarded with disdain.[1]

The disbandment of most of the New Model Army at the beginning of the 1660s did not lead to a recurrence of the troubles that had led to the appointment of 'civil' Provost Marshals a century earlier. Yet the Army was far from popular. Samuel Pepys reflected the views of many of his countrymen when in April 1667 he referred to the fact that the Duke of Albemarle was dining 'with sorry company, some of the officers of his army'. Raw memories of recent events; the cost and constitutional novelty of a standing army; the billeting of troops on inns and private dwellings; the use of the army for 'policing' duties – all of these were factors in the unpopularity of the Army. The primary reason for the antipathy of most civilians was probably the arrogance of the officers and the appalling behaviour of the common soldiery towards the rest of the population. Drunkenness, theft, assault, vandalism, and even murder were not uncommon. These anti-social habits continued well into the 18th century. In Tony Hayter's words, 'The swaggering and bullying habits' of the late 17th century soldier 'had probably been tempered a little', but his successor's 'off-duty amusements did little to endear him to innkeepers and inhabitants'.[2]

This level of indiscipline is partly explained by the absence of an effective military police force in time of peace. The Provost Marshal was relatively powerless. It has been suggested that strong patrols of soldiers commanded by officers might have helped to prevent brawling in taverns, but officers were unlikely to lower themselves to carry out this duty. Even if soldiers were arrested for misbehaviour, there remained significant legal problems, as the powers of courts martial were limited in England under common law. Provost Marshals themselves were not always models of rectitude. In the 1690s the dwellings of Michael Tooley, the Provost Marshal of the Coldstream Guards, and his counterparts in the lst Foot Guards, Robert Davis and John Bright, were used to imprison men who had been enticed in these houses by various nefarious means. Some were simply kidnapped. All found themselves as recruits to the Army, the Provost Marshals receiving payment from officers who were willing to go to any lengths to keep their regiments up to strength. Such banditry appears to have been a common practice, connived at by military and civilian authorities.[3]

The legal framework within which Provost Marshals operated had been established before the end of the 17th century. The new Standing Army was given a law officer (the Judge Advocate, later known as the Judge Advocate General) responsible for the administration of military law. His duties included arranging courts martial and preparing the prosecution's case, recording the results of those courts and bringing them before the sovereign for confirmation. At this period, the line between martial law (summary justice applied in times of crisis to both soldiers and civilians) and military law (a code of discipline and justice within the Army) was still indistinct. The first Mutiny Act of 1689 began the process of codifying military law, which had previously rested on the various articles of war drawn up for each campaign. However, articles of war did not simply pass from the scene. Until 1718, the Mutiny Acts did not apply to offences committed overseas and even after that date articles of war retained an essential role in the discipline and justice of the Army. Ninety years after the first Mutiny Act had been passed, the newly founded American Continental Army turned to British articles of war, believing that 'a more complete system of military discipline' could not be found.[4]

The long-service British Army of the 18th century was relatively well disciplined for the time, but discipline was maintained by the harshest of measures. The unpromising material from which it was recruited and the nature of the close-order tactics of the period called for stern discipline. Most of the attention of the Provost Marshal was focussed on the common soldier, but officers too fell foul of the authorities. During the Jacobite rebellion of 1745–46, Captain Archibald Cuningham was made a scapegoat for the poor performance of the Royal Army at the battle of Falkirk, and was cashiered with infamy. Cuningham was publicly humili-ated:

> his sentence being read, his commission was cancelled, his sword broken over his head, his sash cut into pieces and thrown in his face, and lastly, the provost-martial's (sic) servant giving him a kick on the posteriors, turned him out of the line.[5]

Despite the continuing need for the service of provost, the Army still lacked an effective military police force. William III's armies in Flanders and Ireland possessed provost troops, but in Ireland in 1690 these amounted to a mere 24 men. Fifteen or so years later the Provost Marshal of the Marlburian wars had the modest total of two (sometimes four) men permanently at his disposal.[6] Later in the century, Provost Marshals could call upon rather larger bodies of military police. The army serving in Germany during the Seven Years War had a Provost Marshal General, Deputy Provost Marshal, officers, and 'Constables', a term more usually applied to civilian policemen. At the beginning of the American War of Independence (1775–83), the Provost Marshal's basic entourage con-sisted of a sergeant and 18 men, but he was allowed an additional 30 men, one sergeant, a drummer and a fifer, and a lieutenant when he had to take care of prisoners. If the evidence of the fictional memoirs of

'Mother Ross' can be relied upon, a similar force for gaoling duties was provided in Marlburian times. According to the good lady, the Provost Marshal:

> attends the camp, and all offenders are put under his care, for which reason he commands a strong guard which goes everywhere with him; and the camp colour-men who always precede the army, escorted by the forlorn hope, choose the strongest house they can meet with for his quarters . . . When we march, the less criminals are handcuffed in the middle of the guard; but notorious ones are chained hand and foot, and put into the breadwaggons.

In 1786, Francis Grose commented that the Provost Marshal 'seems to have been formerly an office of much greater rank and authority than it is at present'. Marlborough's staff had included a number of specialist officers who ranked as 'general officers of the army', including the Provost Marshal General, Quarter Master General, and Waggon Master General. The Provost Marshal General's duties resembled those of his Elizabethan predecessor. In addition to the maintenance of discipline and administration of justice, he controlled the organisation and building of camps, organised the order of march, and controlled foraging parties. The latter was a particularly important role, for foraging expeditions were prime opportunities for private soldiers to loot and desert. A Marlburian infantry officer wrote of one such foraging party in Picardy in 1712. A 'strong detachment was sent out under the command of a general officer [almost certainly the Provost Marshal], to keep the foragers within bounds, to cover them from the enemy, and to prevent irregularities and abuses'. By the 1770s the Adjutant General had taken over the role of forming the army into columns and organising the order of march, and the Quarter Master General had the job of organising foraging, although the Provost Marshal seems to have retained some control over the regulation of provisions supplied for the army. The highest rank given to a Provost Marshal in this period was that of a captain, which was sometimes (but by no means always) awarded to bolster his authority.

The Provost Marshal was now mainly concerned with discipline in the army as a whole, dealing with problems which could not easily be handled at unit level, such as keeping order in camp. In 1761, Ferdinand of Brunswick, the allied commander-in-chief in Germany was faced with a rising tide of indiscipline. He caused an order to be issued through the Provost Marshal that men found 'after 10pm in the tents or huts of vivandiers, or in public-houses, will be arrested without regard for his person'. Furthermore, the Provost Marshal was to inflict on 'prostitutes or "*filles de joie*" . . . a withering punishment'. A more mundane duty for the Provost Marshal or his deputy was to notify the officer forming a

General Court Martial of its time and venue. He had also to summon witnesses, to attend the trial and generally place himself at the disposal of the convening officer, the commander-in-chief. Interestingly, provost staff were specifically mentioned in the Treaty and Conventions of Ecluse, signed in 1759, which dealt with the sick, wounded and prisoners of war. If taken captive, they were to be exchanged as soon as could be arranged, along with other non-combatants such as chaplains and surgeons. The Provost Marshal also had responsibility for female camp followers and army wives. Women as well as men were expected to know the articles of war, and female malefactors could be summarily punished, and even executed, by the Provost Marshal. In 1755, a British general ordered that 'The Women of each Regiment are to march with the Provost and none upon any acct (sic) are to appear with the men under arms'.

Alongside the 'field' role of the Provost Marshal must be set his role as a gaoler. Not all those incarcerated in military prisons were actually criminals. In 1718 it was claimed that some newly recruited soldiers were kept in the notoriously disease-ridden Savoy gaol 'by the Provost Marshal or Military Hangman'. Soldiers destined to be shipped abroad were also kept in this prison, lest they be tempted to desert.[7] One particularly notorious gaoler was Captain William Cunningham, who was appointed Provost Marshal by General Gage during the American War of Independence, and placed in charge of the provost gaols in Philadelphia and New York City. Cunningham allegedly starved 2,000 POW to death and hanged a further 250 without trial. He was described as an 'infamously cruel scoundrel . . . a burly, ill-natured Irishman of sixty years whose conduct as Provost Marshal . . . has connected his name with all that is detestable'.

As was the case in the Boer War 130 years later, it is possible that the starving of POW was the result of logistic incompetence rather than deliberate cruelty. In 1794 the Provost Marshal or his deputies were instructed to purchase for his prisoners in Dublin 'wholesome Provisions' of meat, vegetables, and bread to the value of 3s 0½d. The Provost Marshal was forbidden to imprison anyone but a deserter, of which there were large numbers. One conservative estimate is that the mid-18th century army suffered a desertion rate of five per cent per year, a total of perhaps 3,950 men. From 1753 onwards, Provost Marshals were forbidden to hold men for more than eight days before trial, and were compelled to submit to the commander-in-chief, within 24 hours of their arrest, the names of prisoners received.[8]

The period from 1660 to 1800 saw British soldiers deployed all over the globe as Britain carved out an overseas empire. While some of the foreign stations, such as Tangier, were to have fairly brief periods of occupation by British troops, others, such as India and Gibraltar, were to be familiar to British soldiers well into the 20th century. It should not be forgotten that England's first colony was Ireland, and that Provost Marshals had been active in Ireland since the 16th century. Provost Marshals were also appointed in such far-flung places as St Helena (1687–90), Virginia, where a Provost Marshal was appointed as early as 1611, and India, where, in 1678, Thomas Lott, 'eldest sergeant' was appointed at Madras. Problems of maintaining discipline were not, of course, confined to European wars. The future Duke of Wellington recorded that he was forced to use his Provost Marshal to bring looting troops under control after the storming of the Indian city of Seringapatam in 1799, and 'by the greatest exertion, by hanging, flogging &c., &c.' he succeded in restoring order among the soldiery.[9]

Despite the increasingly widespread deployment of British troops, only a very small number of Provost Marshals appeared as such in the Army List. In 1778, at the height of the American War of Independence, only Gibraltar is recorded as possessing a Provost Marshal, the holder of the office being John Medlycott, who was paid £73 per annum. A Provost Marshal was apparently provided for in Minorca, but the post was vacant. In 1799 the post was obviously occupied. According to a staunchly Protestant soldier, in that year a Spanish priest tried to treat the hangman's rope with acid, so that it would break under the strain and prove the lack of authority of 'heretic laws' over the local Catholic population. Unfortunately for the priest, the British Provost Marshal arrived with his own halter and put paid to his plan. Provost Marshals on half pay included Thomas Hawthorn, 'Provost Marshal to the troops' in Germany, Christopher Hewitt 'At the Havannah', John Thompson 'On the late expedition to Guadaloupe' and H Collyer at Belleisle. The absence of Provost Marshals known to be active in the American War, such as William Cunningham (who does however appear as a half-pay Provost Marshal for North America in the 1786 Army List) demonstrates the *ad hoc* nature of the appointment of Provost Marshals on active service in the late 18th century.[10]

3

Wellington's Army

When, in 1808, the Portuguese and Spanish turned and rose against the French Empire of Napoleon, a small British army was sent to Portugal. It was to be the beginning of one of the greatest triumphs in British military history. It was also a period in which a recognisably modern provost organisation emerged for the first time. In 1809, Sir John Moore led the army into Spain. The appearance of Napoleon himself with a superior force compelled Moore to carry out a nightmare retreat over the mountains to the Spanish port of Corunna. During this retreat, Provost Marshals were frequently in action as the discipline of the army all but collapsed. Moore was an extremely enlightened soldier for his day but he was compelled to use floggings and executions to keep the army from disintegrating altogether from drunkenness, looting, straggling, and mutinous behaviour. A General Order of 6 January 1809 declared that Moore was 'forced to order one soldier shot at Villafranca [for looting a rum store] and he will order all others to be executed who are guilty of similar enormities . . .'.

Generals Robert Craufurd, commanding the Light Brigade, and Edward Paget, commanding the rearguard, had few scruples about inflicting harsh punishments. At one stage on the retreat, Paget sought to restore order by holding drumhead courts martial virtually within sight of the advancing French. With the Provost Marshal's men preparing to hang two condemned men from a tree, news was then received that the advanced British picquets had been pushed back by the French. Paget spared the lives of the condemned men on the condition that his division mend its ways. One ordinary soldier, Rifleman Harris, had no doubt that violent punishments were necessary. If Craufurd 'flogged two, he saved hundreds from death by his management'.[1]

Moore's army escaped from Corunna in January 1809 but Moore himself was killed. On 22 April 1809, Sir Arthur Wellesley took command of the British forces that remained in Portugal. One of the first problems that Wellesley dealt with was that of discipline. He was very conscious of the need to maintain good relations with the local civilians and had no wish to deflect Spanish guerrillas from resisting the French invaders to fighting against maurauding British troops. Wellesley had no illusions about the scale of the problems he faced. British officers too often neglected their duty and the ranks contained a fair proportion of the 'scum of the earth'. Wellesley clearly recognised that an effective provost service was essential in enforcing discipline. Within a fortnight of arriving in Lisbon in April 1809, he appointed Provost Marshals to divisions and to important garrisons such as Lisbon. Since there could be only one Provost Marshal, these men were styled Assistant Provost Marshals (APM).

At the beginning of the Peninsular War, Provost Marshals were held in low esteem by the rest of the Army. In 1809, an officer of 95th Rifles was appalled at being ordered to flog some 'delinquents', thus having to lower himself to become 'a provost-marshal (sic) for the occasion'. A fellow Rifles officer described the Provost Marshal on campaign, somewhat inaccurately, as 'a character of considerable pretensions, as he can flog at pleasure . . .' A ranker compared the social acceptability of an APM to that of Jack Ketch, a notorious hangman, claiming that they rarely returned to their own regiments. There is certainly evidence to support such views of the character of APMs. On the retreat from Talavera in 1809, one fell foul of Craufurd and was marched as a prisoner with the provost guard. Sergeant Crane of the 74th Foot, whose frequent bouts of insobriety rendered him 'incapable of doing his duty' was returned to his battalion in 1810, and Sergeant William Conder was sent in disgrace back to the 34th Foot in October 1811 for taking a bribe from a defendant in a court martial for sodomy. Such instances occurred throughout the Peninsular War.

Against such a formidable array of hostile evidence it might seem perverse to suggest that the calibre of many provosts in the Peninsular army was probably quite high. Commanding officers were expressly ordered to recommend NCOs that were 'worthy and capable of performing the duties' of Assistant Provost Marshals, although no doubt some took the opportunity to dispose of an unwanted sergeant. APMs, although sergeants, were paid as ensigns at 5s 3d per day, and given an extra allowance of £18 to pay for a horse. An APM would think twice about abusing his authority for fear of losing such a sum. Paradoxically, the fact that a number were sacked indicates that a high standard of behaviour was expected of APMs. One suspects that most APMs in the Peninsular army were not ruffians but steady, sober NCOs: men such as the splendidly-named Sergeant Xenophon Mosscroft of the 48th Foot. Executioners, no matter how personally worthy, are never likely to win a popularity poll.[2]

In 1809, the Anglo–Portuguese Army threw the French out of Portugal, and made an abortive advance into Spain. In the following year, they weathered a major French invasion of Portugal, before following the retreating French back to Spain in 1811. In 1812, Wellesley (who was raised to the peerage as Viscount Wellington after the victory at Talavera in 1809) seized the initiative. Advancing into Spain, he took two major fortresses, Cuidad Rodrigo and Badajoz, won a crushing victory at Salamanca, and entered the Spanish capital, Madrid. Although at the end of the year Wellington was forced to retreat to Portugal, amid scenes which rivalled those on the retreat to Corunna, the 1812 campaign inflicted irreparable damage on the French position in Spain. In 1813 Wellington struck north, defeated the French at the battle of Vittoria, and moved up to the French frontier and over the Pyrenees. All these campaigns gave much employment to provost.

The exact number of British soldiers executed and flogged by courts martial during the Peninsular War is unknown. The Judge Advocate General estimated that 41 were put to death in a spell of 14 months in 1812-14. Although not every punishment of death or flogging awarded by courts martial was overseen by a Provost Marshal, the practice was so common that in General Orders it is reduced to a formula, which rarely varied:

> The sentence of the General Court Martial on the trial of Walter M'Cann, is to be carried into execution tomorrow morning, the 10th inst. under the direction of the Assistant Provost Marshal attached to 2d Division, in the presence of the troops in camp at Talavera, to be paraded for that purpose.

M'Cann, a private of the 28th Foot who had deserted to the enemy, was shot. In 1811, Private William Wheeler of the 51st Foot recorded the details of an execution. The division was drawn up in a square formation, with a line of condemned men forming the fourth side of the square. A short distance in front of the prisoners was the firing squad, who were drawn from their own regiment. The sentence of the court martial was read, the chaplain gave what comfort he could, and then the prisoners'

> eyes are bound and they kneel down. When they have made a signal, the firing party – who are ready loaded and firelocks cocked – watch the Provost Martial (*sic*) who stands with a handkerchief. At the first signal the firing party presents, and at the next they fire.

The division was then paraded past the corpses. On one occasion in 1812, two men remained alive after a volley, and the Provost Marshal finished them off by firing a musket at their heads.[3]

Provosts still had the power of summary punishment. In a General Order of 1811, Wellington stated that 'Whatever may be the crime of which a soldier is guilty, the Provost Marshal has not the power of inflicting summary punishment for it, unless he should see him in the act of committing it'. Wellington was obviously concerned to prevent abuse of provost authority. If a Provost Marshal merely suspected a soldier of an offence, he had to submit a report to Wellington himself, who would order further investigation or summary punishment. APMs, who, unlike the Provost Marshal, could not carry out summary capital punishments 'require[d] the constant and watchful attention' of senior officers, who were to allow summary punishment only if it was deemed necessary *pour encourager les autres*. Finally, Wellington made it clear that no officer, not even the Iron Duke himself, could order a Provost Marshal to punish anyone. Sometimes this code of practice was ignored. General Picton once threatened to have Wellington's butler flogged by the Provost Marshal for blocking the road – a rare case of a Provost Marshal of the Napoleonic period becoming involved with traffic control – but this was clearly an abuse of authority.[4]

In June 1809, Wellington wrote that there was 'no authority for this practice [of summary punishment] excepting custom, which I conceive would hardly warrant it; and yet I declare that I do not know in what manner the Army is to be commanded at all, unless the practice is not only continued, but an additional number of provosts appointed'. He likewise acknowledged that extending the powers of British Provost Marshals to the British-officered Portuguese Army was 'quite irregular' but nonetheless essential. The aftermath of the storming of the fortress of Badajoz in April 1812 can only have reinforced Wellington's views on the importance of provost. After one of the toughest battles of the entire war Wellington's troops went on a drunken orgy of raping, looting and pillaging. Faced with the collapse of discipline, Wellington sent his Provost Marshal into the town with orders to restore the situation by executing soldiers caught plundering. No lesser measure could have brought the battle-crazed troops under control.[5] Other duties of the Provost Marshal were less controversial. Many would have been immediately familiar to Henry Guylford or a modern day member of the RMP. They had to police wine shops, carry out discipline patrols in camp, check improperly dressed soldiers and round up stragglers, handle prisoners of war, and guard prisons. They continued to have special responsibilities for army women, although summary punishment of women seems to have been a rare occurence. One woman was apparently hanged for stealing flour in 1810, and women were occasionally flogged. On one memorable occasion a Provost Marshal punished the wife of a soldier in the 34th Foot by shooting her donkeys.

As one historian has recently remarked, the most Provost Marshals could do was to confine the army's looting 'within acceptable limits'.

Wellington was well aware of the problem. In 1809 he complained of 'the irregularities and outrages' committed by his troops, and of the inadequacies of regimental courts martial in dealing with them. One solution was, he suggested, the formation of 'a regular provost establishment' on the lines of those existing in the French and Spanish armies, 'of which a proportion should be sent to every army sent abroad'. The British had nothing beyond 'a few sergeants' of whom Wellington said, possibly unfairly, 'were probably not very fit for the duties which they are to perform'. Wellington might have added that there were also provost guards attached to the Provost Marshal, and that officers commanding guards or detachments of troops were supposed to aid the Provost Marshal in the course of his duty.

A small addition to the men available for provost work was provided by the Corps of Mounted Guides, (CMG) first raised in 1808. They were mainly used for gathering intelligence, but also sometimes aided the Provost Marshal – one soldier referred to them as 'the police of the Army'. However, they were an evolutionary blind alley as far as provost were concerned, although they can be counted among the forebears of the Intelligence Corps. Similarly, the Royal Staff Corps were sometimes used for traffic control, but their modern day equivalent is the Royal Pioneer Corps, not the Royal Military Police. [6]

Four years later, Wellington's plan for an effective police force to serve the Army was finally realised. In March 1813, commanding officers of cavalry regiments were ordered to submit the names of NCOs and privates to serve in the two troops of the Staff Corps of Cavalry (SCC). This unit was 'to be employed in the duties of the police of the army, and in others of a confidential nature'. Not surprisingly, such men had to possess exemplary characters. As with the post of Assistant Provost Marshal, service with the SCC was financially advantageous. Sergeants received one shilling per day extra pay, while corporals and privates received eight pence and sixpence extra respectively. Two troops were also raised in Britain and Ireland. A detachment was allotted to each division of the Peninsular army, much in the fashion of the modern divisional provost company.

Britain's first standing military police force came into being as the result of a letter from the Duke of York, Commander-in-Chief of the British Army, to the Secretary of War in January 1813. The former proposed 'that the duties hitherto attached to the office of Provost Marshal shall be placed on a more efficient and respectable footing' by the formation of a Staff Corps of Cavalry to be attached to the department of the Adjutant General which should supply orderlies to general officers and 'patrol the camp or cantonments, to take up stragglers, and to protect the authority of the inhabitants, whether the army shall be halted or on the march'. George Scovell, who had previously commanded the CMG, was appointed Major-Commandant, with the rank of lieutenant colonel in the army. He commanded 10 officers, 6 sergeants, 6 corporals and 20 privates.[7]

Some contemporary documents give the occasional tantalising glimpse of the new 'Police Corps', as it was sometimes described, in action. During the battle of the Nivelle on 10th November 1813, Sergeant Hinchcliffe of the SCC was searching a house when he discovered a private of the 83rd Foot. The private, William Woodcock, had absented himself from his unit to go in search of plunder. Hinchcliffe tried to force Woodcock out of the house and eventually disarmed him, but not before Woodcock had threatened to shoot the military policeman. Woodcock was tried by court martial and executed. The affair suggests that the SCC were deployed just behind the frontline troops, perhaps as a form of straggler post. The 83rd took part in an assault on the village of Amotz on the 10th, and as Woodcock is described as deserting 'during the attack', that is almost certainly where he was arrested by Hinchcliffe. Four months later, we find the SCC in a completely different role, at headquarters, escorting a captured French official. On occasion they were described by the Judge Advocate General as *'gens-d'armes'*. The SCC were disbanded at the end of the war in 1814.[8]

When Wellington's army crossed into France in October 1813, the need for strict discipline became even more important. Wellington feared Allied indiscipline might stir up a French guerrilla campaign. He sent home most of his ill-disciplined Spanish troops, and punished looting severely. Four or five men were hanged for being caught in the act after the battle of the Nivelle in 1813. One regimental officer believed that the improvement in relations between Allied troops and French civilians in late 1813 owed much the 'strict discipline' imposed by Wellington and to the activities of the divisional APM, for without the Provost Marshal's powers of summary execution plundering troops might 'arm an exasperated population' against the British. In the event, the British Army's behaviour compared so favourably with that of the French – who had routinely pillaged their own people – that many French civilians preferred the British. The activities of Provost Marshals and the SCC played a significant role in ensuring that Wellington's march into France was not hindered by French guerrillas snapping at their heels.[9]

It is likely that Wellington was thinking along similar lines as he prepared to advance into France after his victory at Waterloo on 18 June 1815. On 20 June he ordered that France was to be treated as the country of an ally. However, reluctant to rely solely on the political sensitivity of his troops, he re-raised the SCC, from 'the best and steadiest Men' of the army a day later. Interestingly, Wellington initially called it the 'Gendarmerie' in an attempt to overcome the prejudice of foreign troops towards the Corps. Scovell once again commanded the SCC and, when recruiting for it, preference was given to men and officers who had served in the old SCC. One novel feature was the presence of foreign troops within its ranks.

The distribution of Provost Marshals in the 1815 campaign followed the pattern established during the Peninsular War. Important garrisons, such as Brussels, were given provosts, and various formations received an APM: thus Sergeant-Major David Davis of the 51st Foot was appointed APM to II Corps on 8 May 1815. A General Order of February 1815 referred simply to 'Military Police' of towns.[10] After the occupation of Paris, a Provost Guard was stationed there. A soldier who served with this unit recalled the Provost Marshal, Captain F Stanway as 'a keen fellow' who punished transgressors ruthlessly by flogging. Belgians, in particular, were notorious for looting. On one occasion a Belgian unit attacked the provost building to release some of their comrades, which resulted in a pitched battle with the Provost Guard (while Stanway calmly continued with the flogging!). It is interesting to note that, according to one officer, Stanway was a kind man when off duty.[11]

General Picton still seems to have been abusing the authority of the Provost Marshal during the Waterloo campaign. At the battle of Quatre Bras (16 June 1815) he is said to have been carrying out a drumhead court martial when the Provost Marshal arrived and cut short the proceedings by flogging the prisoner 'instantly who joined his ranks and assisted in defeating a very sharp attack of Ney's'.[12]

Wellington was far ahead of his time in recognising the importance of provost; on the formation of the SCC he complained that numbers were insufficient, and argued for retention of the CMG in a police role. On another occasion Wellington showed his understanding of the difficulties of provost work. A soldier was sentenced to death for assaulting a sergeant of the SCC in 1813 (as Tyler notes, the first known death sentence for an assault, on campaign, on a military policeman) but with a recommendation for mercy. Wellington referred to the danger of weakening the authority of the SCC, recognising that the Corps was already held in low esteem by the rest of the army, and recommended that the court should 'allow the law to take its course'.[13] His foresight and his understanding of the problems of provost work surely places the Duke of Wellington high in the pantheon of patron saints of the Royal Military Police.

4

The Crimean War, 1853–56

The defeat of Napoleon at Waterloo brought an end to 22 years of war. With no European enemy in sight, the government took a sharp axe to the army. One of the victims of the cuts was the Staff Corps of Cavalry, which was disbanded in 1818, after the occupation of France came to an end. Wellington appears to have accepted the disbandment of the SCC as inevitable, however regrettable. The post of Provost Marshal General was abolished as a sinecure in 1829. However, as some compensation, Queen's Regulations laid down in 1844 that a 'provost marshal of the Army' was to rank as a captain in the Army.

The period from 1815 to 1854 became known as the Long Peace. In reality these years were anything but peaceful for the British Army. One fairly typical colonial operation was General Sir Charles Napier's Sind campaign of 1843. Napier's use of Captain Pope, his Provost Marshal, to flog plunderers caused a storm of controversy. One journalist even incited the troops to mutiny and thus 'put an end to this fellow's [Pope's] breaches of law'. Flogging had been abolished for Indian soldiers in the 1830s but Napier believed that corporal punishment was still necessary on campaign, and he placed a 'detachment of horse' at Pope's disposal to keep order.[1]

In 1854, Britain went to war with France and Turkey against Russia. The major land campaign of the war was fought to destroy the Russian fleet and base of Sevastopol, although there was also significant activity elsewhere, notably a naval campaign in the Baltic. Initially, the British force (commanded by Lord Raglan) was sent to Bulgaria, but in September the British and their French allies invaded the Crimea. The campaign turned on the long, costly, but ultimately successful siege of Sevastopol.

The Crimean army was dominated by the ghost of the Iron Duke, who had died in 1852. In July 1854, that pioneer military policeman, Sir George Scovell (who was by this time a lieutenant general) drew up a memorandum on the formation of a Staff Corps, which reflected his experiences in the Napoleonic Wars. Sir George Cathcart, the Adjutant General and a veteran of Waterloo, also wrote on the subject. He believed that although such a corps was desirable 'for the performance of Police with an army in the field', the invidious word 'police' should be avoided.

The name 'Mounted Staff Corps' (MSC) would, Cathcart claimed, be more easily understood, and it followed the practice of Wellington himself. Lord Hardinge, the Commander-in-Chief, approved of the formation of the MSC, once again quoting a Wellingtonian precedent. The suggestion that the establishment of the MSC was a political response to press criticism undoubtedly contains a good deal of truth, but the precedent of the Peninsular is clearly discernable in the provost arrangements for the Crimea.

Cathcart's ideas regarding the functions of the MSC are important because attention has recently been drawn to the fact that the duties and even the status (whether military or civilian) of the MSC were unclear to many in the Crimea and in London. No less a person than the Secretary of State for War, the Duke of Newcastle, was forced to admit in December 1854 that he did not know whether the MSC was supervising the cleaning of camps, as he had intended, because he had 'never heard from anyone of its arrival'. On 19 July, Newcastle had informed Raglan of the dispatch of the MSC to the Crimea. Newcastle promised that Cathcart, who was being sent out to command the 4th Division, would brief Raglan on 'the formation and duties' of the Corps. Cathcart was a competent Adjutant General and his memorandum of 17 July sets out the MSC's role reasonably clearly, although it assumes a knowledge of the activities of the SCC of the Peninsular campaign. In view of the fact that the MSC did not arrive in the Crimea until 24 November, it is likely that he gave Raglan only the most sketchy of briefings on the Corps, if indeed he briefed him at all. The MSC paid the price for this breakdown in communication, in that they were never properly employed.[2]

In theory, the MSC should have been admirably suited for their tasks. Fifty strong, they were raised from members of the Irish Constabulary and the Metropolitan Police. Before the MSC departed for the war, Newcastle commented upon the 'high characters' and 'intelligence' of its members. They were paid much more than the ordinary soldier, as befitted the greater weight of their individual responsibility. In practice, the MSC suffered from the indifference of high command – Raglan had not asked for such a force to be raised – and ignorance as to their role. The MSC were disliked and envied by the rest of the army. In January 1855, they were described as being dressed 'in fanciful helmet, red tunic braided with black cord . . . looking very much as if they . . . were the advanced guard of some equestrian troop coming to open a circus in the village'. They pranced about in the mud or stood sentry, sword drawn, at a ruined house at the entrance to Balaklava 'in the vain hope of preserving some order among the multitude of travellers'. *The Times* correspondent, William Howard Russell, claimed they were hated because their pay was equivalent to that of an ensign. In the middle of December 1854, the MSC received the unwelcome reminder that as they were earning over £100 per annum, they were liable to income tax![3]

The MSC were eventually used for a variety of tasks. From early December 1854, parties of mounted and dismounted men were deployed to police the port of Balaklava, which was situated a mile from the MSC camp. On 14 December, this system was changed so that an NCO and five mounted men paraded daily at 0845, and proceeded to the residence of the Provost Marshal 'for the purpose of assisting him in his duties'. From 3 January 1855, the PM's party was increased to six men and permanently stationed in Balaklava. An important duty in the port was the prevention of theft from ships in the harbour, by enforcing the order that forbade soldiers to go on board vessels unless accompanied by an officer with written authority. The MSC were on parade for the funeral of Lord Raglan, where they were used 'to close the procession' and 'subsequently to act as a flying squadron on the flanks of the procession'.[4]

A letter of 7 December 1854 indicates that the MSC were also used for traffic control in the Balaklava area and also in the movement of supplies to the positions before Sevastopol. This letter, written by an Irish constable from Kilkenny then serving with the MSC, gives a fascinating glimpse of the situation in late 1854. He wrote that the handful of horses that remained were very weak, as were the men, who were suffering from the cold and from other hardships:

> The Russian army . . . are encamped about three miles away . . . we can see . . . the Cossack sentries . . . The roads are knee deep in mud, and to see poor men and horses dragging and pulling along the road it would strike pity into any person's heart . . .

If the fortress of Sevastopol was not taken soon, he warned, the British Army would face the fate of the French invaders of Russia in 1812. He also wrote of the poor rations, but ended by saying that some of the MSC had good health and morale, and only two men had died.[5]

The winter soon took its toll of the MSC. By 13 February, it was reduced to only 28 effectives. It was further weakened by the stationing of eight privates and two NCOs under a subaltern at Kamiesh Bay 'for the purpose of the conveyance of letters'. In September 1855, Russell commented that latterly the efforts of the MSC had been 'almost exclusively' devoted to this task 'and indeed, their diminished numbers did not render them available for any further service'.[6]

There was a provost presence in the Black Sea theatre before the arrival of the MSC. Captain W D MacDonald of the 93rd Highlanders was Provost Marshal, with Deputy Provost Marshals (all of the rank of sergeant) appointed to the divisions and to headquarters. In late July, two Turks who tried to sell two stolen British horses to British infantry were summarily flogged by the provost, cheered on by a crowd of Bulgarian onlookers. The siege of Sevastopol provided provost with plenty of work. Thefts and murders were investigated, and camel-drivers and sutlers roamed the camp 'much perplexed', wrote Russell, 'by the conflicting emotions of fear of the Provost-Marshal (*sic*) and love of plunder'. Indeed, Russell later wrote that 'the office of that worthy and active person and of his myrmidon sergeants has been by no means a sinecure between "navvies", Greeks and scoundrels of all sorts'. Russell clearly disliked the well-paid civilian navvies who were sent to the Crimea to construct a railway, and hinted that the Provost Marshal was needed to instill discipline into them. On one occasion provost was used to break a strike. One navvy was flogged for robbery, although it was questionable whether the Provost Marshal actually had the authority to punish the navvies.[7]

How successful were the MSC and provost in the Crimea? Russell, the scourge of incompetence and inefficiency, seems to have been favourable impressed by provost, and on the disbandment of the MSC stated that they had 'performed a good deal of severe work during the winter'. On the other hand, the military police aroused the ire of the ordinary soldier. This may, of course, simply indicate that they were doing their job properly. By contrast, Raglan complained about the inefficiency of the MSC and Newcastle, frantically covering his back, proposed as early as February 1855 to disband the Corps and replace it with 100 men from the line regiments, organised into two troops. In the event, the MSC was disbanded in September 1855, perishing largely unmourned.[8]

Military Mounted and Military Foot Police, 1855–1914

The year 1855 marked a turning-point in the history of British military police. On 13 June of that year the War Office authorised the formation of a 'Corps of Mounted Police'. The Crimean campaign had clearly demonstrated the drawbacks of existing arrangements for policing the Army. Cathcart's memorandum of July 1854 had recognised that the Provost Marshal and the MSC should inflict summary punishment on soldiers caught in the act of committing an offence. Cathcart noted uneasily that these powers went 'beyond what is called Law' but were nonetheless 'indispensible', lamely suggesting that 'A Bill of Authority will no doubt exculpate the General, the Provost and the Police for any acts of unavoidable military rigour, when the war is over'. Such sentiments were less acceptable than they might have been 40 years earlier. The Army was not immune to changes in British society. By the 1850s the worst excesses of the 18th century system of criminal law, the 'Bloody Code', had been modified and in 1829 the first modern civilian police force was established. The Army was directly affected by a parliamentary campaign against military flogging which had resulted in limitations being placed on the number of lashes which could be awarded by courts martial. In short, the summary punishment of British soldiers was looking increasingly anachronistic, and the decision to set the policing of the Army onto a proper footing was very much in tune with the spirit of the times.

Nevertheless, there is little doubt that the immediate reason for the establishment of the Military Mounted Police (MMP) in 1855 was practical rather than philosophical. In 1855 a series of militia riots left a trail of destruction across the country. A large camp was established in the spring of that year at Aldershot, where many militia regiments were stationed along with Regular units. Given the militia's unenviable disciplinary record and the lack of facilities and poor conditions at Aldershot, it is small wonder that in June 1855 the War Office thought it desirable to form a military police force 'for the Cantonment of Aldershot', nor that the military policemen should have at least five years service and possess 'sober habits' and be 'intelligent, active and capable of exercising a sound discretion'. In July, 21 NCOs and men arrived to form the new corps, drawn from the 2nd Dragoon Guards, 15th Hussars, 7th Hussars, and 3rd Light Dragoons. Initially, the military police at Aldershot were also used on military prison duties. The Military Provost Staff Corps (MPSC) were formed to take over this responsibility in 1901, but even today the Provost Marshal (Army) is head of the MPSC as well as the RMP.

The numbers and role of MMP grew gradually over the next few years. In 1865 the establishment was increased to 32 all ranks, and seven years later military police were deployed on exercise for the first time. The dominant figure in the MMP was Thomas Trout, who arrived (as Troop Sergeant Major) from the 7th Hussars in October 1855. He was appointed acting Provost Marshal later that year, and was commissioned as Provost Marshal in 1869. APMs were provided for each brigade, and units in the garrison supplied men to serve with the MMP. A further reorganisation took place in 1877. Numbers of MMP grew to 75 other ranks. Responsibility for records was now passed to the MMP and promotions were made within the Corps, thus establishing the MMP on a firmer footing. The venerable Major Trout died in 1881, and was succeeded by Captain W Silk, who was also promoted through the ranks of the Corps, as were Silk's successors, Major C Broackes (1885), Major J E Emerson (1894) and Major J W M Wood (1898). After a protracted bureaucratic battle, Emerson, while Quartermaster and APM at the Curragh in 1889, succeeded in persuading the War Office that he should be considered as belonging to the MMP. Thus, the Quartermaster became the only officer commissioned within the Corps, a situation which endured until 1954.[1]

In the 19th century, units of 'Military Police' were raised in India, such as the Assam Military Police and the Oudh Military Police. These were not provost troops, but para-military units of native soldiers raised for service in frontier regions and in other unsettled areas and cannot be counted among the forebears of the RMP.

* * * *

In May 1857, the 3rd Bengal Cavalry mutinied at Meerut. This began the Indian Mutiny, a major war which took on the character of a popular uprising against the British and was fuelled on both sides by racial and religious fear and hatred. The British fought not only to restore their grip on northern India, but also to revenge the atrocities inflicted by the rebels. In an atmosphere in which a private was given a punishment of a mere two days confinement to barracks for 'Hanging a native without permission', the Provost Marshal's noose became one of the principal instruments of retribution.[2]

One of the heroes of the siege of Lucknow was Captain John William Carnegie of the 15th Bengal Native Infantry, head magistrate and chief-of-police of Lucknow at the outbreak of the Mutiny. After the siege began, he added leadership of the Intelligence Department and Provost Marshal to his list of responsibilities. Carnegie took a prominent role in organising the defences of Lucknow during the uneasy days of May and June 1857. On 31 May, he succeeded in halting an attempted insurrection in the city. A substantial party of Indians from the city staged a religious rising and tried to join up with the mutineers. They were opposed by Carnegie's police, and dispersed. On 28 June, with the rebel army advancing on Lucknow, he was one of a party who raided the palace of the King of Oudh. This risky expedition yielded a considerable number of jewels and, of more immediate importance, a 24 pounder gun and a large number of firearms. Carnegie's reputation spread among the rebels to such an extent that it was rumoured that his head had been displayed on a public gateway. Carnegie survived both the mutiny of his native police and the siege itself.[3]

The most notorious massacre of British women and children took place at Cawnpore in 1857. The British Army took a terrible revenge for this and other atrocities. The killing of Indians, guilty and innocent, was a frequent occurrence, and the harshest of 'justice' was legalised by the Legislative Council of India's Act XIV. Brigadier General Neill, on reaching Cawnpore in July 1857, sentenced mutineers to clean up the scene of the massacre. In accordance with Neill's orders to make the task 'as revolting as possible', many were forced to lick the bloodstains from the floor. A Provost Marshal flogged those who held back. Victims were then hanged. 'No doubt', wrote Neill, 'this is strange law, but it suits the occasion well . . .' Other rebels were blown from the muzzles of guns, with a Provost Marshal often presiding over the execution.

The Provost Marshal's responsibilities towards British soldiers were not forgotten. At Cawnpore, troops were threatened with summary execution by the Provost Marshal if they were caught looting. Such threats seem to have had little result at the storming of Delhi in September 1857, which was followed by widespread looting and murder by British troops. Judicial retribution followed the capture of the city, with an APM on one occasion hanging ten Indians simultaneously. Provost Marshals were not the only officials able to exercise such formidable powers of punishment. Attached to the Oudh Field Force was Mr Power, a civilian magistrate. When the troops halted, Power would hold 'a court of summary jurisdiction' and the condemned rebels and mutineers were summarily dispatched. At Mhow on 8 January 1858 some 100 were hanged from the branches of a large pipul tree. Not surprisingly, the magistrate, who was popular with the men, was nicknamed 'Hanging Power'.[4]

* * * *

The newly raised MMP did not serve in the Mutiny, but first saw service in the Egyptian campaign of 1882. Their original commander was Major Broackes, but he was appointed Provost Marshal at base on 11 September 1882, shortly after his arrival in Egypt, and his place was taken by Captain C E Beckett, 3rd Hussars. The MMP's baptism of fire came at the battle of Tel-el-Kebir (13 September 1882). In the aftermath of the battle, the Provost Marshal and the MMP sought to prevent the looting of the camp of the defeated enemy.

In July 1882, the Military Foot Police (MFP) were formed in Cairo from reservists who had experience of service with the Metropolitan Police. The initial strength of the MFP was one sergeant major, 13 sergeants, 17 corporals and 59 privates. The MFP were established as a permanent corps in 1885 and stationed in a number of garrison towns in Britain, with a detachment remaining in Cairo. From 1896 onwards, military police were also posted to Malta. The Provost Marshal doubled as the commandant of both military police corps, which were often referred to collectively as the 'Corps of Military Police' or 'Military Police Corps', even in official documents. Strictly speaking, the Corps of Military Police (CMP) did not come into being until the MMP and MFP were amalgamated in 1926.[5]

Expeditions mounted from India in the latter part of the 19th century were often well equipped with Provost Marshals, although there was a tendency to combine the post with that of Deputy Judge Advocate General. This, of course, gave the individual a formidable array of legal authority. Colonel G F Beville served as Deputy Judge Advocate in the second campaign of the Afghan War of 1879–80 with Roberts' Kandahar Field Force. He also, of necessity, carried out the duties of Provost Marshal during the siege and battle of Kandahar. The 'Principal Provost Marshal' on the staff of the Tirah Field Force of 1897 was Lieutenant Colonel E Balfe. Like Beville, Balfe also acted as DJAG. The 1st and 2nd Division of the Main Column had a captain as Provost Marshal, while each of the divisions' four brigades had also had a Provost Marshal, apparently drawn from the units of the brigade itself. Two subsidary columns and the Rawalpindi Reserve Brigade received Provost Marshals in the same way. A major acted as a Provost Marshal on the lines of communication. The sheer numbers and relatively high rank of senior provost officers deployed in this campaign is noteworthy.[6]

For the most part, late-Victorian Provost Marshals carried out their tasks fairly unobtrusively. However, the activities of one particular Provost Marshal, a keen amateur photographer, in the Burma War of 1885, caused a major political scandal. A journalist reported that Colonel W W Hooper of the Madras Army had photographed executions of Burmese guerrillas. It was alleged that Hooper was so intent on recording the exact moment that bullets struck the condemned men that some minutes might elapse between his first order to the firing party, and the final order to fire. This lurid tale gave the Opposition at home ample ammunition against the government. It eventually emerged that the Provost Marshal had indeed pursued his hobby during executions, but he had not prolongued them for the sake of a better picture. His APM, Lieutenant Burrows, had however extracted information from a Burman at the point of a firing party's guns. These incidents must be set against a background of, in Hooper's case, personal courage and morality, and an ugly war in which guerrillas murdered and mutilated Burmese and British alike.[7]

* * * *

Until the Second World War, military policemen in India did not belong to the CMP but were drawn from soldiers seconded from their units. W H Davies of the York and Lancaster Regiment served as a garrison military policeman in Deolali and Agra between 1897 and 1903. Much of Davies's duties were concerned with the control of prostitution, principally ensuring that the women operated only in certain areas. New arrivals at Agra railway station were scrutinised by the military police, and European women who could produce a certificate from their previous town were given a list of bungalows, rented from particular landlords, where they could ply their trade. These duties were not without their dangers. Anti-prostitution operations sometimes provoked fights, and prostitutes had to be 'persuaded' to attend periodical medical examinations. 'By Jove!' Davies remarked, in his unpublished memoirs, 'this job had to be done tactfully or you soon burnt your fingers'.[8]

By 1914, provost presented a much more modern picture than had been the case 60 years earlier. The Army Act of 1879 had removed the power of provost marshals to inflict summary punishment on wrongdoers, who were subject to military law. In Britain there were three varieties of military policeman: Regimental Police, (RP) Garrison Military Police (GMP) and members of the CMP. The first were simply soldiers chosen to perform police duties on a temporary basis in their unit, and as we have seen garrison police were somewhat similar. Only members of the CMP were entitled to wear the red cap cover, which was supposedly chosen by the wife of Major Broackes, although Tyler cites an Indian military police unit which had worn a red turban during the Mutiny. Standing orders detailing the duties of military policemen were first issued in 1875.

It is clear that appreciation of the importance of their role was growing in the rest of the Army. In 1883 a treatise entitled *The Lines of Communications* was published which argued that military police were essential, especially on the field of battle (possibly reflecting the experience of Tel-el-Kebir the year before), and that another body of military police, quite separate from those deployed with the field army, should be used on the lines of communication. This foreshadowed the pattern that emerged during the First World War, 30 years later. In 1911, a number of senior officers placed on record their belief that trained military police represented far greater value than untrained garrison police. It was reckoned that 82 'attached men' could be replaced by a mere 29 NCOs of the Corps.[9]

Some surviving reports and letters written by the Provost Marshal, Major R J A Terry, gives an insight into the work and lives of military policemen on the eve of the Great War. From 1892 military policemen no longer faced competition from outside the Corps for promotion to sergeant, but it could still take a man 19 years to achieve that rank. Worse, because the Garrison Sergeant Major was responsible for the discipline and interior economy of the military police of a garrison, NCOs of the Corps had little opportunity to show their administrative ability. The Provost Marshal was thus 'compelled to promote chiefly by seniority – an undesirable system in the Military Police Corps'. Messing also presented problems. In some garrisons they had to share their mess facilities, where they rubbed shoulders with NCOs of other units. At Dover, CMP NCOs had a mess of their own, which Terry much preferred: '[if] they do not see too much of the other NC officers of the Garrison, they are more likely to do their duty in a businesslike way without partiality or favour'.

NCOs of the Corps sometimes fell foul of paragraph 477 of King's Regulations, which restricted the ability of the NCO to arrest private soldiers, ordering that he should call upon private soldiers to 'conduct the offender to the guard-room and will himself avoid coming into contact with him'. While this regulation was promulgated from the best of motives (an assault on an NCO would only aggravate the original offence), Terry pointed out that MP generally worked single-handed, often in circumstances where no privates were on hand to offer assistance. Military police in Britain had only the powers of arrest conferred by their rank, therefore they could not arrest wrongdoers of superior rank.

This anomaly was not rectified until the middle of the Second World War.

At the outbreak of the First World War the CMP was a small and efficient body of men consisting of 3 officers and 508 warrant officers, NCOs and men with high *esprit de corps*, who had chosen provost work as a career. Minimum entrance requirements to the Corps were four years service in the Army, an exemplary character, and a recommendation from their Commanding Officer. Men were accepted on six months probation as acting lance corporals (there were no privates in the Corps). The drop-out rate was high, with many men being rejected or requesting to be returned to their units. Not only were the standards of the CMP extremely exacting, but the nature of their duties, patrolling garrisons at home or abroad alone or in small groups, thrust a great deal of responsibility onto relatively junior ranks; this in an army in which initiative was not encouraged. The inevitable unpopularity of military policemen with the rest of the army demanded a high degree of commitment from the men. By comparison with their duties in later years, the role of the military police was a limited one, mainly confined to the enforcement of discipline.[10]

6

The Boer War

When the 19th century drew to a close, the British Army was fighting the forces of the white South African republics of the Orange Free State and the Transvaal. The Second Anglo-Boer War of 1899–1902 began with a series of humiliating British defeats. It ended in a fashion which was to become all too familiar to British soldiers in the second half of the 20th century, as the Army came to terms with the problems of counter-insurgency.

Initially, the Boer forces had a number of advantages over the British. They were fighting, in their eyes, for national survival. They fought in small groups known as 'commandos' which were composed largely of farmers who made excellent mounted infantry and unlike the British, were at home on the South African veldt. Only 20,000 British troops were present in South Africa when the war began, although this figure was to rise to nearly 250,000 by the end of 1900. The early British campaigns were characterised by an ineptitude which, in part, can be blamed on chaotic staff work. Writing in December 1900, Colonel Wolfe Murray complained that he, 'an officer who had never previously set foot in the country and of comparatively junior rank' had been placed in command of the lines of communications in Natal. To make matters worse, his chief staff officer had changed three times in 17 days.[1] As we shall see, confusion also existed over the exact role of the Provost Marshal and the military policeman.

By the time substantial British reinforcements began to reach South Africa at the end of 1899, British garrisons had been surrounded and besieged at Mafeking, Kimberley and Ladysmith. General Sir Redvers Buller's response was to send columns to relieve these garrisons. Each formation had its complement of military police. Eleven MFP had sailed from England with Buller's staff on 18 October, and in late 1899 150 military policemen were deployed with the British forces. They were somewhat thinly spread. Ten MFP were deployed on the lines of communications, and detachments of ten or eleven MMP were attached to each of the three infantry divisions then present in the theatre. Groups of ten MFP were similarly attached to each of the five infantry brigade headquarters. A further brigade, the 5th, had only eight MFP. In addition the Cavalry Division had four MMP and 1 and 2 Cavalry Brigade each had five MMP and 26 MMP respectively. MMP were attached to Army headquarters and staff. Each division had an APM, who wore the red tabs of a staff officer, a practice which apparently caused some confusion.

This large-scale deployment was only achieved by sending virtually the entire CMP to South Africa, and 45 men from outside the Corps had to be drafted in to keep a skeleton military police presence in Aldershot. Later reinforcements, including military policemen from Malta and Egypt, brought the total provost strength up to over 300, which allowed increases in the numbers of military policemen allocated to formations. It was the largest force of military policemen that the British Army had deployed up to that time.[2]

In July 1900, Major Poore, the Provost Marshal in South Africa (described in the press as a 'famous cricketer and Man-at-Arms') complained that 'The functions of the Provost Marshal are very numerous and have never been officially defined'. As a result, '[I] had to gather experience for myself as I went along, and to find out not only what properly came within my province but also how best to deal with it with the men at my disposal'. Poore stated that the Provost Marshal had five major functions: supervision of police work; custody of POW; guarding important places on the march or in towns; granting of permits and passes and the collection of arms. According to a report written in July 1900 by the Deputy Adjutant General, Major W F Kelly, the discipline of British troops in South Africa had been relatively good up to that time. The difficulty of obtaining alcohol was, in Kelly's view, a very important factor in the absence of crime. This reflected the effective work undertaken by the Provost Marshal and his military police, since the 'closing and picketing' of places where the demon drink could be obtained was a provost responsibility. However, it is clear that drunkenness did become a problem later in the war, which in turn led to disciplinary problems.

Soldiers who misbehaved and were awarded punishments by a court martial could be handed over to a provost officer for punishment, or the punishment could be inflicted regimentally. However, no set pattern was followed, with the result that punishment varied greatly in its effectiveness. Provost Marshals could arrest a man but could only request that the man be tried by court martial. In some cases this made a mockery of the disciplinary system. If there was no officer available with the power to convene a court martial, it was not unknown for the prisoner and witnesses to separate and never to be brought together again.

After the British had relieved their besieged garrisons, they advanced into the Boer Republics. In the guerrilla phase of the war, which lasted from the end of 1900 until May 1902, the British found themselves chasing a highly mobile and elusive enemy. General Lord Kitchener (commander in South Africa from November 1900) responded by constructing defended blockhouses linked by wire fences, thus dividing up the veldt into sectors. British units, many of which had been converted into mounted infantry, launched drives to hunt down and destroy the Boer guerrilla bands who were trapped within these 'nets'. The policing of anti-guerrilla columns on the march presented provost with a difficult set of problems.

Looting was perhaps the worst of these. Looting was far more sophisticated than simple rifling of corpses; it was 'a collective activity' which took place far from the field of battle. One contemporary suggested that in the earlier part of the war loot was likely to consist of food and fowls. This problem was exacerbated by Kitchener's tactic of destroying Boer farms, partly to intimidate the guerrillas and partly to deny them food. The main offenders were widely believed to be Colonial troops. Men operating ahead of, and on the flank of the main body also caused problems since it was difficult for their officers to exercise tight supervision. Some officers, complained Poore in 1900, were inclined to 'wink at' looting and even shield their men from justice. Other officers simply abdicated their responsibility for controlling looting, considering it 'entirely the business of the Provost Marshal'. For all the efforts of provost officers, they had little impact on the problem because it would have needed a 'whole army of provosts' to eradicate looting.

Looting was often linked to the problem of straggling. As columns advanced, large numbers of men, including those with sick horses, drifted to the rear of the column. Hundreds of men from many different units might congregate around the transport wagons. On occasions, transport officers found these men impossible to control and looting resulted. Sometimes an officer would be made responsible for keeping stragglers in order, but such efforts were rarely successful, since he might have a column four miles in length to patrol. During the guerrilla stage of the war, small mobile columns operated, which made the prevention of looting even more difficult.

The Provost Marshal was also responsible for keeping POW in custody until they were sent down to base, and this proved to be one of his major duties. Frequently, his job was made more difficult by line officers who sent a prisoner back with no instructions as to whether he was to be detained, or sworn to neutrality and released. Another duty was the collection of arms from POW. As the British forces moved across Boer territory, some burghers were allowed to remain in their homes if they swore an oath and surrendered their weapons. Often, on these occasions, the Provost Marshal had to take a difficult decision, for a surrendered

Boer had 'only to take up his rifle and bandolier to become a combatant'. If such people lived beyond the protective reach of the army, they could be forced to go back on commando by Boer 'Bitter Enders'.[3]

One aspect of the British campaign which cannot be ignored is the concentration camps. Unlike Nazi death camps, the purpose of the camps of the Boer War was to concentrate Boer families into guarded camps to cut off the guerrillas from their sources of supply and to place further pressure on hostile Boers. Conditions in the camps were bad, which led to a high death toll from disease and malnutrition, but this was in large part the result of administrative incompetence. Conditions improved somewhat when their administration passed from military to civilian control. Although the concentration camps do not seem to have been a provost responsibility, because of the habit of giving provost officers duties which lay outside their province, it is possible that some may have served as concentration camp commandants. Certainly, one APM arranged for milk from impounded cattle to be delivered to a camp at Klerksdorp.[4]

When British troops first entered a town, it was the Provost Marshal's duty to seize and mount guards on key buildings such as the telegraph office and gaol, as well as detaining leading citizens. In these duties he had to work closely with the Intelligence Department, who would often provide relevant information. The Director of Military Intelligence issued orders that 'Every assistance should be given to the Provost Marshal in carrying out the instructions as to clearing the country' although it appears that Provost Marshals were apt to annex Intelligence personnel for other duties, for the DMI goes on to say that 'the herding of cattle is *not* an intelligence duty'. Major H F Coleridge, Loyal Regiment (North Lancashire) was in fact awarded the DSO while serving in a dual role as APM and Intelligence Officer. This was probably the first such award to a provost officer. Provost tasks included the maintenance of order in newly captured towns until a police force was organised, issuing various types of pass, and traffic control. All sorts of other duties came the way of the Provost Marshal and the CMP. Major Coleridge was once ordered to collect 'all forage, cut chaff etc' from around Klerksdorp. Anticipating problems with the Boer population, Coleridge was informed that 'It is essential that your intentions should be kept as secret as possible to the last moment, and the work then thoroughly carried out'.[5]

The Boer War was the first major test of the provost branch in a modern, large scale, sustained conflict. Many lessons emerged, most of which had been forgotten by the time of the First World War. There were never enough military police, and untrained men drafted in from other units were an unsatisfactory substitute for the genuine article.

Military policemen and Provost Marshals were frequently misused. At one extreme, a military policeman acted as General Buller's orderly; at the other, the APM at Capetown acted as a camp commandant, drawing rations, forage and other supplies, while his opposite number at Pretoria 'became an office man entirely and performed the duties of head of the local police, to the detriment . . . of his more legitimate duties'. These were tasks which someone had to do, but they did not lie within the province of the Provost Marshal. During the South African conflict, both the Adjutant General's Department and Major Poore recommended that the duties of the Provost Marshal should be more clearly defined. Unfortunately, the outbreak of the next major war demonstrated that these wise counsels had not been heeded.[6]

Part Two:
The First World War, 1914–18

Mons to Neuve Chapelle, 1914–15

Corps orders for 31 July 1914 reflected the routine of peace-time soldiering. The commanding officer announced his intention of inspecting the barracks at 1100 hours on the following day. A request was made for members of the Corps bicycle club to pay their subscriptions. Three probationers arrived from the Essex Regiment, the Buffs, and the Royal Garrison Artillery. Within a week, Britain had declared war on Germany, and was preparing to send an army to fight in Western Europe for the first time since Waterloo. The scenes at the depot at Stanhope Lines, Aldershot in August 1914 were similar to those being enacted at regimental depots all over the country. Reservists poured in, needing to be fed, equipped, and deficiencies in their uniforms and equipment repaired.

Five days after the declaration of war on 4 August, the British Expeditionary Force (BEF) of one cavalry and four infantry divisions began to embark for France. The move to the continent had been a considerable triumph for British staff work. 1800 trains had been used over a period of five days, and the CMP played an important role in the process of moving the BEF to its positions in France. MFP were sent to the channel ports such as Southampton where they helped to ensure the smooth embarkation of the force. The exclusion of civilians from the dock area, apart from enhancing security, also prevented tearful farewells.

At this time Captain A G Ruttledge, one sergeant and six other members of the MFP left Southampton for France. (Ruttledge had been appointed APM on the Lines of Communication). They were the first of many MFP (who were mainly used for rear area duties) to be deployed behind the lines. It has been said that the percentage growth rate of the CMP was greater than that of the army as a whole. It would be wrong to view this simply as a response to an increase in disciplinary problems. By 1918 the BEF had evolved from a relatively small, uncomplicated body into 'the largest and most complex single organisation created by the British nation up to that time'. Provost was one of a host of bodies with highly specialised roles that developed. The forward areas became a mass of trenches, roads, headquarters and administrative units amongst which were sprinkled a liberal profusion of billets, estaminets and brothels, located in the battered remnants of towns and villages. All presented a wide range of tasks and responsibilities for the military police. In addition, it was necessary to police the Lines of Communication and in the Base areas, a web of dumps, workshops, transit camps and hospitals served by a network of roads and railways and numerous ports. It calls for little imagination to realise how complex the role of the military police had become.[1]

On 23 August II Corps came face to face with German First Army at Mons. The British won a defensive victory but were forced to retire, as the neighbouring French formation had fallen back. The 'Retreat from Mons' had begun. A second defensive action was fought at Le Cateau three days later. The retreat ended on 6 September, when the BEF turned and advanced towards the Marne. At the beginning of the war, the BEF's divisions had an establishment of an APM and 25 MMP, with a further six MMP attached to I and II Corps. In addition, French gendarmes under the control of an officer were attached to some divisions. At this stage, the role of military policemen in the field had not been properly defined. It was the Crimea and South Africa all over again. There was no manual which laid down provost duties, reflecting the fact that the provost requirements of an expeditionary force had not been considered in the years leading up to the war. This was extremely unfortunate. Most of the APMs appointed in August 1914 had no previous experience of provost work, and had to pick up the job as they went along. A problem that constantly reoccurred was that staff officers often did not understand the role of the military police. Redcaps were much in demand as orderlies and APMs frequently found themselves responsible for finding guards and security patrols for formation headquarters.

Military policeman needed to exercise tact when dealing with senior officers. After a skirmish near I Corps HQ at Landrecies on 26 August, one military policeman wisely refrained from interfering when a colonel emptied a revolver down a street which contained nothing more threatening than officers' horses. The military policeman explained that the colonel was 'very excited and it may ease him'. Some staff officers simply refused to believe that the APM served a useful purpose at all. Major-General Snow, the commander of 4th Division, ordered his GSO1 to send on a dangerous reconnaissance an officer he considered expendable. The officer chosen, naturally enough, was the APM.

Captain H S Rogers of the King's Shropshire Light Infantry was one of these officers 'who suddenly found themselves saddled with the strange and almost unknown appointment of Assistant Provost Marshal', in his case, of 6th Division. Rogers, who ended the war as Provost Marshal, BEF, and later became the Provost Marshal in the War Office, left an account of his experiences. The 6th Division did not arrive in France until 9 September 1914, when it fought in the later stages of the Battle of the Marne; but his account of the duties of the military police on the march can stand as representative of this period. One of Rogers's problems was that on the march to the Marne, the 6th Division was

> going forward into an unknown area with an unknown destination . . . one didn't know where one was going, as the General Staff might expect to get orders to divert at any moment. The length of an Infantry Division [on the march] was fourteen miles. It was my practice on these marches to remain behind until all the headquarters had cleared the village. Together with several MPs the place was searched for absentees. We left when we had cleared up the situation.
>
> The distribution of our personnel was as follows:- Two [MP] in front of a Brigade and three in the rear. With [the] Headquarters of a Division there were usually three in front some way ahead to ensure a clear road. There were three in the rear and the remaining six were split amongst the Artillery. The duties varied according to the circumstances; MMP were warned that they had to be ready to cope with any situation, but ordinarily those in front of Divisions and Brigades were responsible for a non-check march – to clear the roads. When near the destination to ride forward with the Staff Officer responsible for billeting, to put up sign boards. The MPs in the rear had a much more difficult task. They were continually riding forward to check some fault or to give some help. They were responsible for the collection of all stragglers.
>
> After one of our marches a Brigade Major came up to me and said that he thought that I ought to be continually riding up and down the column. I pointed out to him that I always did ride up the column, but as it was fourteen miles in length, by the time I got to the head it was time I went on to the billeting area and saw to things there.

The strain of the Retreat from Mons placed a very heavy burden on the slender resources of the CMP. The discipline of the BEF never collapsed entirely, but as early as the second day of the Retreat, the APM of the 5th Division recorded that 'March discipline was bad' and he had charged 'many men with entering cafes and drinking while on march'. On 3 September, several cases of looting and robbery, and one of attempted rape were recorded. Earlier men had been charged for entering cafes on the line of march and stealing fruit. The handful of men of the MMP made a significant contribution to the maintenance of discipline. The distressing duty of clearing the roads of French and Belgian refugees often fell to provost. As the retreating troops neared villages on the route of march, the APM and MMP rode ahead to warn the inhabitants. Estaminets were watched, to ensure that alcohol did not add to the troubles of the retreating troops.

In the confusion of the Retreat, many men became separated from their units, and it was often the military police who had the responsibility of rounding up weary men and propelling them in the right direction. Some men simply sank to the ground through sheer exhaustion, too tired to care whether they lived or died. Handing out emergency rations, or leading men in drill, or even singing, was often found to be sufficient to motivate exhausted men; occasionally, the MMP had to resort to the threat of force. The small size of the provost force limited their usefulness, but the efforts of the MMP probably saved many hundreds of exhausted men for the BEF.[2]

As we have seen, the military police of the BEF had no clearly defined battlefield role in August 1914. At the end of that year, GHQ found it necessary to issue guidance on provost duties, based on the experience of the 5th Division. These instructions amounted to a mere 14 paragraphs, of which only one referred to duties on the line of march, and none gave any indication that the CMP might be of use on the battlefield.[3] This is strange, because the MMP of the 5th Division had played an active role at the Battle of Le Cateau on 26 August 1914. The APM was positioned on the edge of Reumont, a village to the rear of the battlefield, to regulate traffic moving down the main road to Maretz. The MMP were being used to collect stragglers, organise them into sections and platoons, and dispatch them back to their units. At about 1400 hours, the APM sent 200 stragglers forward into Reumont itself, only to see a large number of troops falling back through the village. The 5th Division had been under very heavy pressure as the Germans forced back the units on their flanks. Men had begun to leave the front line, the decision having been made to withdraw. The APM rode forward to find Sir Charles Fergusson, the Divisional commander, who was watching the battle from the roof of a large house in Reumont. The APM asked for help with traffic control, for he recognised that it was essential to keep the line of retreat from becoming blocked with men, vehicles and guns. He worked for the rest of the afternoon at this task, before riding with two other staff officers to find an area where the retreating division could rally. Open ground south of the village of Estrees was chosen. The MMP then worked until 0100 hours on the morning of 27 August, diverting men and vehicles off the road to their bivouacs at Estrees, which had been organised by the brigades.

These interventions were important. Although the APM of II Corps believed that no soldiers had wilfully shirked, the 5th Division's retirement was disorderly. However, as a prominent historian of the battle has noted, 'there was no irremediable disorder, no panic'. Part of the credit for this can be awarded to the CMP. Without their work it is doubtful whether the 5th Division's retreat could have been as smooth as it was.[4]

A grim side to provost work emerged in the autumn of 1914. A 19 year old private deserted from the 1/Royal West Kents (5th Division) and was later arrested by French gendarmes. He was tried by a British Field General Court Martial (FGCM) on the day of his arrest, 6 September. Two days later, the acting APM, Captain Monteith of the Bedfords, told the soldier that he was to be shot. 45 minutes later, the private had been executed. From the earliest days of the war, it had become obvious that modern weaponry had made warfare more dangerous and more stressful than ever before. Psychiatric casulaties were nothing new, but they occurred on an unprecedented scale on the Western Front. The West Kent private, it was alleged, said at his FGCM 'I have had enough of it. I want to get out'.

Under these conditions, an effective military police force became more necessary than ever to prevent men from obeying their natural instincts and running from the danger. Today, psychologists recognise that few men can survive under intense strain indefinitely. However, for much of the war High Command clung to a policy of executing deserters *pour encourager les autres*, although in fact only about 10 per cent of death sentences were actually carried out. It was the military policeman who manned the straggler post that acted as a barrier between the killing zone and the rear area; it was the military policeman who apprehended the deserter; it was the APM who oversaw the execution. The CMP helped to enforce this policy, but they did not initiate it.[5]

The German retreat on the Marne was followed by a confused period of manoeuvre. After the Marne, the BEF was moved from the Aisne to the Ypres area in Belgium, where the last spasm of the war of movement spluttered out in the second week in November 1914. The Allies and the Germans had fought each other to a standstill, and a more or less continuous line of trenches snaked across Belgium and eastern France remaining substantially unchanged until March 1918. The Battle of the Aisne, in October 1914, was the first occasion in which provost were deployed on a large scale, albeit on an *ad hoc* basis, to round up battle stragglers. On this occasion the straggler problem was a relatively minor one.[6] The story was very different during the First Battle of Ypres in October–November 1914.

'First Ypres' pushed the men of the BEF to the very limits of their endurance. The BEF fought the Germans to a standstill and was all but destroyed in the process. The stragglers posts of the CMP suddenly assumed a greater significance than ever before. Understandably enough, men seized upon any excuse to leave the front line. The commander of I Corps noted in his diary on 4 December 1914 that 'we have to take special precautions during a battle to post police, to prevent more unwounded men than are necessary from accompanying a wounded man back from the firing line!' The last major action of First Ypres provided a further example of the usefulness of having a line of military police at the forward edge of the battle area. On 11 November, a division of the Prussian Guard attacked along the Menin Road and broke clean through three weary and understrength battalions. At this moment of crisis, it was the proverbial line of 'cooks and bottlewashers' that saved the situation. Among the forces that were hastily assembled to drive the Germans back were a field company of Royal Engineers and parties of infantrymen – and a group commanded by Captain Graham of the 2nd Battalion, the Welsh Regiment, APM of 1st Division. Graham's party consisted of both military police and stragglers, and he was awarded the DSO for his part in pushing the enemy back and stabilising the line. This was one of the first occasions on which straggler posts had been called upon to serve the function of a last-ditch fighting reserve, but it was not, by any means, to be the last.[7]

Before moving on to examine later battles in which the CMP was involved, it is appropriate to examine the use of straggler posts a little more closely. The primary task of a line of straggler posts was to act as a barrier to men attempting to leave the front line. One APM wrote in 1918 that they were placed so as to make it 'practically impossible for soldiers to stray out of the front line system without coming into contact with these posts'. It would be wrong to see them simply as a way of ensuring that reluctant warriors remained in the killing zone; 'In many cases soldiers lose their way accidentally and are put on the proper course by these posts'. A post-war report went so far as to recommend that the terms 'Battle Stop' and 'Collecting Post' be used rather than 'Straggler Post', as the latter was 'one of often undeserving reproach to a soldier, frequently only anxious to discover his unit'. A Battle Stop was defined as the forward Straggler Post, which was located just behind the front line. Collecting Posts, as the name would suggest, were the positions where stragglers intercepted by the Battle Stops were sent, ready to be returned to their units. From First Ypres onwards, it was the usual practice for an APM (who was responsible for the organisation of Straggler Posts) to place one military police NCO in command of each Battle Stop, and to allocate two or three to each Collecting Post. Under their orders would be placed three or four soldiers drawn from other units (often regimental policemen), which were found by brigades. Thus members of the CMP were usually significantly outnumbered by draftees on the straggler post lines.[8]

Given the ferocious reputation of the Redcaps, it is interesting to find that one of the functions of the Straggler Post was to re-equip and refresh stragglers, a policy reminiscent of modern ideas about the treatment of battleshock. Food, water, gas masks and field dressings were held at police posts. Field Ambulances were found to be useful sources for rifles and helmets, which had been discarded by wounded men. Whenever possible, Collecting Posts were supplied with hot tea. To take a typical example of their role, in May 1918 we find a retreating gunner wandering into a Straggler Post consisting of several lorries and tents. He was given food and a hot drink and told to wait until the military police could find the whereabouts of his battery.[9] It is important to realise that an essential function of Straggler Posts was to help restore order to the inevitable chaos of the battlefield; they were not simply a means of enforcing military discipline. As we shall see, military police were to play an increasingly important role on the battlefield from early 1915 onwards.

Straggler Posts also proved themselves useful in a number of secondary roles. Being conveniently situated in the rear of the trenches, military policemen on Straggler Post duties were well placed to guide parties going forward towards their units, and to direct traffic. Walking wounded could be directed to the nearest dressing station and POW and their escorts could be put on the right road to the nearest cage. One of the greatest assets of the military policeman in these circumstances was his local knowledge. He was expected to be able to tell Royal Engineer units how far forward their wagons and limbers could move, and to know which positions or parts of a road were dangerous; whether they were liable to be shelled, or exposed to sniper fire. Sometimes, mainly as a result of the fluid conditions prevalent in 1914 and 1918, Battle Stops served as what was described as 'civilian stopping posts'. When the fighting spilled over into inhabited areas military policemen had the unwelcome duty of clearing the roads of civilian traffic.[10]

The first independent British offensive of the war begun at Neuve Chapelle on 10 March 1915. The preparations for this battle were thorough and included the first properly organised system of Straggler Posts the BEF had seen. Haig's First Army was to make the attack, on a frontage of 2,000 yards. Once the town had been seized, the British were to push on to take Aubers Ridge, a mile and a half away. First Army issued instructions that traffic circuits were to be organised, and traffic posts were to be set up by IV Corps and the Indian Corps, and by the newly arrived Canadian Division. These were also to have the function of blocking the path of inquisitive civilians who might have wanted to move into the battle zone, and of preventing stragglers from moving out of it. In addition to the CMP, IV Corps deployed 40 French Gendarmes and two troops of the South Irish Horse on traffic control and Straggler Post duties.

Haig and the First Army staff radiated confidence that the Neuve Chapelle offensive was going to be a success. Accordingly, it was anticipated that the major role of the Straggler Posts would be to collect, process and distribute captured Germans, not straggling British. Three days before the battle began, First Army issued instructions for the guidance of APMs on how to deal with POW. This document is worth examining at some length, for it provided a blueprint for the treatment of POW that was to be adhered to for the remainder of the war. Three key principles were identified. First, POW were to be evacuated from the battlefield as soon as possible. Secondly, escorts drawn from the infantry were to be relieved at the first opportunity, to allow them to get on with their primary task of fighting the enemy. In practice, many escorts were changed at the lines of Straggler Posts. It was recommended that the escort should number between 15 and 20 per cent of the number of prisoners. Above all, the Instructions emphasised that POW were to be handed over to the General Staff for interrogation as a matter of priority. Prisoners were a prime source of intelligence. Since the trench raid specifically aimed at seizing prisoners was in its infancy, it is not surprising that the intelligence-starved First Army General Staff stressed that APMs were to 'assist in every way' to ensure that POW reached the hands of the General Staff with all possible speed.

The Straggler Post represented the first level of control exercised by the Army over POW. Military policemen manning these posts had to ensure that prisoners were not denuded of personal effects by their captors, and that any documentation was forwarded to the proper authorities. They were also responsible for passing on wounded prisoners who were unable to march to a Field Ambulance. The APM also had a strict code of instructions to follow. Divisional APMs had to send prisoners on to Corps HQ, and keep meticulous records of all enemy captives that passed through their hands. The main burden fell onto the shoulders of the APM at Corps HQ, who as well as ensuring that prisoners were searched in the presence of an officer, had to make arrangements for their custody, accommodation and feeding, and provide fresh troops to relieve the initial escort. He also had to arrange with the Railhead Commandant for POW to be transported to the various headquarters, as well as apprising the Provost Marshals at GHQ and First Army of all details. Clearly, the military authorities placed a high premium on receiving prisoners for interrogation as soon as possible after capture – with good reason, for the sooner they were examined, the more likely they were to 'spill the beans'. Later in the war, the processing of POW was further refined by the appointment of 'Intelligence Police' (see page 82) to interview captives near the front line.

In the event, Neuve Chapelle proved to be the first of many battles in which the BEF learned the difficulty of converting an initial tactical success into a breakthrough. As anticipated, the numbers of British troops handled by the Straggler Posts was minimal, but they did have to handle significant numbers of POW. First Army captured 1687 German prisoners in the three days of the battle, including 30 officers. The arrangements for coping with this influx worked smoothly. The prisoners taken by IV Corps were initially accommodated on two barges moored on the canal at Merville, guarded by the 'Corps Infantry Detachment'. They were escorted on part of their journey by men of the Inland Water Detachment. In later years, the CMP clearly recognised that Neuve Chapelle represented a turning point in the fortunes of the Corps. This action demonstrated beyond all doubt that the military policeman had a vital role on the modern battlefield. In the words of a post-war report 'the question of the necessity of Straggler Posts was settled and further events proved how necessary they are'.[11]

8

Second Ypres and Loos, 1915

At about 1700 hours on 22 April 1915, German units advanced behind a cloud of chlorine gas through a four mile breach in the Allied lines created by the rout of two French divisions near Ypres. A major disaster was avoided because of a number of factors, including the failure of the Germans to exploit their success and the stubborness of some of the defenders. Another, hitherto overlooked, reason was the prompt and decisive action of a British Assistant Provost Marshal.

The town of Poperinge, which lies a few miles behind Ypres, was the Forward Base for the salient, and also the headquarters of the APM of V Corps, Major G M H Stirling. On the day of the attack, Stirling received garbled acounts of the happenings in the salient, from which he gathered that the French had suffered a reverse. Even more alarmingly, Stirling became aware that a large number of refugees and soldiers were streaming back from Boesinghe, towards Poperinge. Poperinge was a frontline town, packed with troops, wagons, guns, horses, and all the impedimenta of trench warfare. It does not take much imagination to realise the catastrophic confusion that would be created had a panicking mob been permitted to enter Poperinge unhindered.

Stirling took prompt action. He deployed strong picquets along the roads leading into the town, thus preventing the crowd from spilling into Poperinge itself. Having gained control of the roads, Stirling was in a position to bring order to the chaos. He used British troops to march French stragglers to pre-arranged camps, and billeted civilian refugees in the churches overnight. On the following day, Stirling arranged for the refugees to be evacuated by rail to Hazebrouck. This action by APM V Corps at Second Ypres is a fine example of the importance of having a disciplined body of military police behind the front line to restore order to confusion, to halt and reorganise retreating troops, and ultimately to return them to their units. Without Major Stirling's foresight and very effective actions the roads which passed through Poperinge leading up to the Salient might have been swamped by French stragglers and refugees, starving the defenders of reinforcements at a vital moment in the battle.[1]

In September 1915, Haig's First Army once again took the offensive, this time amidst the pit villages and slag-heaps of the Loos area. According to the plan, once the crust of the German defences had been broken, the 21st and 24th Divisions of XI Corps would be committed to exploit the breach. The problem with this plan was that Sir John French, the Commander-in-Chief, was holding XI Corps under his own control, 16 miles behind the front line. It was to arrive in the immediate rear of the battlefield only on the actual day of the assault. Thus, two inexperienced 'Kitchener' divisions, which had only recently arrived in France, were condemned to a punishing approach march to be carried out over a period of three nights. It was the responsibility of First Army's APM, Major E R Fitzpatrick, to ensure that the roads were clear so that XI Corps would be at the right place at the right time. It was to prove the greatest test of military police traffic control to date.

The resources at Fitzpatrick's disposal were limited, although he was able to deploy A Squadron of 5th Dragoon Guards, and some divisional troops such as the Cyclist Battalion of the 24th Division. Fitzpatrick's plan was to establish 'control points' at crossroads and road junctions on the Beuvry-Annequin road, on the Beuvry-Sailly Labourse-Noyelles-Philosophe road, and on the Noeux-Les-Mines roads. At the most important positions were stationed the APMs of the 1st, 7th, 9th and 15th Divisions and XI Corps, while their counterparts of I and IV Corps patrolled the main roads in motor cars.[2]

The initial British attack made some progress at the cost of heavy casualties. Sergeant Major H Smyth MMP was a horrified witness of the results of the attack. 'Ye Gods' he wrote in his diary for 25 September,

> have seen the sight of Vermelles and the poor unfortunate wounded, hundreds and hundreds of . . . [them, one] was nearly a goner from loss of blood . . . I was not sorry to leave the place not hardly a house standing, the fighting of the French for that place must have been terrific.[3]

The 21st and 24th Divisions, tardily released to Haig by French, found their routes congested. They arrived on the battlefield exhausted, too late to attack that day, and the opportunity to exploit the early success passed, never to return.

Haig and his supporters subsequently claimed that the late arrival of the reserves at Loos was due to their belated release by French and their poor march discipline, while French and GHQ blamed poor staff work which had created congestion within First Army's rear areas. In a letter to French, Haig flatly denied that an 'unavoidable delay' had occurred in First Army's rear areas on 25 September. The APM's report to GHQ, based on the evidence of officers and men on traffic duty that day, supports Haig's argument. Fitzpatrick claimed that at noon there was 'No other traffic' on the 21st Division's road. Likewise, at 1530 hours 'The

roads were clear of traffic'. He also stated that the progress of 64 Brigade
was assisted by holding up all other traffic at Noeux-Les-Mines. One
officer on traffic duty at this town stated that 'the only interference with
the march of the infantry through the town was due to motor ambulances
being pushed through the column to go to the dressing station'. Similarly,
on the 24th Division's route it was claimed that the total time lost because
of blockages along the route was a mere 45 minutes.

How can these claims be reconciled with the Official Historian's
damning verdict that traffic control at Loos was reminiscent of an attempt
'to push the Lord Mayor's procession through the streets of London
without clearing the route and holding up the traffic'?[4] Haig saw the
reserves controversy as a heaven-sent opportunity to replace French.
Haking, the commander of XI Corps and a protege of Haig's, having
initially blamed congestion in First Army's area for the slow progress of
his Corps, altered his story three weeks later and laid the blame on poor
march discipline, proffering a series of feeble excuses in order to explain
his earlier mistake. It is possible that Fitzpatrick, whose report was
submitted on 12 November, a day later than Haking's recantation, also
came under pressure from Haig. It is likely that Fitzpatrick's report was
substantially true. The roads were very likely clear at the times he stated,
and he admitted that there were some examples of poor traffic control.
However, the major problems appear to have occurred during the previous night. The Staff Captain of the 64 Brigade 'spent the whole night
[of 24/25 September] trying to get the battalions through a mass of traffic
that was absolutely uncontrolled', his brigade having been held up for
one and a half hours at Bruary railway crossing. The frequent disruptions
to the march caused large gaps to open in the columns, which had to be
closed by halting the leading columns – which wasted yet more time. This
gruelling night march made the men tired and hungry, factors which
contributed to the ragged march discipline on the following day.

Mistakes were also made in the policing of the rear areas. An over-
enthusiastic military policeman halted the 72 Brigade for five minutes at
Bethune because the Brigade Commander did not have the correct pass
to enter the area. Similarly, a military policeman caused serious delay to
the 62 Brigade at Noeux-Les-Mines, by ordering the Brigade to change
into an open formation at a level crossing, which was normal practice in
trench warfare, but wholly inappropriate in the circumstances.[5] However,
as several (non-provost) sources make clear, the major cause of delay to
the reserves was not the occasional over-zealous military policeman or
incompetent APM but bad staff work. The 24th Division, in ignorance
of normal procedures, established Ammunition Refilling Points on a
traffic circuit. Worse, the routes were badly designed by the Q Branches

of First Army and XI Corps. Moving up the road to Mazingarbe, the 21st Division was faced with 'seven cross and entering streams of traffic' and five level crossings. This exacerbated GHQ's military unsound decision to insert an inexperienced corps into the area of another two corps. In 1920 a member of the Operations Staff of GHQ admitted that the failure to ensure adequate traffic control was 'a bad oversight on my part'.[6]

XI Corps belatedly attacked on 26 September. The assault was an utter failure. The demoralised remnants of the 21st and 24th Divisions fell back through the advanced British positions until they reached the straggler posts, where most were halted and then dispatched to the Corps Collecting Post. From there they were reorganised, and marched in bodies back to their battalions. In order to cope with the large numbers of men drifting in from the battlefield, the first stragglers were retained at the Battle Stops. There they found themselves enrolled as temporary military policemen, and were used to man additional posts set up to control the floods of stragglers.

The Battle of Loos was one of the few occasions before March 1918 when Straggler Posts had to cope with large numbers of British soldiers in retreat. The flat terrain at Loos had caused Straggler Posts to be positioned in front of the villages of Philosophe and Vermelles, which provided virtually the only cover in the landscape. Stragglers were not going to be allowed to skulk in the semi-ruined buildings of the villages. Forward positions gave the military police manning the Straggler Post a number of other advantages. Because the ground allowed excellent observation over the battlefield, retrograde movements could be spotted at an early stage, which gave time for reinforcements to be brought up and for the military police to prepare themselves to deal with numbers of stragglers. The Straggler Posts of IV Corps were pushed up to within 800 yards of the line, with the main post being located in Le Routoire Farm. Those of the 7th Division were situated 'at the end of every communication trench'.

Exposed positions so close to the trenches were vulnerable to artillery and long-range machine gun fire but the decision of APM IV Corps to place his men well forward was vindicated by the success of the military police in controlling stragglers. A neighbouring corps did not fare so well. Its posts were placed further back, but this only delayed the moment when the military police were able to re-impose the grip of discipline on the disordered and frightened men. Other problems resulted from neglecting to situate Straggler Posts as far forward as possible. In the words of a post-war report 'the further back stragglers get, the longer is the journey to rejoin their units'.

The Battle of Loos brought about the birth of modern traffic control in the British Army. The high level of success in traffic control in campaigns since Loos can be attributed in large part to the CMP learning from their mistakes on 25 September 1915. As a Guards officer was to write after the First World War, 'I have always understood that the afterwards excellent system of traffic control was evolved as a result of the lessons of that day'.[7]

9

Battles of Attrition, 1916–17

On 1 July 1916, Britain committed her army, the largest she had ever raised, to the battle on the Somme. This army, consisting mainly of wartime volunteers, suffered 57,000 casualties on that disastrous day, and the Somme rapidly evolved into an attritional struggle which lasted until November.

Provost arrangements were included in the plans issued before the offensive. VIII Corps attacked on 1 July around Beaumont Hamel and Serre and suffered 13,500 casualties, yet the Provost Officer of the 4th Division saw only one straggler;

> an extremely small Seaforth Highlander named Doig who came in with seven German Prisoners taken by his brigade ... [and after] some refreshment at the Divisional Collecting Station nearby started off to rejoin his Unit again, though he did not believe that any of the Seaforths were left alive, for so many had fallen during their first advance.

Private Doig's gloom was well justified. The 4th Division sustained 4,692 casualties on 1 July 1916.

The lack of stragglers did not mean that Straggler Posts were redundant. They were used for traffic control, and a large number of walking wounded passed through them on their way to the Field Ambulances. By 1916 most soldiers were aware of the existence of Straggler Posts. Some men attempted to pass through the CMP's cordon and reach safety by claiming that they were carrying important messages to headquarters in the rear. However, military policemen would only let through men who had some form of identification. Men lacking such credentials were, as a provost officer drily commented, 'returned to their units for a chit and did not often reappear again'.[1]

The 4th Division was not unusual in having few stragglers. The 7th Division, who suffered losses of 3,410 in capturing Mametz on 1 July reported that only 'four or five men were arrested for straggling' during the whole of July, and expressed satisfaction with the placing of Straggler Posts. Similarly, the 30th Division's military police had handled only seven stragglers on 1 July. The Straggler Posts of this division, like their counterparts in the 4th Division, spent most of their time dealing with the walking wounded and prisoners of war. The 30th Division and its neighbouring formation, the 18th Division, were unique in succeeding in taking all their objectives on 1 July. The 30th Division's Straggler Posts processed 12 enemy officer prisoners and 489 other ranks. On this occasion, the MMP threw themselves into their work with the wounded with an enthusiasm which did them credit but got them into trouble. They were reported to XIII Corps for diverting lorries from other work to ferry wounded soldiers back from the line, and it was decided that only empty lorries returning from the front were to be used for this purpose.

As the summer of 1916 wore on, the British Army struggled to gain possession of a series of woods, hills and other tactical features. The Germans defended doggedly. When the battle was halted in November, the British had captured a narrow band of land, some seven miles deep, at the cost of 420,000 casualties. Yet the morale of the BEF continued to hold, and little straggling occurred. ' . . . with the exception of one or two large parties which had to be stopped', recalled the compiler of the post-war report on straggler posts, 'the behaviour of the troops was exceedingly good'. During the fighting of 23 July, the 30th, 35th and 3rd Divisions established a joint Collecting Centre where it was intended that POW and stragglers would be taken, although in the event the Centre was not much used. The policy of placing the Straggler Posts just behind the lines, which had proved so successful at Loos, was repeated. Another lesson learned from Loos was the inadvisability of giving reserve divisions long approach marches. All these factors helped to keep straggling to a minimum, but the most important factor was the resilience and amazingly high morale of the British infantryman.[2]

By 1916, the front, support and reserve trenches were connected by a maze of lateral communication trenches, and these labyrinths needed to be policed. The primary purpose was to ensure that the routes along which men and supplies had to pass were clear. Struggling along a trench fully laden was difficult at the best of times; if one had to contend with two streams of traffic the problems were greatly multiplied. Thus a layer of military policemen was deployed in front of the main Straggler Posts. This task was usually given to Corps cavalry, cyclists and regimental police. The 30th Division seems to have had a highly developed system of trench policing. On 16 June 1916, the GOC ordered that the main communication trenches were to be policed by a detachment of the Northumberland Hussars, apparently under the control of the Divisional APM. No men would be allowed to pass along these main arteries 'in the wrong direction under any pretext whatever'. The Northumberland Hussars were supplemented by a platoon of cyclists, who were to be used for traffic control. Strict regulations were also applied to forward areas, with brigades being made responsible for policing their own sectors. During the battle, the 'Brigade and Commn. (sic) Trench police', as they were described, were given the secondary role of turning back stragglers. As we have seen, the 30th Division's forward provost arrangements worked well under the stress of battle.[3]

As a staff officer of the 23rd Division commented, it was essential for the Q [administrative] staff to liaise closely with the APM to ensure that the traffic on essential supply roads was properly controlled. In July 1916, the 18th Division had 15 yeomanry and 25 MMP trained in provost duties, in addition to 50 cyclists under two officers, and an officer and 20 men of the Northumberland Hussars sent from Corps. 37 yeomen and MMP were used on traffic control. The cyclists were split into two parties, each under an officer, one to guard and escort POW and the other to man static traffic control posts and straggler posts. At the request of the French, three MMP were sent to the village of Suzanne. Divisional provost assumed responsibility for four and a half miles of road from Bray to Carnoy on 23 June. Traffic control in this sector was relatively sophisticated. The traffic scheme included diversionary tracks, roadside bays and a breakdown lorry for the clearance of wrecked vehicles. On one occasion, the breakdown lorry removed a wagon in the midst of a bombardment of tear gas shells, which not surprisingly caused the breakdown gang considerable annoyance. The majority of traffic was moved during the hours of darkness. From 6–7 July, 34 guns, 175 limbers and 300 wagons were counted on the road going east, most traffic returning later. Intermingling with the motor traffic were horse-drawn vehicles and the columns of marching infantry – an everpresent feature of any road near the front.[4]

One of the most controversial aspects of provost work on the Western Front was the use of 'Battle Police'. Various claims have been made about the use of military police to threaten, or to actually shoot, men who refused to go 'over the top'.[5] However, the terms 'military police', 'police' and 'Redcap' tended to be used very loosely. Infantrymen rarely bothered to distinguish CMP from regimental policemen or other men acting in a provost role. The official provost regulations stated that regimental policemen were most suitable for manning straggler posts. Genuine Redcaps, that is members of the CMP, were usually husbanded as a precious resource and used to man rearward straggler posts and for traffic control. For the attack on Flers-Courcelette on 15 September 1916, 122 Brigade (41st Division) ordered 'Regimental Police Posts' to be established as Battle Stops in the trenches. Thus the military policeman, the villain of popular mythology, would in all probability not have been a 'Redcap' at all. The posting of battle police, who can be defined as provost troops operating in a coercive role in the trenches, as distinct from military police manning the line of straggler posts, does not seem to have been a universal practice. Regimental police were often used in this role. During Third Ypres in 1917, the 3rd Australian Division were using their regimental policemen in this way. Since battle police were also used to guide the walking wounded and POW towards the rear, it would appear that their role was not simply coercive.[6]

The execution of men for cowardice and desertion was intended to act as a deterrent to others. Details of death sentences were published in Routine Orders and regularly read out on parade. For men to be summarily shot in a trench, out of the sight of the majority of their fellows would not only have been illegal but would also have defeated the purpose of providing an example to would-be fainthearts. Clearly, some summary executions did take place, but it seems that the drastic decision to shoot one's own men was taken only under extreme pressure by harassed officers or NCOs attempting to stem a rout. In spite of the claims of some writers, usually drawing on the claims of one, atypical, 'fire-eating' commander, the author has uncovered no evidence that this practice was officially sanctioned on the Western Front. Indeed, when in May 1918, in a time of extreme crisis on the Aisne, the commander of the 19th Division asked to be allowed 'to confirm, and have carried out, any death sentence which might be inflicted on a straggler and which I might think it necessary to have carried out in order to make an example' the request was turned down by GHQ.[7] In short, the idea that brutal Redcaps were deployed by cynical generals to force the 'Poor Bloody Infantry' into action at the point of a revolver is a misleading caricature of the truth.

On 9 April 1917, the BEF began a major offensive around Arras. An elaborate series of tunnels had been bored under Vimy Ridge which allowed men and material to reach the front line trenches free from shellfire. Effective traffic control in the tunnels was, as the Corps Scheme of Operations stressed, vital especially for the evacuation of wounded. Above ground, provost arrangements reflected the experience of the Somme. The 2nd Canadian Division made their brigades responsible for providing 'Trench Police' for traffic control, while the Corps Cyclists under the APM manned Battle Straggler Posts at the exits of the communication trenches. The dramatic advances made by the BEF on the first day, which included the seizure of Vimy Ridge by the Canadian Corps, could not be sustained, and the Arras campaign settled down into another attritional battle. During the fight for Bullecourt, the advantage of having straggler posts well forward was demonstrated. 70 men, led by a corporal, fell back 'saying it was too much for them and they could not go on'. They were halted at a Battle Stop, which was within 700 yards of the trenches. An officer persuaded the men to return to their unit, and the corporal was arrested.[8]

A major French offensive had been launched in conjunction with the BEF's Arras attack. It ended with large numbers of French divisions in a state of mutiny. Henceforth, the main burden of the Allied effort passed to the British, who on 7 June carried out a masterly limited offensive against Messines Ridge, south of Ypres. IX Corps deployed 44 men, including nine MMP, on straggler post duties, but these men had to deal with only 19 stragglers. In all, 14 officers and 433 ORs were 'exclusively employed' by IX Corps on traffic control. Each divisional area was divided into two sections, each under the command of a Traffic Control officer. Section HQs were linked by telephone with each other, and with the Divisional APM. Each divisional area was allocated half a troop of a Traffic Control squadron, and 10–12 MMP divided among the two sections for traffic patrols. Section commanders were allocated two cyclists, and APMs three, for keeping communications open. In addition, each traffic control post had at least one cycle, and nearly all had been provided with splinterproof shelters. A reserve stock of signs was kept at Traffic Section HQ. Haig, who clearly recognised the importance of traffic control, fought a rearguard action against the War Office in August 1917 to retain adequate numbers of traffic control personnel.

These traffic control arrangements worked reasonably well, but some problems were encountered. Some lorry drivers lost their convoys and were discovered to lack the faintest idea of where they were supposed to be heading; the map reference of their destination was chalked on the lorry. Traffic Control Units, which had been formed as recently as April 1917 from personnel of the Corps Cavalry unit, proved particularly useful*, although some troops were inclined to pay them little heed. IX Corps APM's refrain in June 1917 was one which has been repeated by successive provost officers down the years: too few men, too little equipment.[9]

The BEF's next offensive was the Third Battle of Ypres, popularly known as 'Passchendaele' from its last phase. It began on 31 July with an unsuccessful attempt to achieve a breakthrough, but soon developed into another attritional slogging match, which lasted into November. Although the British came close to inflicting a serious defeat on the Germans, the name 'Passchendaele' has come to symbolise all the horrors of attritional trench warfare. The men of the CMP were, of course, spared the worst horrors of the battle, but the main Straggler Collecting

---

*The Provost Marshal BEF ruled that traffic control personnel could carry out non-traffic related provost work at the discretion of the APM. (WO 154/8, 14 May 1917).

Station, located at Ypres Prison, was a far from healthy spot. On arrival, a number of stragglers asked to be sent straight back to the trenches, 'where more effective cover was obtainable' from shelling. On 31 July, about 800 prisoners of war were rounded up by the straggler posts on the outskirts of the town. It seems that they had been captured, brought back and simply abandoned by their escorts. The orders issued by the APM, Ypres three weeks before the offensive indicates that soldiers manning 'Battle-Posts' were expected to differentiate between men on the one hand who had been gassed, were severely wounded, or were suffering from shellshock, who were to be sent to an Advanced Dressing Station, and 'ordinary' stragglers on the other. Posts also had a traffic control role, being tasked to see 'that cross roads are kept clear for reinforcing troops' and essential vehicles. In general, military policemen were to keep a check on men leaving the battle area, and to prevent civilians from gaining access to it.

According to Lance Corporal G W Durham, a Canadian cyclist who served as a military policeman, Ypres was 'not a dull town to do duty in' even in the absence of a major battle. 90,000 British soldiers died in the Ypres Salient, where the Germans held the high ground on three sides. Durham manned a traffic post on the southern flank of the Salient. There he saw little movement during the day, because of the risk of attracting German artillery fire:

> but at night Piccadilly isnt in it. We are swamped, but have to string out wagons and guns to one per 50 yds and troops in file at one platoon per hundred. We get lots of cursing, but are usually obeyed as Shrapnel Corner has a reputation of its own, and lives up to it as it rarely fails to take its toll every night . . . Odd men . . . are stopped and questioned very closely and do not get out of our hands till we are quite satisfied.
>
> It is curious to see the difference between those going in . . . and those coming out. Those going in are grim . . . and seldom speak, whereas those outward bound are cursing the delays . . . we have to challenge all comers in and get the password. We try to save the halts by meeting the leader outside and going along beside them. No one who has not gone through it knows how heartbreaking even a short stop is to men coming out of the line under such conditions, and stopping the head of a column in the [Lille] gate means that the tail is stopped at Shrapnel Corner.
>
> About dawn there is no one going either way except the odd ambulance, silent as a cat, creeping in with the night's casualties.[10]

Durham was writing of a relatively quiet time. In the autumn of 1917 the situation was far worse.

A typical divisional provost layout during the fighting for Broodseinde in October 1917 had three straggler posts, each commanded by an MMP NCO with four regimental police drawn from the infantry. There was a six strong straggler post co-located with the walking wounded post at Vlamertighe, to the west of Ypres. Some MMP were also used at the main collecting post at Ypres Prison. Five traffic control posts, manned 24 hours a day, were located along the Ypres-Broodseinde road and the parallel Ypres-Menin road. One post was situated at the infamous Hellfire Corner. Each was manned by four men. In August, some Corps traffic control responsibility had been transferred to the division, and the divisional APM had received additional personnel. In addition there were four 'Flying Traffic Patrols' mounted on cycles. For the operations of 4–12 October a total of 16 officers and 249 men were at the disposal of the divisional APM – a number which was not far short of the strength of an infantry battalion on active service.[11]

10

Retreat and Victory:
The Western Front, 1918

The growth in the importance of straggler control during the Great War can be gauged by comparing the thin Redcapped line of 1914 with the sophisticated provost arrangements behind Fifth Army's front in March 1918. At the beginning of the 1918 German Spring Offensive, Fifth Army had three separate lines of Straggler Posts organised by Division, Corps and Army, each comprising forward Battle Stops and rearward Collecting Stations, and mobile patrols of MMP visited the posts at regular intervals. Behind these three lines were to be found both Traffic Control units and more military police patrols with orders to round up stragglers. Further back were to be found two lines of 'Examination Posts' manned, from early 1916, by two garrison infantry battalions of the King's Own Yorkshire Light Infantry and the Oxford and Buckinghamshire Light Infantry. Examination Posts were permanently deployed, while the full range of Straggler Posts was only put into place immediately before action.[1]

Apart from serving as a general deterrent to would-be absconders, the importance of Straggler Posts varied with the circumstances of battle and the morale of the Army at any given time. To give an example, a total of 67 men were arrested as absentees from their units at the Examination Posts manned by an infantry company between 1 April 1917 and 11 November 1918. As one might have expected, there is some correlation between the numbers of arrests and dates of battles. The two worst months coincide with the battles of Arras and Amiens, although records for the vital March–April 1918 period are incomplete. Generally speaking, straggler posts were most used during unsuccessful, defensive operations. The German offensive of March 1918 – a battle in which the BEF was on the defensive and which was, in its early stages at least, unsuccessful – gave the system of straggler posts its greatest test of the war.[2]

On 21 March 1918, the Germans mounted a massive assault on British Fifth and Third Armies on the Somme. Using new infantry and artillery tactics, the attackers punched through the British lines and reopened mobile warfare. The experience of British XIX Corps gives a very good idea of the traumas and problems of provost work on what became to be known as the March Retreat. This corps, commanded by Sir H E Watts, held a frontage of about 13,000 yards on 21 March, and was sandwiched between Congreve's VII Corps to the north and Maxse's XVIII to the south. Two divisions, the 66th and 24th, were stationed in the front line. Their Divisional Straggler Posts were established on a line between 3,500 yards and about 6,000 yards from the front line. This was much further back than had been the practice in earlier battles, and is probably a reflection of the fact that defence-in-depth had been adopted by this stage: the Divisional Straggler Posts ran down the centre of the Battle Zone. Four Collecting Posts had been established, the furthest lying about 6,500 yards behind the front line.

The Straggler Posts were manned at about 0600 hours, and by 1100 hours the enemy were attacking the Battle Zone, having cleared the obstacle of the Forward Zone. This brought chaos to the British line. At about 1230 hours Captain Westmacott, APM 24th Division, arrived at Vermand, where a Straggler Post and a Collecting Post were both situated. He found a body of wounded and unwounded men from the artillery and infantry, many without their weapons, streaming back, with the Straggler Posts doing little to prevent them crossing the bridge. Westmacott held up the crowd with his revolver, helped by a sergeant of the North Staffords. They then armed 40 men with rifles taken from the wounded, and pressed them into service as temporary military policemen. As soon as Westmacott's back was turned, these men ran away. He then took more drastic action, pressing another 20 stragglers into service and, arming his military policemen with rifles (normally, they only carried revolvers), he ordered them to shoot the 'draftees' should they attempt to abscond. Westmacott and his military policemen then served under the commander of the 13th Battalion the Middlesex Regiment until the APM was ordered to retire, having been lightly wounded by shellfire. This was the pattern for the remainder of the retreat: men manning Straggler Posts fell back to fresh positions, resuming their duties until the approach of the enemy forced them to retire. They shared most of the discomforts and many of the experiences of the infantry. On 27 March, the situation was so critical that Westmacott was forced to send most of his police to fight in the front line. On other occasions, he was able to distribute much needed rations to the infantry. From Westmacott's reports, it is clear that the military policemen were not always as efficient as they might have been. On 1 April, he was extremely critical of the leniency of Corps Straggler Posts, and he used his divisional police to conduct a house-to-house search in rear villages to flush out stragglers, even though this should have been a Corps responsibility. Nevertheless, it is clear that XIX Corps provost generally

coped well with the enormous responsibilities placed upon them by the
retreat.[3]

One soldier who, clearly, was no admirer of the Redcaps, recognised
the importance of military police during the March Retreat:

> I remember seeing several men leaving their trench after being shelled and
> retiring through the cavalry, to be intercepted by military police and sent back
> at revolver point. [Military policemen] on the battlefield – It seemed incredi-
> ble! But when one considers that many of these soldiers had been taken, in
> this desperate situation, from the administrative side of the Army, and had
> never before seen "a shot fired in anger", it is not so hard to understand.[4]

At least 25,000 stragglers were collected, fed, and put back into the
fighting by Straggler Posts. This estimate almost certainly understates the
numbers involved. XIX Corps alone collected 11,214 stragglers (of which
four were officers), or roughly 50 per cent of the grand total from 21
March to 5 April. Third Army too suffered a number of stragglers: for
example, IX Corps collected 200 stragglers in the first two days of the
battle. Where possible, stragglers were directed back to their original
units, but sometimes they were formed into composite battalions along
with men newly returned from leave, and other assorted odds and ends.
Traffic control was not neglected. An infantry private recalled the stream
of traffic behind the front on 22 March: 'Amidst it all, at intervals on his
stationary horse sat the military policeman, directing and regulating that
long procession'.

The effectiveness of the provost arrangements is indicated by the fact
that, according to DPM Fifth Army's report, less than 100 men from the
fighting arms got back as far as Fifth Army HQ, and the DPM was able
to state categorically that 'At no time during the retreat was the straggler
position out of hand, and much larger numbers could have been dealt
with'. In effect, the CMP maintained a tight cordon behind the Fifth and
Third Armies, a cordon which undoubtedly helped materially to maintain
cohesion during the retreat. The problems which would have resulted if
the BEF had not developed relatively sophisticated provost arrangements
by 1918 is demonstrated by the situation which arose when the Guards
Division neglected to deploy Straggler Posts, claiming that they did not
need them. As a provost officer of the 31st Division, a neighbouring
formation, commented,

> This sounds very well in theory but in practice it broke the continuity of the
> Straggler Post lines, and allowed the leakage of a number of troops from
> various divisions. Had these stragglers been directed to their units by posts
> well up behind the front lines, they would have never have wandered as far
> back as they . . . did.

In fact, relatively few Guardsmen were separated from their units, but those that did wandered a considerable distance before reaching military policemen who could direct them back to their unit. The absence of straggler posts behind the Guards Division allowed stragglers from neighbouring formations to get much farther back than would otherwise have been possible, and valuable time was wasted in getting troops, fit and ready to fight, back into the firing line.

It has often been said that the Fifth Army were routed in March 1918. It is thus interesting to find that provost sources are unanimous in agreeing that the majority of stragglers in the early stages of the battle were not drawn from front line units. DPM Fifth Army wrote in his after-action report that 'During the first two days fighting Battle stragglers from the firing lines were few and were chiefly those who were genuinely lost and anxious to rejoin their Units'. Many stragglers were non-combatants who had been working on British defensive positions. A special collecting post specifically for labour personnel had to be established at Villers Bretonneux. 'From a spectacular point of view', wrote DPM Fifth Army, 'anyone might well think these men were stragglers from the firing lines but the Deputy Provost Marshal and other Officers well qualified to speak maintained that stragglers from the fighting troops did not get away . . .'

The real problems of straggling amongst frontline troops did not set in until they had become exhausted by days of retreat. At the beginning of the battle, most stragglers were simply directed back to their units, and went back often unescorted: 'they didn't get to the Army back areas, nor did they attempt to after receiving their directions'. Later, stragglers had to be rested and fed at straggler posts and taken (sometimes by bus) to central collecting points, that for artillery stragglers being at Villers Bretonneux, for instance, and then distributed to various units. Statistical evidence reveals that the largest daily number of stragglers collected by the Straggler Posts of the 8th, 24th, 50th, 66th and 16th Division were collected in the period 27–30 March 1918, thus at least six days after the battle began, when weariness was setting in. The evidence is probably incomplete, but figures from the 24th Division certainly support the contention that the worst period for stragglers came towards the end of March. 40 Stragglers were collected on 21 March; 15 on 22 March, 10 on 23, 6 on 24, 50 on 27, and 227 on 30 March.[5]

The German offensives petered out by the early summer of 1918. The Allies then seized the initiative. On 18 July, the French struck on the Marne, and on 8 August, the BEF attacked at Amiens. These twin blows began a series of offensives in which the Allies advanced steadily, taking large numbers of guns and prisoners and severely damaging German morale. The crushing victories, achieved mainly by British and Dominion divisions, forced the Germans to sue for peace in November.

In the second half of 1918 the CMP, like the rest of the BEF, had to learn how to conduct offensive operations under the conditions of open warfare. The stunning success of the tanks at the beginning of the Battle of Cambrai (20 November 1917) had shown the BEF that surprise could still be achieved. On this occasion, tanks were brought up to their start-lines at night, without lights. This was an operation which called for the most careful traffic control: a tank crewman recalled 'road police, and wagons on the move, and the passing shadow of troops, and an occasional surreptitious electric torch'.[6] The Battle of Amiens of 8 August 1918 was preceded by a similarly effective traffic control scheme. The tightest possible security was maintained, heavily policed by the provost. Once again, the Germans were taken completely by surprise. The preliminary administrative orders issued by Rawlinson's Fourth Army, which included details of traffic control, encapsulated, in the words of the British Official Historian, 'the experience of four years of war'. The Traffic Control Officer of 31st Division (nicknamed 'Sleuth', an indication of the close relationship between traffic control and provost work) was told on his first morning in the post 'If you catch Haig breaking traffic regulations, run him in!'[7] In contrast to 1914, traffic control was taken very seriously indeed four years later.

The experience of the mobile operations in the spring of 1918 had been invaluable in weaning the CMP from the habits of trench warfare, but now new problems arose, such as the policing of newly captured towns. At the end of September, the Allies broke through the formidable Hindenburg Line and on 8 October, the Germans evacuated Cambrai. Preparations had been made for the policing of the town as early as 5 September – an indication of how 'provost-minded' the British Army had become by 1918. Captain Strachan was notified that when Cambrai fell he would become APM of Cambrai, operating under the Town Commandant. Strachan was allocated a clerk, 30 NCOs of the MFP under a CSM, and 18 cyclists under a sergeant for traffic control. In addition, 30 French gendarmes would be sent from Third Army. All patrols in the town were to be undertaken jointly by the CMP and the French.

Three major problems faced Strachan and his military police. Firstly, Cambrai was an important communications centre, through which much traffic would inevitably pass. Secondly, the town was a tempting target for looters. Thirdly, the town was being heavily shelled. Accordingly, on 9 October, Cambrai was placed out of bounds to troops not on duty in the town. On the same day, traffic posts were set up to the north and south of the town, which from 1700 hours onwards, was being heavily shelled. Strachan put in an urgent request for extra MFP and Traffic Control men, and, to place temptation out of harm's way, commenced to seal up houses. (He requested 400 long strips marked 'OUT OF BOUNDS BY ORDER' to paste on doors of sealed houses). Over the next few days the shelling diminished but both the traffic flow and the number of military sightseers increased. A few cases of looting were reported; an artilleryman was caught trying to take away a table and three pillows, while a random search revealed a piano stool and two chairs concealed on lorries. To add to Strachan's problems, French and American dignitaries visited Cambrai in the week following its liberation, while 323 civilian refugees arrived from Avesnes on 17 October. However, ensuring the flow of the traffic was Strachan's prime concern, with fresh routes and diversions being brought into operation throughout the week.[8]

During the Allied offensives of autumn 1918, Battle Straggler Posts continued to be deployed, although the number of stragglers picked up seems to have been quite small. On 21 August the 42nd, 37th, 2nd, Guards and New Zealand Divisions launched an ultimately successful offensive towards Bapaume. Judging from the one APM's War Diary that has survived, the MMP were mainly used to collect and escort enemy POW. The Straggler Posts of the New Zealand Division, which had been established on the day preceding the attacks on a line from Fonquevillers to Sailly-au-Bois, received just 13 stragglers, of which only three were New Zealanders. During the period from 1 September to 21 September, when the Australian Corps was spearheading the Allied advance, the 3rd Australian Division reported that no stragglers had been received.[9]

Apart from the ever present problem of traffic control, the biggest headache for the CMP in the 'Advance to Victory' was the vast numbers of enemy prisoners that were taken. On 4 November, the military police of the 24th Division handled 326 German prisoners drawn from 22 separate units. Over 186,000 German other ranks and nearly 5,000 officers were captured between 6 August and 11 November 1918. Never before in the war had such large numbers been taken in such a short period. During 1917 comprehensive instructions for dealing with enemy POW had been issued. An order from GHQ had stated 'The Provost Staff is the responsible authority for the safe custody and disposal of Prisoners of War from the time the Prisoners are received from the fighting troops until they are handed over at the Railhead or transferred to P. of W. Companies'. Furthermore, POW enclosures were commanded by a provost officer. Searching of prisoners was to be carried out jointly by Provost and Intelligence Police.[10]

Captain E A MacKechinie, APM Arras, recalled the arrival of POW as the result of one British victory:

> They were rather a motley lot, but all the same still with a certain amount of spirit . . . One [officer] . . . seeing a bed that belonged to one of the intelligence Officers, said that it would do for him. For that he got a clump on the face from one of the NCOs. Altogether, that day, nearly four thousand arrived. The following day, the same thing happened, only the men had that look on them that all was up.

A party of 84 POW arrived,

> The guard to that crush being one very undersized Canadian. In several instances prisoners arrived on their own, and it was nothing to find batches of them being driven up to the prison by Frenchmen who had found them wandering about the Town trying to find the place where they had to go, one Frenchman being in front, and another behind with a large knife as a weapon.[11]

10,310 German soldiers were taken prisoner in the last week of the war. On 11 November at 1100 hours, an armistice came into effect. The First World War had ended. In the four years since 1914 the Corps of Military Police had come of age. On 2 April 1918, Haig had handsomely acknowledged the part played by provost in the operations of the previous month in a message of congratulation which ended 'The orderliness which has prevailed behind the front is directly attributable to . . . [provost's] efficiency and devotion'. In his final dispatch, Haig wrote of the importance of traffic control 'In the battle zone, where [provost] frequently had to do duty in exposed positions under heavy fire and suffered severe casualties', and attributed the good relations that existed between the civilian population and British troops in large part to the 'vigilance and zeal' of the military police.[12] Haig, a truly 'provost-minded' commander, spoke no more than the truth. The BEF of August 1914 had foreseen no role for the CMP on the battlefield. By 1918 the CMP had a vital operational role which was understood and appreciated at the highest level.

11

Behind the Lines, 1914–18

The vast and complex infrastructure that developed in France and Belgium to support the BEF provided many roles for provost. Military police first arrived in France in August 1914, and by December of that year, in addition to men attached to field formations, a total of 206 were deployed on the Lines of Communication at Havre, Rouen, Boulogne, Paris, Abbeville and Marseilles. 32 of these men were MMP, 75 MFP, and 99 were men attached from other units. On the eve of the battle of the Somme in 1916, these figures had grown to 50 MMP, 612 MFP, 138 permanently attached men, and 424 temporary attached men, and Calais, Dieppe, Etaples and St Omer had been added to the list of stations. These figures undoubtedly had grown even further by the time of the Armistice, when the Provost Marshal, BEF had a total of approximately 270 officers and 12,000 men under his command. Worldwide, perhaps 25,000 men served in a provost role during the Great War.[1]

Military police were also posted to GHQ, where they were supposed to memorise over 60 different armbands worn by personnel ranging from the Signal Service to Divisional Gas Officers. Provost officers and military police had their own armbands, although interestingly, the most distinctive item of provost apparel, the red cap cover, came under threat in the spring of 1915. The custom of wearing the red cap in base areas originated at Rouen, and MFP at other bases soon followed suit. Although some provost officers were in favour of it, because it made MFP more conspicuous, the Provost Marshal BEF, Colonel V Bunbury, stated that 'this was exactly what he does not want them to be'. The fact that 'Redcap' (or as a variant, 'Cherry Nob') was in use as a universal nickname for military policemen in World War One would seem to suggest that attempts to ban this most familiar item of military headgear were unsuccessful.[2]

Many men engaged on provost work were not, in fact, entitled to wear the red cap. Some units were transferred *en bloc* to provost work, without becoming members of the CMP. Paradoxically, considering the strictly limited opportunities for cavalry on the Western Front, the mobility of the mounted military police made them an extremely desirable asset for patrolling behind the static front. Three parties from the Bedfordshire

Yeomanry were transferred in the autumn of 1914 to serve as the divisional police of 48th Division, while in January 1917 it was reported that 460 men of the Hants Yeomanry were trained in (dismounted) traffic control duties, of which 51 were so employed at any one time. Cyclist units were also much used in this role.[3]

While yeomanry and cyclists had other duties in addition to provost work, some units were transferred permanently to this work, such as the garrison infantry battalions used from early 1916. (See page 70.) From 1916 onwards, substantial numbers of men who had been serving as Garrison Military Police were temporarily transferred to the CMP, and the CMP also received a small number of conscripts. It has been calculated that in 1914 the ratio of military policemen to soldiers stood at, 1:3306. In 1918 the ratio was 1:292. Impressive as these figures are, they exclude the large number of men who were used on provost work but did not wear the badge of the CMP.[4]

Although the CMP expanded to a peak of 151 warrant officers and 13,325 other ranks in 1918, the Corps could boast only three officers actually on its permanent cadre. Other officers were appointed as varying grades of Provost Marshal to command detachments of military police. In October 1918, 175 of these officers were serving in France. The most common variety of APM were those graded as staff captains. An analysis of the provenence of those 64 officers appointed to this position from August 1914 to May 1915 reveals that about a third were appointed from Regular officers who had retired or were on the reserve. If one adds in other categories of reserve officer, one arrives at a figure of approximately 75 per cent of APMs drawn from reserve sources.[5]

The First World War saw something of a leap in social quality of Provost Marshals. R J A Terry, the Provost Marshal in 1914, had ranked as a major. By 1918 there were two brigadier generals who served as Provost Marshals in France and at home respectively. Officers of socially exclusive regiments also served as provost officers, Captain Viscount Powerscourt of the Irish Guards (APM 16th Division) being a case in point. Many provost officers were older men, or had been wounded. During training at Bedford, the APM of the 51st (Highland) Division was the only member of the divisional staff who had trench experience. Captain E B H Cunnington, who served as APM to the 25th and later the 68th Divisions in Britain from 1914 to 1917 (when he finally got to France at the age of 56) had been a voluntary dispatch rider at Tel-el Kebir as far back as 1882. In short, most provost officers were not taken from teeth arm units, but were 'dugouts' or men who, for one reason or another, were no longer fit for front line service, and service as a provost officer allowed them to fulfil a valuable and increasingly socially acceptable role.[6]

One of provost's most visible and least popular roles was the policing of ports, railway stations, and towns frequented by British soldiers. APM Paris was Captain Maurice Brett, and it was said that his father, Lord Esher, did a distinct disservice to his son in arranging this position for him. On arrival in Paris, every frontline soldier said 'a little hymn of hate' against Brett. APMs were also supposed to be models of moral rectitude. One wrote a 'lament of the APM' which began

'Oh! the life of an APM my friends
Begins with sorrow, with sorrow it ends'

and went on to catalogue the fun they were not allowed to have.[7]

Normal disciplinary duties included the interviewing of VD patients by APMs to discover where they had picked up the disease. Estaminets had to be patrolled, crimes investigated, absentees and deserters apprehended. By the end of 1914, a system had evolved whereby absentees were reported to a central body and their descriptions regularly circulated on the Lines of Communication.[8] The tracking of deserters was an unending and frequently dangerous task. Deserters were often desperate men; desertion was an offence punishable by death. An officer, a deserter from 1/Essex, was executed in 1918 for the murder of Sergeant H Collinson MFP. Another victim of trigger-happy deserters was Albert Eddenden, an MFP sergeant from Camberley, Surrey.

In the early evening of 3 October 1918, two MFP NCOs apprehended two soldiers in a brothel in St Omer. Once in the street, one of the men broke away and fired a revolver at Lance Corporal Brennan MFP, wounding him in the foot. The two men later foolishly returned to the brothel, but as they approached the building a door opened and the doorkeeper recognised one of them, and informed Sergeant Eddenden. Eddenden challenged the men, who ran away. Eddenden pursued them, but one of the running figures turned and shot him with a revolver, mortally wounding him. The two men were arrested on 7 October, after firing further shots and robbing a civilian's house. The men, both infantrymen, were sentenced to death, commuted in both cases to 20 years imprisonment.[9]

As in the pre–war era, military policemen and APMs could not inflict punishment on their own authority. Nonetheless, they played an important role in the execution of punishments awarded by courts martial. An APM generally had charge of the prisoner before a death sentence was carried out, and military police escorted the condemned man. An APM usually oversaw the actual execution, reading the sentence, and sometimes giving the sign to fire, although command of the firing party (which was not composed of military policemen) was normally given to another officer. A much more common punishment was Field Punishment No. 1 or 'crucifixion' where a prisoner was tied to a fixed object for a period of time. This was often carried out regimentally, although MFP sometimes were involved in its infliction. An inexperienced military policeman once tied some prisoners so loosely that they were able to slide down the post, where they were discovered squatting on their haunches and talking. A callous sergeant suggested that the novice Redcap should apply his boot to the prisoner's backsides.[10]

Field Punishment (FP) at Etaples base camp – 'a vast concentration of military police to the square yard' as one officer described it – caused considerable unrest long before the celebrated mutiny of September 1917. In May 1916, the Base Commandant held a Court of Enquiry into the administration of the FP compound, which held about 200 men at any one time. The Commandant found that insufficient personal supervision by the APM had resulted in individual NCOs abusing their authority. The APM was replaced in the following month by Captain E Strachan of the 10th Battalion the Lancashire Fusiliers who appears to have been an unpopular, although efficient, officer. A disturbance took place in August 1916, when 60 to 70 men 'refused to go to work and a struggle ensued while they were being tied up'. This incident was rapidly followed by a concession, when Strachan ordered that in future men were to be tied with their hands behind them, rather than stretched out. Australian troops posed particular problems, and the arrival of dominion provost in June 1916 was welcomed by the APM. Much of the fury of the mutineers of September 1917 was directed against the military police and the 'Canaries' (instructors) rather than their officers, and one of the mutineers' first targets was the Field Punishment compound. On Christmas Day 1917 provost were involved in suppressing another mutiny, among 105 Chinese Labour Company.[11]

Relations between Provost and the rest of the Army reached their nadir in the 1914–18 war. Depictions in novels and on the screen have tended to present APMs and Redcaps as evil psychopaths.[12] Two former infantry privates claimed that military police were never to be seen in 'the danger area', and that 'Redcaps were not usually drawn from the civil police; their job was voluntary and few decent men would undertake it if they realised what it implied'. Most modern historians have accepted such statements at face value. In one article, army doctors were described as being regarded during the war as 'little more than Redcaps with stethoscopes'. For Redcap, it would seem, read martinet, sadist and enemy of the ordinary soldier.[13]

Undoubtedly, some military policemen were officious and unpleasant. G S Chaplin, a yeoman who transferred to the MMP, regarded his APM

1 Major Charles Broackes, Provost Marshal 1885–94 (*RMP Museum*)

2   Military Mounted and Foot Police on manoeuvres, Masebury Camp, 1910

3   Military Foot Police, Malta, December, 1913

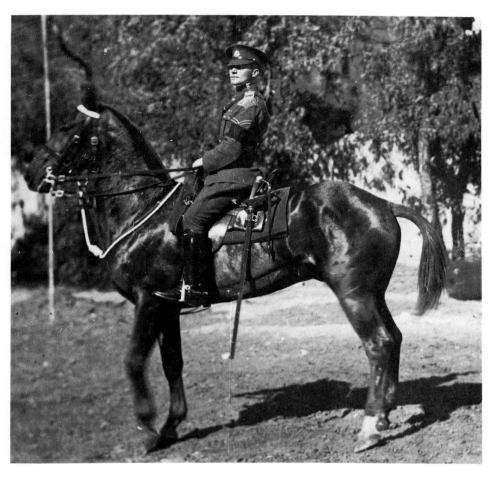

4   Corporal AW Lane MMP, Abbassia Camp, Cairo, 1923

5   Coronation of HM King George VI, 12 May 1937. CMP Depot staff,
Mytchett Hutments, Ash Vale

6   Regimental Sergeant Major FJ Green MFP
Ash Vale Depot, 1921

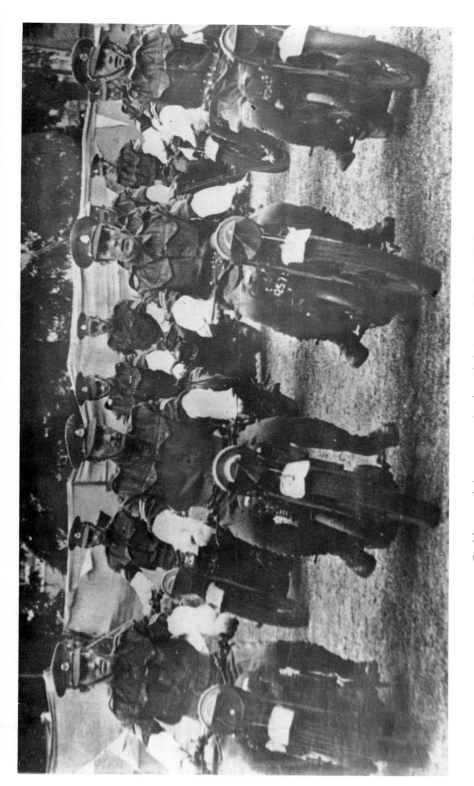

7   Motor cycle instructors going through their paces, Mytchett, 1940

8   Members of a CMP Traffic Control Point comfortably ensconced on the route to Arnhem, 1944 (*Imperial War Musem Neg No BU 4137*)

9   Escorting German prisoners-of-war, 1943 (*Imperial War Musem*)

10   Normandy, July, 1944. Removing German route signs near Aunay-sur-Odon during the
advance to the River Orne (*Imperial War Museum Neg No B8934*)

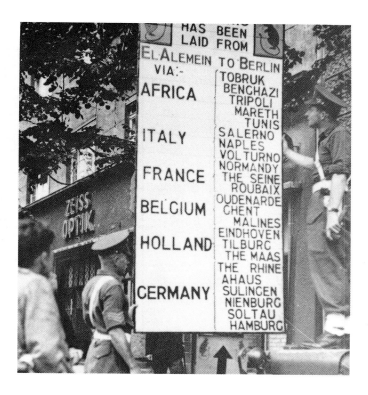

11   Berlin, 1945. Fixing a huge sign recording the divisional axis of
7th Armoured Division (The Desert Rats) from El Alamein to Berlin
(*Imperial War Museum*)

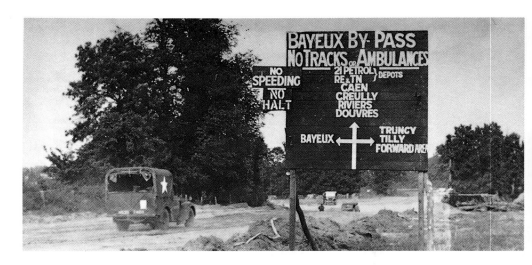

12 Normandy, 1944. On the Bayeux bypass shortly after D-Day (*Imperial War Musem*)

13 CMP search a building on the advance through Italy, 1944 (*Imperial War Musem*)

14 Signing a route for the advancing infantry near Geilenkirchen, 1944 (*Imperial War Museum*)

15   April, 1944. 1st Airborne Division Provost Company at Stubton Hall, near Newark

16 Hamburg, 1945. CMP using a captured German E Boat
for patrol duties on the River Elbe

17 Military Police on mounted duty, Jerusalem, 1947

18   The last mobile patrol in Haifa by the East Palestine Military Police Company, 1948

19   Kure, Japan. British and Indian Military Police, who formed part of the British and
Commonwealth Occupation Force, 1946–52

20 In Tripolitania in the 1950s

21 Cyprus, 1951. During the emergency, RMP dog handlers performed
valuable work on anti-terrorist patrols

22 Korea, 1953. A TCP of 1st Commonwealth Division Provost Unit at Pintail Bridge

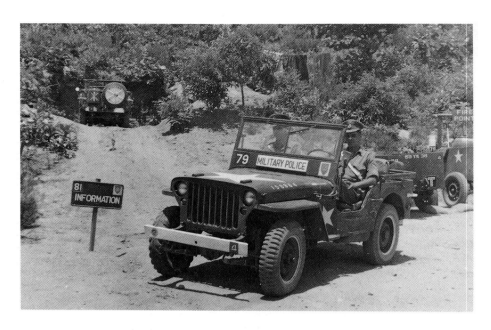

23   An RMP patrol sets out from Headquarters 29 Infantry Brigade in Korea

24   The International Patrol, Vienna, manned by military police from the four occupying powers, was established in August 1945 and remained in being until September 1955

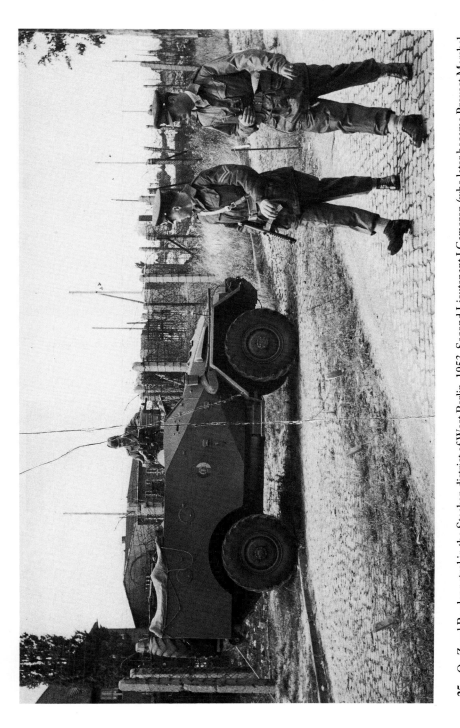

25   On Zonal Border patrol in the Staaken district of West Berlin, 1953. Second Lieutenant I Cameron (who later became Provost Marshal (Army) in 1993) and Corporal E Simpson of 247 (Berlin) Provost Company RMP, keep a wary eye on an East German APC. At that point, the border ran down the centre of the road

26   The effects of a near miss from a 'drainpipe' bomb on the Landrover of an
RMP 'anti-assassin' patrol. Cyprus, 1956

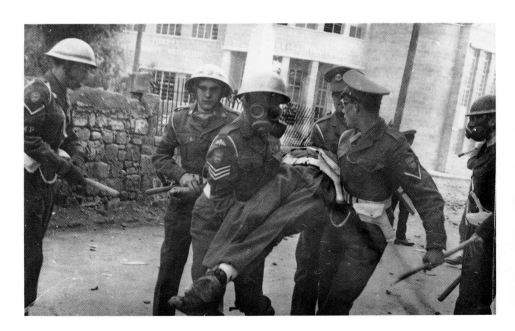

27   Nicosia, 1956. Rescuing an injured person

as over-zealous and described most of his fellow military policemen of the 15th (Scottish) Division as 'a proper shower', but it is noticeable that Chaplin himself claimed to be the only man properly trained in the provost principle that it was often better to warn a man than to put him on a charge. Provost paid the price of rapid expansion: some men became military policemen who would not have been accepted as members of the CMP in peacetime, and who were not trained to CMP standards. It is perhaps significant that while the Etaples Mutiny of September 1917 was sparked off by the shooting of an infantryman by a military policeman, Private H Reeve, he was a camp policeman (a species of garrison policeman) rather than a member of the CMP. Another camp policeman, Private Heeseman, seems to have received little training for his post, being given this job simply because he was too old for trench service in the infantry. It is not surprising that in 1915 an APM claimed that 20 MFP were worth 30 to 35 temporary military policemen attached from other units.[14]

The relationship between an army and its military police is often difficult. The dislike of the working classes for the police was probably simply transferred from civilian to military life. Much of Provost's unpopularity can be explained by their role in enforcing discipline that appeared to many soldiers to be petty and even tyrannical. Although the nature of trench warfare ensured that most infantrymen looked upon the world's population as being divided into two groups (combatants and everyone else) not every military policeman was loathed by the fighting troops. The historian of the 47th (London) Division took the trouble to record the popularity of the division's APMs and the MMP, although he admitted that few other divisions could boast such a harmonious relationship.[15]

From the beginning of the war, military police were used to prevent unauthorised personnel approaching the front line. Journalists were a frequent nuisance, and in November 1914 orders were given to arrest all British civilians who were found east of a line from Calais to Paris without the appropriate pass. The most prominent individual arrested for appearing in the war zone without permission was a Cabinet Minister, F E Smith, (later Lord Birkenhead), who was arrested in January 1916 while on a visit to his close friend Lieutenant Colonel Winston Churchill. Smith was arrested by an APM, and then confined to a bedroom which was guarded by two military policemen.[16]

It is often said that the Special Investigation Branch (SIB) was founded in 1940. However, it is clear that a similar organisation was functioning in the 1914–18 war, which carried out intelligence work in addition to the investigation of crime. Provost work frequently overlapped with that of the Intelligence staff, especially in the early years of the war, partly because of the small size of the fledgling Intelligence Corps and partly because of the absence of a clear definition of provost roles. A slightly ludicrous example of the overlap between the two functions on the home front is provided by the case of a German-born man who was accused of being the leader of a spy ring. The German had allegedly signalled to U-Boats and had predicted the sinking of the *Lusitania*. The APM of the 2nd (Canadian) Division investigated these (unfounded) allegations in concert with Scotland Yard. Provost counter-intelligence work was not confined to Britain. In April 1915, for instance, V Corps MMP arrested a 'spy' just behind the front, who turned out to be nothing more sinister than a deserter from the Royal Garrison Artillery.[17]

On the Western Front, a line of provost Examining Posts controlled entry to the Forward Zone. Military police also co-operated closely with 'Intelligence Police' (IP). These were not provost, but at least in the early stages of the war some seem to have operated under the aegis of APMs. The primary role of IP was to move around the war zone, equipped with passes signed by provost officers, to detect enemy agents and to gather information of use to the military. Intelligence Police did not concern themselves with such provost work as investigating crimes, but they were ordered to give all possible help to provost in the course of their work. As we have seen, IP also co-operated with the military police in the processing of enemy prisoners. IP were also supplemented by military policemen in carrying out work such as checking suspicious characters in the 'Controlled Army Zone', which consisted of the Forward Zone, just behind the front line, and the Middle Zone, where the troops were billeted.[18]

During the Allied advance in the second half of 1918, provost had an important role in the control of civilians in newly liberated areas. Fourth Army orders issued before the Battle of Amiens in August 1918 stressed that APMs of divisions 'must be on the spot at least as soon as the Intelligence' to prevent civilians leaving the area, to arrange for rations to be distributed to civilians, and to organise their evacuation and escorting. Examination of civilians by Intelligence was accorded a high priority, and all military policemen were ordered to 'work closely' with Intelligence counterparts. A line of posts manned by French military police was established to prevent civilians entering the area of the fighting, which was patrolled by both IP and 'Provost Agents'. This role for provost had been envisaged at least as early as 1916.[19]

IP were supplemented by specialist British and French detectives. These divided their time between provost and intelligence work. A spate of thefts at hospitals in Boulogne in the summer of 1915 prompted calls for 'CID' men to be deployed but they were 'fully employed on contra-espionage (*sic*) work'. The fact that the same group of detectives were employed on both intelligence and police work caused some friction between the Intelligence Officer and APM at Boulogne in 1915.[20] A number of Scotland Yard Special Branch men had been sent to France for intelligence work in 1914 and it would be logical to assume that at least some of these men also carried out investigation of crime.[21]

By May 1916, the Provost Marshal was advocating that each Army should be allotted eight detectives, two to be equipped with motor cycles, the rest with bicycles. Later that month, APM Lines of Communication reported that the Provost Marshal hoped to place about 40 detectives at his disposal, which would also report to the APMs of base areas. In June, seven detectives from Liverpool City Police were deployed on the lines of communication. In Britain, plain clothes military policemen were also used for criminal investigations.[22]

Unfortunately, military detectives of the Great War were not always of the highest quality. The two Littlemore brothers, who, with the rank of acting corporal, carried out undercover work at Boulogne, had a mere three years experience of police work and none whatsoever of detective work. Other detectives were transferred from the uniformed MFP, and all had their expenses paid from the melodramatically-named Provost Secret Service Fund. Detectives were used for undercover work at Etaples base camp in August 1916, while Lance Corporal Griffiths investigated the 'doings of officers at Paris Plage', a nearby watering hole. Other detectives were sent on railway journeys through France in an attempt to spot irregularities, while the 63rd (Royal Naval) Division used provost agents to investigate conditions in estaminets in January 1917.[23]

Military policemen continued to carry out intelligence work in the immediate post-war period. A CMP report written just after the war stated that the 'closest relations' were maintained with 'G Intelligence'. Provost obtained much information on 'unrest among troops caused by labour troubles or bolshevists', and in some areas where Intelligence had no representatives 'selected Military Police' were employed as agents. Members of the MFP operated in this role in places as far apart as Brighton and Sheffield. However improbable a British revolution might seem in retrospect, the years immediately following the war were a period when the threat of revolution was taken very seriously indeed.[24]

12

The Great War: Home Front

The strength of the Corps of Military Police on 4 August 1914 stood at three officers and 508 WOs, NCOs and other ranks. On the outbreak of war, 28 probationers were hastily transferred to the Corps and promoted to lance corporal, and mobilisation brought 27 MMP and 56 MFP reservists back to the colours, including one who rejoined in Malta. In addition, the CMP received 177 reservists drawn from cavalry regiments. This raised the grand total to 776. Most of these newly appointed military policemen seem to have given useful service, although eight were sent back to the Eastern Cavalry depot after only 24 or 48 hours service, being euphemistically deemed 'surplus to MMP requirement'. In reality, even in the very first days of the war, the demand for military policemen was outstripping the supply. In September, the officer commanding the hand-ful of military policemen in the French port of St Nazaire reported that they were proving so useful that they were being forced to work very long hours, and he would welcome a reinforcement of two or three times their number. By 2 September the CMP had begun to recruit civilians, tapping the wave of enthusiasm for enlisting in Kitchener's Army. Over 200 men had joined the CMP direct from civilian life by the end of September alone.[1]

The first military policemen began to move to their war stations on 5 August, and all were in position by the 13th of the month. Most military police found themselves attached to the divisions and brigades of the BEF, headquarters, bases or ports of embarkation. Like most other units, the CMP left only a skeleton staff at the depot. In some ways the CMP was more fortunate than the average Kitchener infantry battalion. Many of its recruits were already accustomed to discipline. A number of time-expired old soldiers rejoined the Corps from civil life, and large numbers of civil policemen enlisted, including men from the Manchester, Shef-field, Norfolk, Shropshire, Portsmouth, and Essex forces. The Chief Contable of Essex maintained a close interest in former Essex policemen serving in the forces. Writing in 1917 to Lance Corporal Havers, who had been wounded while serving with the MFP, the Chief Constable noted with regret that '17 constables of this Force have been killed or have died of disease while two have returned for duty. We look forward to the time when we shall see you all back again'.[2]

Nonetheless, in common with many other volunteers for Kitchener's Army in the autumn and winter of 1914, early recruits had to put up with considerable discomfort, as existing facilities were simply inadequate to deal with the large numbers of men. R C Brookes joined the MFP as part of a contingent from Sheffield City Police. On arriving at Stanhope Lines, they had to sleep on the stone floors of empty married quarters. Later, they were moved into barracks, but the living conditions were still far from luxurious:

> It was a bare place, iron bedsteads, straw palliasse and two blankets, never washed, and smelt of stale beer, and sweat. At one end was a fire, and at the other end, a big wooden tub, which served as a chamber pot, it smelt dreadful in hot weather, and at weekends when there had been a lot of drinking, the stench was worse . . . We had one bath, and you had to book it, as it was only heated once a week.

Just as the expansion of the CMP was beginning, the pre-war Provost Marshal, Major Terry rejoined his unit, the Royal Sussex Regiment, with whom he was killed at Loos. He was replaced at Aldershot by a 'dugout', Colonel Darling. On pay day he would address the men:

> It was always the same, 'We are at War, with a great and Mighty Nation and we must always avoid women and wine', which always brought a grunt, or a Raspberry, from the rear rank. Being slightly deaf, he never heard it. He was always mounted when he addressed us, someone once tied a toy balloon to his horse's tail.[3]

The growth of the British Army from a regular force of 250,000 men into a mass army of over two million in a matter of weeks in 1914 created a host of problems which the CMP was ill-equipped to meet. Shortage of barrack accommodation meant that numbers of men equivalent to the combined populations of Leeds and Edinburgh had to be billeted on the civilian population. This was, of course, in a state without a tradition of large scale billeting of troops, in which a mass army was a novelty and in which there was a residual suspicion of soldiers. In addition, the poor conditions in which many of the newly volunteered troops found themselves led to discontent. Add to this the problems of crime which attend the presence of any large group of men in a particular place, and the magnitude of the policing problem which faced the tiny CMP can be appreciated.[4]

The problems of the Provost lay not only in their small numbers, but also in their organisation. APMs were appointed at major training camps, but as in France, their duties were vague and undefined, and they were often given responsibilities that no one else cared to take on. The policing of the army camps and nearby areas rested mainly with regimental and garrison (usually called 'Camp' or 'Town') military police. Later the Garrison Military Police (GMP) were raised. This body (not to be confused with the garrison police mentioned earlier) were paid at CMP rates and had duties analogous to those of the Corps. The usual practice, carried on from the pre-war era, was for patrols of one CMP NCO and one garrison policeman to be sent out. Mounted patrols, normally drawn from yeomanry units, were sent out to patrol country lanes round about army camps.

These arrangements were unsatisfactory. The powers of regimental and garrison police were limited, and the temporary policemen were often unsuitable. The first appearance of one very young garrison policeman on patrol was greeted with hoots of laughter. An officer, on becoming APM at a training camp in 1916, was told that theft was rife but the military police were useless, being old soldiers, 'smart in appearance, but to say the least of it, not very highly educated'. The parent units of temporary military policemen were wont to recall them for medical inspections, musketery practice and the like, and if they were reclassified fit for overseas service, they were rarely returned to police duty. Perhaps even more serious was the fact that, as their name implies, garrison military police were confined to areas where troops were actually stationed. Large industrial centres, where, not unnaturally, military absentees tended to congregate, 'were never visited' by military police of any description.

Many of these problems were remedied by a fundamental reorganisation which took place during 1916. This was inspired by the former DPM, First Army, Brigadier General E R Fitzpatrick who was appointed Provost Marshal, Home Forces on 16 June of that year. The establishment of military policemen was changed in the case of Northern Command from 90 MMP and 115 MFP to 50 and 710 respectively. The numbers of provost officers grew, and their status was improved. Standing Orders and (in September 1918) a 'Manual for Military Police in Great Britain' were published. DPMs of Commands were appointed, and Commands were divided into Areas which were known by letters (Northern Command included A Area, covering Newcastle and Sunderland, and E Area, covering Sheffield and Huddersfield, for instance). An APM was allotted to each area and stationed at the headquarters of the principal formation included in his area. In 1918, the situation was modified further by the appointment of Deputy Assistant Provost Marshals (DAPMs) to formations stationed in a particular area. Previously, divisional APMs had also acted as Area APMs. While this reorganisation was not, initially, popular outside Provost circles, it undoubtedly placed the military policing of Britain on a much sounder footing.[4]

During 1916, except in London District, the GMP was abolished, with the most effective of its men being transferred to the Redcaps. There were also mass transfers of men attached to the CMP in overseas theatres to the CMP proper and in 1917–18 the cumbersome machinery for transferring men in and out of the CMP was overhauled. The position of Dock Police (MFP employed at embarkation ports) was rationalised, although that of Port Police, who were trained by the CMP but then handed over to Intelligence, was not.

The chain of command was clearly laid down, and it was decided that the 'Provost Branch should have nothing to do' with the administration of field punishment or detention barracks in Britain. Unfortunately, the medical standards of the men from whom the CMP were drawn remained low. By the end of the war, all A 1 and most B 1 men who were drafted out, and the remaining men were complimented for the 'plucky way' they carried out their arduous duties. Rather than recruit unsuitable men to make up the numbers, units were often deliberately kept understrength. As some compensation, the training of military policemen improved from 1916 onwards. Courses were run at York and Aldershot, which not only sharpened up the skills of provost NCOs but also created a provost *esprit de corps*. The improvement in training, allied to an increasing emphasis on smartness and drill, meant, one APM believed, that the 'modern Military Policeman was totally unlike his spiritual forebear'.

A newly appointed DPM, arriving at York, the headquarters of Northern Command in December 1916, was greeted by an officer with the words 'I understand that your only experience of Provost work is in France'. On answering in the affirmative, the DPM was told 'Well! You can know nothing about the work in this country as it is all totally different.' The difference lay in the fact that the majority of the provost work at home was concerned with crime and discipline. This was the staple diet of the pre-war CMP writ large. The roles of the CMP in civil defence – enforcing the blackout on military personnel, co-operating with the civil police in cases of civilian panic brought about by air raids, and guarding crashed aircraft – were, until 1917, virtually their only additional 'warlike' duties. The vital experience gained in France of the importance of traffic control and straggler posts was largely ignored. In the words of the DPM 'no machinery existed for directing our efforts away from crime into other directions should the occasion arise', 'the occasion', of course, being a German invasion of Britain. One APM, for example, had been told to report to HQ in the event of a German landing when he would be told what to do. Almost the only role allotted to military police in case of an enemy landing was that of collecting officers and men on leave in the major cities, which was scarcely the most efficient use of provost manpower. Perhaps through overconfidence, perhaps through apathy and inexperience (not one APM in Northern Command had any first hand knowledge of traffic control in France), but most likely through lack of direction from above, the provost lessons learned on the Western Front had not been evaluated and disseminated to units at home.

During 1917 and 1918 this began to change. The appointment of an influential brigadier at GHQ for whom 'traffic control was almost a hobby' was extremely helpful, as was the keenness of DPM Northern Command for spreading the gospel of modern provost work. It was probably the inspired idea of sending UK-based APMs on traffic control courses in France which did most to stimulate interest. The home defence scheme proposed in October 1917 envisaged the use of special constables as traffic control personnel, with the military traffic scheme being grafted onto existing plans for the control of the civilian population. Unfortunately, the enthusiasm displayed by the DPM was not shared by the General Staff, who proved unable to provide rulings on certain basic matters (such as the roads that would be needed for military purposes) until August 1918. In fact, the operational plan for the military police in the event of a German landing in Britain was not finally approved until the week in which the Armistice with Germany was signed.[5]

Alongside the tardy development of an operational role, from mid-1916 MFP in Britain were expanding their normal policing duties. Military policemen were posted to cities which had previously been *terra incognita*. Three MFP NCOs were, for instance, posted to Sheffield in January 1917. Their presence on duty caused 'quite a commotion' in the city, with the local civilians invariably taking the part of any soldier stopped by a Redcap.

Eventually 30 men were stationed in Sheffield. Outlying regions were visited by bicycle-borne travelling patrols, who liaised with the local civil police. Close co-operation with the civil police was found to be absolutely vital. In 1918, Britain was scraping the bottom of the manpower barrel, and provost and civil police raided places of public entertainment to catch draft-dodgers. A raid on a music hall in north London resulted in a number of men hiding behind scenery, in lavatories, and under furniture. The impact of the extension of the role of provost was considerable. In the words of one APM, 'Both soldiers and civilians began to get the "Wind Up". Legs of mutton no longer disappeared in swill tubs. Civilians felt uncomfortable when wearing Army boots . . .'

Harmonious relations with Railway Police and officials were also essential, for railway stations were prime spots to catch absentees. A big city such as Sheffield might have more than 1,000 soldiers arriving by train each day on leave. The large concentrations of Redcaps at main railway stations caused considerable resentment among ordinary soldiers; in August 1918 a party of infantrymen attacked two MFP NCOs and rescued a sergeant who had been arrested. MFP also gave considerable help to Railway Transport Officers and hospital authorities in entraining and detraining troops and convoys of wounded soldiers.

The apprehension of men masquerading as officers was not uncommon, but the majority of police work was unspectacular, dealing with prostitution, absentees, drunkenness, theft, blackmarket activities, and of course, officers and men who were improperly dressed or behaving in an unsoldierly manner. On Armistice night an APM encountered a Highland officer at the Savoy who came into both of the last two categories. In explaining his reasons for overstaying his welcome, the officer complained: 'Mon, I canna move. Some ----- has stolen ma kilt!'[6]

The origins of female provost can be traced back to November 1914 when two members of the newly formed Women Police Volunteers were invited to come to Grantham. A major army camp, Belton Park, had been established, which brought all the attendant problems of prostitution and breaches of public order to the town. The APM looked favourably on the WPV's activities and indeed they soon proved to be extremely useful, the camp commandant writing to tell them that they had dealt with problems involving women in a fashion which would have been impossible for male military police. The success of the WPV and other women's police bodies led to women from the Queen Mary's Auxiliary Army Corps being sent to the school at Bristol which had been set up to train women in policing duties. These QMAAC 'military patrols' can be regarded as the ancestor of ATS and WRAC Provost.[7]

13

The Great War: Secondary Theatres

On 25 April 1915, an Anglo-French force landed on the Gallipoli penin-sula. The seizure of Gallipoli was to be followed by the passage of Allied ships through the Dardanelles *en route* to Constantinople. The seizure of the Turkish capital would, it was believed, knock Turkey out of the war. The Honourable Clive Bigham (later Viscount Mersey), the Provost Marshal, Mediterranean Expeditionary Force (MEF), had a grandstand view of the landing from the deck of the SS *Arcadian*, anchored a mile from the shore. When daylight came he could see the whole coastline: 'scattered groups of men slowly fighting their way over the sand and stones of the beaches, or climbing the lower slopes of the hills'.

However, the *coup de main* failed and the Allies were left holding two precarious toeholds, at Helles on the southern tip of the peninsula, and at Anzac further up on the west coast. In attempting to circumvent the deadlock in Flanders the Allies found themselves fighting an attritional struggle depressingly similar to that on the Western Front.

Initially Bigham was stationed on the island of Tenedos, where with a small force of provost, he prepared to receive Turkish prisoners. MFP were also stationed at the base on the island of Mudros. After three days of idyllic living, Bigham returned to GHQ on *Arcadian*. From there he commuted daily to the Helles beaches where he had a tent as an office. Bigham, who had a mainly administrative role, made a point of liaising regularly with his APMs and the French Provost Marshal. Provost duties on Gallipoli – traffic control, policing of vital points such as wells and bridges, handling of POW and disciplinary work, were similar to those on the Western Front. From 10 May, Bigham lived permanently on W Beach, also known as Lancashire Landing. On one occasion, a shell ripped a coat which was hanging up in his tent. Living in such close proximity to the enemy helped Bigham to appreciate the strain endured by the front line soldier. Returning from the trenches one day, he saw a man deliberately shoot himself in the hand. However, it emerged that the man had witnessed two of his brothers killed next to him the previous night, and so he escaped a court martial. In late May, Bigham was summoned to take up residence with GHQ on the island of Imbros. In late June, he was visited by the novelist Compton Mackenzie, who found that, as befitted an old campaigner, Bigham had made himself comfortable. As in France, provost and intelligence work overlapped. On Imbros, Bigham not only supervised the policing of the island but also investigated alleged cases of spies signalling to the Turks by means of hill-top fires.[1]

As early as 28 April, an ASC officer noticed military policemen forming 'battle posts' just behind the lines at Helles, which also served as useful landmarks. At Anzac Cove, Colonel Bowler, the APM of the Australian and New Zealand Division armed himself with a whistle, which he blew when the shelling grew so intense that it was necessary to get the men under cover. This called for fine judgement and a calm demeanour. A fellow officer compared Bowler's deliberations with a man consulting with the porter of his club whether the rain was heavy enough to warrant calling for a taxi.[2]

The one resounding Allied success of the Gallipoli campaign was the withdrawal. Under the cover of an elaborate deception operation, the northern beaches were evacuated in December 1915. In January 1916, it was the turn of the troops at Helles. Prior to the pull-out, confusion reigned on the beaches, where piles of stores had simply been abandoned. Although the Principal Military Landing Officer, General O'Dowda, had set military police to guard these makeshift dumps, one general overruled him and permitted troops to loot the piles, with the result that soldiers arrived at the evacuation boats loaded with all sorts of useless impedimentia. This was bad for discipline, but even worse was the fact that large numbers of bottles of alcohol had been abandoned, which resulted in some soldiers apearing at the beaches distinctly the worse for wear. O'Dowda sent his military police to smash the bottles. The alcohol fumes given off from the fizzing stream that flowed on to the beach had the wholly unexpected effect of intoxicating the military policemen, many of whom were teetotallers, much to the delight of the officer in command of the bottle-smashing party. On the night of the 8–9 January, military police were among the last troops to be evacuated, along with the party of sappers who had set explosive charges in the abandoned British positions.[3]

* * * *

The British campaign against the Turks in Mesopotamia (modern day Iraq) began in November 1914 when troops dispatched from India were landed at the head of the Persian Gulf. The Force Provost Marshal, Lieutenant Colonel Macmullen, arrived in April 1915. A Base and Lines of Communication provost establishment, distinct from Force Provost, was organised in the same month.

The city of Basra was captured in November 1914 and became the main British base. Advancing inland, the British eventually appeared before Kut-al-Amara on 28 September 1915 when General Townshend defeated a Turkish force. Macmullen entered the city on 30 September with a handful of military police and was given the duties of military governor. The Arabian Nights city of Baghdad now beckoned, and the main body of Townshend's force had already moved on. On 8 November, Macmullen and his military police left Kut to move up the Tigris river on a steamer, arriving in time for the assault on Ctesiphon on 21 November. The attack, mounted against an entrenched Turkish force, was a disaster and Townshend ordered a retreat. A sizeable number of Turkish POW went with the British, guarded by provost.

The British limped back into Kut at the beginning of December, the provost arriving on the 2nd. After disembarking POW from barges, they began clearing the hospitals of sick and wounded prisoners and sent them down the Tigris. The Turks invested Kut on 7 December. Five of the prisoners died *en route* to Basra and four escaped. 'This loss I consider quite unavoidable' noted Macmullen, 'the difficulties in marching this number of prisoners in a retirement with fighting going on, and with dust and darkness prevalent, were considerable'. On 29 April, after a prolonged siege, Townshend surrendered Kut to the Turks.

Townshend's capitulation did not end the campaign. More troops were sent to Mesopotamia. In July 1916 Macmullen died and Major E Percy-Smith assumed the position of 'Principal Provost Marshal'. The provost establishment grew considerably; among other developments, an APM was appointed on the lines of communication to combat pilfering and military police were deployed on the railway. The APM at Saik Saad was Lieutenant Victor McLaglen, remembered by one of his military policemen as a 'real Tough Guy'. McLaglen later became a Hollywood film star, specialising in military roles, and in fact in 1934 he starred in *The Lost Patrol*, a psychological thriller set in the Mesopotamian desert. McLaglen later became APM Baghdad.[4]

* * * *

At the end of 1916, the new commander in the theatre, Sir Stanley Maude, took the offensive and, in the following February, smashed a Turkish force. 3,000 POW were handled by provost during that month; most 'gave no trouble', it was noted, indeed many were 'only too glad to be in our care'. Baghdad was taken, for the 13th time in its history, on 11 March 1917, Percy-Smith entering the same day. In the absence of any military police, 90 infantrymen of 36 Brigade and a troop of cavalry policed the city. Fortunately, in the early days of the occupation there was little trouble between soldiers and civilians. 75 MP arrived in Baghdad on 20 March.

With Townshend avenged and Baghdad captured, the main aims of the campaign had been achieved. Fighting continued, however, and in September 1918, the British won an overwhelming victory at Mosul. The small divisional-sized force of November 1914 had grown to an army of 500,000 men, and the provost contingent had expanded accordingly. Initially, all personnel appear to have been men attached from infantry regiments, but CMP members later arrived. As in other theatres, many temporary military policemen were transferred to the CMP in the course of the campaign. One such was Sydney Blythman of the 5 Wiltshires, who was posted to the Depot Police at Basra in February 1917. The Depot Police were later transferred to the MFP.[5]

The Anglo-Turkish conflict also spilled over into Egypt, one of the original homes of the CMP. In February 1915, a Turkish attack on the Suez Canal was beaten off, and for the rest of the year Egypt was used as the main base for the forces in Gallipoli. Egypt saw its fair share of disturbances during the war years, with Australian troops in particular causing much trouble. In April 1915, Redcaps were called in, unsuccessfully, to quell a serious riot which became known as 'the battle of Wazzir'. British soldiers and native Egyptians also caused provost trouble. The letters of one mounted military policeman give a taste of the incidents. In May 1915 he recorded a round-up of trouble makers in Cairo which resulted in the incarceration of 80 soldiers, although the MMP did not escape without injuries. Early in the following year he was involved in a pitched battle with Egyptians in Cario.[6]

In 1916, the British forces, swollen by troops evacuated from Gallipoli, advanced into Sinai against the Turks. The two armies met at Romani on 4 August. The British won a defensive victory, taking 4,000 prisoners, which were escorted to Cairo by 50 MMP.[7] The key to Palestine was the city of Gaza. This was attacked, unsuccessfully, in March and April 1917. After 'Second Gaza', General Sir Edmund Allenby arrived to command in Palestine. His forces consisted of seven infantry and three mounted divisions. This large body of cavalry, formed into the Desert Mounted Corps (DMC), was to play an important role in the Third Battle of Gaza. In this battle, provost operated under very different conditions to those of the Western Front or Gallipoli.

Previous offensives had been tied to the coast, where the British had the use of a railway and a water pipe-line. Allenby intended to strike inland against Beersheba and thus turn the flank of the Turkish position. The capture of the wells at Beersheba was vital. Without them, the

DMC's offensive would fail for lack of water. The attack began on 31 October and Beersheba fell rapidly. Military police, who had a major role in traffic control before the battle, were kept busy directing stragglers, escorting enemy prisoners and conducting watering parties to the newly-captured wells.

Allenby's plan was remarkably effective. It was the beginning of an operation which resulted in the capture of southern Palestine and, on 9 December 1917, the surrender of Jerusalem. On 8 November, an Australian APM of the DMC set off in pursuit of a Turkish spy, eventually taking two lightly-armed Ford vans to Bethlehem, 15 miles behind Turkish lines. The party encountered two enemy cavalry patrols, which they dispersed, and on 9 November they returned home, motoring straight through the Turkish positions, unchallenged, at Hebron. All in all, November 1917 was, as an APM commented, 'a very trying month' for provost.

Shortly before the offensive, the Desert Mounted Corps' APM issued a document setting out the role of provost during the forthcoming operation. Corps MMP were to patrol roads and dumps in the rear areas, and assist the APM at the POW Collecting Station. Divisional and Brigade MMP performed similar duties in areas further forward and formed straggler posts. At the end of November, the Australians compared the theory of these instructions with the reality of what had actually occurred in the heat of battle. The original instructions had very sensibly stressed the need for military police to know the whereabouts of main roads, supply dumps and watering places, and to be issued with written instructions concerning the traffic priority of vehicles, hours for convoys and the like. However,

> Owing to the rapidity of the advance it was found quite impossible to adhere strictly to [these] instructions . . . Movements have, to a large extent, been carried out at night, and it has been very seldom that Brigades or D[ivisional] H[ead] Q[uarters] have spent more than 24 hours in the same place. At Beersheba, watering duties were carried out very systematically but elsewhere arrangements had to be improvised very quickly, and it was impossible to give all police definite instructions as to what units would be watering or using certain roads or areas.

The instructions concerning straggler control, echoing the experience of the Western Front, had called for organised straggler posts on the main roads, manned by three or four MMP, who would feed, rearm and escort stragglers. In reality, the sheer speed of the advance made it impossible 'to form regular posts . . . Police were, however, occasionally able to direct men who had lost their way and assist them to rejoin their units'. The orders to clear the ground of abandoned material after battles, action, and prevent looting in captured settlements were carried out. However, contrary to instructions, formations found it necessary to use MMP as POW escorts because of the shortage of men and the speed of the advance. Third Gaza was one of the greatest cavalry operations in history. The problems faced by provost were to be repeated not only during the Megiddo offensive in Palestine in September 1918, but in the fast-moving mobile campaigns of later wars, when horses had been replaced by motor vehicles.

Allenby's forces operated at the end of a tenuous logistic chain. Shortage of water was a particular problem, and an important task of provost was to ensure that existing water supplies were managed properly. No washing was allowed within 50 or even 100 yards of drinking water, while in May 1917 Anzac MMP were instructed that their 'principal duty' was to protect the water supply in the Wadi Ghuzza. The fall of Jerusalem was accompanied by operations in the Judean hills, which were a far cry from the mobile operations of early November. This stage of the campaign imposed considerable traffic control problems. Motor lorries could be used on only two roads. An infantry officer recalled seeing a military policeman attempting to control 'the mass of men and vehicles passing or stuck before him'; a large native cart drawn by oxen contributed considerably to the confusion.

Provost played an important role at the beginning of a major raid into enemy-held territory. During the night of 22/23 March 1918, the Turks were driven back from the bridgehead at Makhadet Hajla. The crossing of the River Jordan, swollen by recent rains, began. A mixed party of Anzac and British military policemen controlled the traffic over the bridges, which were clear by 1600 hours on 24 March, provost having laboured for 36 hours to move troops across the river.[8]

* * * *

Military police were to be found in every major British theatre of the First World War. Soldiers transferred from the Western Front to Italy in 1917–18 found that they had not escaped from the Redcap, who controlled traffic, made the usual patrols of cafes (and sometimes provoked the fury of the infantryman), while officers came across APMs in a warning and advisory role.[9] Similarly, provost served in the longest running 'sideshow' of them all, the East African campaign against German guerrillas.[10] The pattern of provost work in France was repeated in the Salonika theatre, where Lieutenant General G F Milne, the British commander, mentioned two military policemen in his dispatch of December 1916.[11]

The years 1914 to 1918 were crucial in the development of military police in the British Army. At the beginning of the First World War, few if any senior commanders recognised that military police had any useful role to play on the battlefield. By the end of the war, provost were seen as an essential part of a modern army. In the First World War the Corps of Military Police came of age.

Part Three:
The Second World War, 1939–45

14

From War to War, 1919–1940

Although Germany was defeated in November 1918, the Great War petered out in a number of smaller conflicts. From 1919 to 1921, Britain fought a bitter campaign in Ireland. Colonel George Cornwallis-West, who served as APM in the south of Ireland, covered some 10,000 by car in a four month spell in the autumn of 1919. His memoirs make it clear that he had a low opinion of the discipline of the 'Black and Tans', an armed gendarmerie noted for their ruthless conduct, and that their activities were counterproductive – an interesting judgement from a senior officer very much concerned with discipline. The CMP were among the last British troops to be withdrawn from Ireland after the end of the war in 1921.[1]

British military police also served in Russia, where British forces were supporting the White Russian forces against the Bolsheviks. Sergeant J H Moore MFP was awarded the Meritorious Service Medal in March 1920 in recognition of his work as a detective operating against thefts of government property. Members of the CMP also served with the Allied occupation forces at Constantinople and in Germany. Most unusually, Allied police officers had powers to inflict minor summary punishments. Provost activities in the Turkish capital included the covert escorting of the last Sultan to a British warship, in which he was carried into exile. British forces occupied the Rhineland from 1919 to 1929 and the CMP maintained an important presence there. The SIB (sometimes referred to as 'Special Investigation Bureau') was active, but appears to have been disbanded when the 'first BAOR' withdrew. Provost Headquarters was located at Connaught Barracks, Wiesbaden. Women police served under the DPM from 1923 to 1925, but do not appear to have been thought a great success. Provost had some brushes with members of the fledgling Nazi party, and military policemen continued to have a secondary role in collecting political intelligence, but on the whole relations with the local population were correct, and on occasions friendly.[2]

In the 1920s and 1930s, British military authorities slowly absorbed the lessons of the Great War, and in these years various reforms of Provost were put into effect. As early as 1919 a committee concerned with reorganisation of the Army had recognised that the experience of

1914–18 had clearly demonstrated the need for the establishment of permanent provost companies and traffic control units, and in January 1927, a provost company was formed for service with the Shanghai Defence Force. This was, as Lovell-Knight states, the first ever 'self-contained and self-administered' military police unit formed 'for a specific purpose overseas'. Earlier, on 27 February 1926, the MMP and the MFP were formally merged to form the Corps of Military Police.

In the 1930s the CMP underwent some of the most radical changes in its history. 1935 saw the formation of provost companies and sections with fixed establishments. Previously, in time of peace, the CMP provided detachments of varying strength which were distributed to the various commands. Under the new system, stations received provost companies and detachments according to a policy laid down by the Army Council. Direct enlistment into the Corps from civil life became possible in 1938, and in February 1939 provost companies were allotted to Territorial divisions. Guards reservists with civil police experience were earmarked for posting to the CMP on mobilisation. In May 1937 the Field Security Wing was formed, although in 1940 it was transferred from the CMP to the Intelligence Corps. Largely as a result of the enthusiasm of Sir Stenson Cooke, Secretary of the Automobile Association, some 800 AA scouts joined the Supplementary Reserve of the CMP between 1938 and the outbreak of the war. Thus the association of the AA and the CMP began, which continues today in the form of 163 (Ports) Provost Company (V), which will form 251 Provost Company (V) under the reorganisation of the Army in the 1990s. At the outbreak of war with Germany in September 1939, the CMP were able to deploy some 3,500 men from all sources.

In comparison to its predecessor of 1914, the British Expeditionary Force of 1939 was extremely 'provost-minded'. 'Field formation' provost units served at Army, Corps and Divisional level, and on the Lines of Communication, and static companies served at home. Since the late 1920s the CMP had recognised the importance of mechanisation. Initially, progress towards this goal was slow but by 1939, non-L of C field formation units were completely mechanised. Lance-corporals of divisional provost companies were mounted on solo motor-cycles, and in addition the company had a number of motor cars, 15 cwt and 30 cwt trucks and lorries, and motor-cycle combinations. Even more significantly, the CMP went to war in 1939 with clearly defined roles, set out in the 1936 *Manual of the Corps of Military Police* and other documents. This view of the proper place of provost in the modern army was based on the lessons of 1914–18 and, naturally, by 1945 it had undergone considerable modification. Nevertheless the fact that military policemen of 1939 went to war with some form of doctrine meant that they possessed a priceless asset denied to their forebears of 1914.

However, CMP units did face some problems on the outbreak of war. The mobilisation experience of No. 3 Provost Company was perhaps typical. On 1 September 1939, the Company was formed around a nucleus of 22 WOs and NCOs at Bulford, under the command of Captain C M L Clements of the 4th Hussars. Four days later, 84 reservists arrived from the CMP Depot. The Company compiled a depressingly long list of War Equipment Deficiencies, which ranged from 'Rattles, Trench Mk II – 7' to 'Ointment, anti-gas No. 1 (2 oz tins) – 468'. No. 3 Provost Company eventually joined the BEF in France.

The BEF crossed to the continent in September 1939. During this operation the CMP played a key role by signing routes and controlling the traffic as the force moved from the Channel ports to the concentration areas in northern France. The mechanisation of the British Army in the inter-war period meant that the CMP's traffic control role was now even more important than in 1918. Once the BEF was in place, the CMP began normal policing duties. Maintenance of good relations with the local population was vitally important, and a sound working relationship with the French police was patiently constructed.

Perhaps the most significant development in the months that followed – the so-called 'Phoney War' – came about as the result of a visit to Britain by the Provost Marshal, BEF, Colonel S V Kennedy, in early December 1939. Kennedy reported that there was a high incidence of theft of stores in France. Chief Inspector Hatherill was despatched by the Home Office to report on the situation. As a consequence of his report, a War Establishment for 'An Investigation Section of the Corps of Military Police' was drawn up. The Metropolitan Police provided 19 detectives, all volunteers, for this new body. On 29 February, the first detachment of detectives joined the BEF in France. They were commanded by an APM, Major C E Campion, who had previously been in charge of the Criminal Records Office at New Scotland Yard, with the rank of detective superintendent. The detachment was split up into small parties, which were deployed at key points such as the port of Brest, where a party of two other ranks commanded by Lieutenant H Dibbens was in post. Thus, the Special Investigation Branch (SIB) was reborn, and in 1990 celebrated its 50th year of continuous existence. In the 1970s, the SIB adopted an emblem featuring 19 twigs, symbolising the pioneers of 1940.[3]

* * * *

The British Army fought its first campaign of the Second World War far from France. On 9 April 1940, the Germans attacked Norway. The British landed hastily-assembled and ill-equipped forces in Norway at Namsos, Aandalsnes and Narvik. The ADC to Lieutenant General Sir Adrian Carton de Wiart VC, commander of the Central Norwegian Expeditionary Force, signalled that his command lacked, among other essentials, military police. However, 'Rupert Force', which landed on 14 April at Harstadt, prior to the attack on Narvik, included No. 6 (L of C) Provost Company. An advance party of 10 men landed, who patrolled Harstadt docks, policed the disembarkation of the infantry, and even acted as stevedores.

The duties of the CMP at Harstadt were unexciting but demanding and dangerous. The usual round of picquet duties on the docks, maintaining discipline and traffic control were carried on against a background of frequent German air raids. As early as 16 April the DAPM, Captain P C Wardle reported that 'One MP killed in carrying out his duty ie, trying to get soldiers under cover who would persist in coming from under cover to see what was happening'.

Wardle was concerned at the excessive workload being placed upon his men, who at the end of April numbered 51 WOs and NCOs, plus two attached privates. The Company, Wardle warned, were 'working at full capacity, and there is no margin of reserve'. It was immensely difficult to find time for the men to relax or even to sleep. At least two full sections of 'fully trained' military policemen were needed for provost work to be carried out in a fully effective fashion.

On 27 April provost carried out a reconnaissance of the road running south to Lilleengen to determine its suitability for traffic. But it was in organising an evacuation rather than an advance that No. 6 (L of C) Provost Company performed some of its finest work. Although Narvik was only weakly held by the Germans, overcautious British generalship delayed its capture until 27 May. By this time the Germans had attacked France and the Low Countries and the Allies were being defeated in central and southern Norway. The decision was taken to recall Rupert Force. The CMP organised the embarkation of the wounded and the destruction of equipment. During a search of the town many weapons and documents were recovered. Finally, the CMP played an important role in a deception plan to cover the final evacuation. The local inhabitants had come to regard the sight of a CMP policeman situated just outside the town as 'a visible symbol of British presence.' As the last troops pulled out a corporal maintained his usual post, resplendent in red cap and white sleeves. 'Just as enemy tanks appeared three miles down the road the signal was given on the destroyer's siren. The corporal then calmly removed his traffic sleeves, neatly folded them and placed them on the roadside as though for his successor, mounted his motor-cycle, rode to the docks, and was the last man to leave Norwegian soil'. No. 6 (L of C) Provost Company returned to Glasgow on 2 June 1940.[4]

* * * *

This day was also the penultimate day of Operation *Dynamo*, the evacuation of the BEF from Dunkirk. The world had awoken on the morning of 10 May to find that German forces had invaded the neutral states of the Netherlands and Belgium. The Allies promptly put into action their preplanned response, which was to move two French Armies and Lord Gort's BEF into Belgium to take up position on the River Dyle. The advance was led by the armoured cars of the 12th Lancers, with the CMP close behind. Six hours later 'the main body were able to move forward over a controlled routing system – signed right through to their positions'. It was another quiet triumph for carefully planned and well executed traffic control. Unfortunately, the Allies discovered that their advance into Belgium had simply played into the hands of the enemy. Powerful German forces, including most of the panzer divisions, attacked through the Ardennes, a hilly and wooded region to the south of the main Allied forces. On 14 May, the Germans broke through the weak Allied defences and began to race to the north. Such was the speed of the German advance that it was said that an Allied military policeman in Arras held up the traffic as he saw tanks advancing, only realising that they were German when the panzers opened fire. Colonel Kennedy, the Provost Marshal, deployed his military police as part of Petreforce, which attempted to defend Arras.[5] By 20 May, the Germans had reached the Channel coast, cutting off the main Allied forces in Belgium.

The rapid change in Allied fortunes is illustrated by the operations of the 2nd Division Provost Company. On 11 May, Company headquarters were established in a chateau on the outskirts of Brussels. The next few days were spent in preparations for the coming encounter battle on the Dyle Line; building a POW cage, keeping pedestrians at bay during a bridge demolition, and setting up stragglers posts. By 28 May, the 2nd Division Provost Company were in full retreat, acting on official instructions to destroy its documents and part of its transport. On the following day, on the outskirts of Dunkirk 'the remainder of the Company's transport was put out of action and abandoned. The Company in groups marched on foot to DUNKIRK'. Lance Corporal V V Tozer recalled the officer commanding giving the men a short talk, telling them that they were now on their own and had to make their way to Dunkirk as best they could. A huge stack of motor-cycles was doused in petrol and ignited. That was the end of the 2nd Division Provost Company as a formed unit.[6]

One of the many problems encountered by military police on the retreat was the large numbers of refugees who had fled from the advancing Germans. The flight of these unfortunates severely congested the roads, and one of the many examples of provost dealing with this problem occurred on 19 May when Lieutenant General Sir Alan Brooke, commander of II Corps, used his military police to shepherd refugees into Lille, where they were cared for by the Prefet.

Traffic control too was vitally important. In Major Crozier's words:

> Everywhere in France and Belgium [military] policemen were standing unrelieved at cross-roads while the armies rushed back to escape the closing German pincers. When the last vehicle had passed him the 'Redcap' would discard his white traffic sleeves and, taking a rifle, would join the infantry covering the retirement.

An incident which neatly illustrates the importance of traffic control occurred on the night of 27/28 May. In order to plug a gap in the Allied line created by the Belgian surrender, Major General B L Montgomery's 3rd Division was ordered to carry out a move of 25 miles, at night, across the rear of three other divisions, with the troops sometimes travelling as close as 4,000 yards to the front line. Any student who had dared to put forward such a scheme at Staff College, Montgomery wrote in his memoirs, would have been written off as a madman. Yet such was the desperate position of the BEF that the manouevre was attempted. The CMP played a crucial role in ensuring its success. Operating well ahead of the main body, the Redcaps signed the routes and then controlled the movement of nearly 13,000 men and several thousand vehicles, in conditions of near total darkness. The 3rd Division was in place on the following day.[7]

Dunkirk was not the only port to become a battlefield. The historian of the battle for Calais stated that the CMP contingent played 'a splendid part' in the defence of the town, which fell to the Germans after bitter fighting on 27 May. Corporal W S Calvert of the 23rd Division Provost Company recalled the final days of Calais as 'just pure hell, under continuous fire, bombing shell-fire, small arms. Our duties were many and varied – parking vehicles, rounding up stragglers, stretcher-bearing'. Calvert's active military career came to an end at 1630 hours on 26 May, when, along with the section of the Rifle Brigade with which he was fighting, he was taken prisoner. He was to spend the next five years in a POW camp in Poland.[8]

The loss of Calais underlined the desperation of the British position.

The BEF and French forces formed a perimeter around Dunkirk, and the evacuation of Allied troops began on 27 May. An historian of Operation *Dynamo* has criticised the organisation of the evacuation, arguing that the lack of a 'proper and permanent beach organisastion' was partially 'due to a breakdown of the Provost Service'.[9] How valid is this criticism?

As a blanket criticism of the CMP it is clearly unfair. Individual military policemen performed well during the evacuation. A French soldier recalled seeing a British military policeman on traffic control duty in Dunkirk on 29 May. Nearby lay the bodies of four other Redcaps. They had remained at their post until killed. Likewise, individual provost units did sterling work, such as the 46th Division Provost Company, which formed straggler posts on the canal bridges in the Rosendael suburb on 1 June, rounding up stray soldiers and taking them to the beach.[10] It is, however, sadly true that the CMP was largely leaderless during the evacuation. This situation stemmed directly from a mistake made by a very senior officer who had no appreciation of the value of provost. On 19 May it was decided to evacuate 'useless mouths' to England. Unfortunately, the Adjutant General, Lieutenant General Sir Douglas Brownrigg, chose to include senior provost officers among this category, decapitating the provost organisation at exactly the moment that leadership was most needed. To be fair, even if the leadership had existed, the enormous problems of traffic control posed by the movement of French and Belgian troops and refugees, over which the CMP had no control, would have remained.[11]

Thus chaos reigned. One provost officer serving on the La Panne/Bray dunes was told that a naval officer was in command of embarkation, and yet he never caught sight of him. The bulk of the 2nd Division Provost Company was evacuated on 30 May, 48 hours before the last men were lifted from the beaches, leaving only small parties behind to assist with embarkation. These, and other incidents such as the earlier diversion by a 'person unknown' of military police from the La Panne–Dunkirk road, at a time when traffic control was all important, highlight the chaos that existed throughout the BEF at Dunkirk, and the magnitude of the mistake that was made in evacuating the Provost Marshal and much of his staff at an early stage in the operation. Brownrigg paid the price for this and other errors. He was never given active employment again.[12]

In the event, it was left to local provost commanders to work out their own salvation. Military policemen carried out patrols, maintained discipline and controlled the embarkation of men onto the vessels that would ferry them to safety while enemy aircraft constantly bombed and strafed the beaches. One victim of the Luftwaffe was Major Campion of the SIB, who was mortally wounded during a raid on Rear HQ at Boulogne on

19 May. At Dunkirk Lance Corporal Tozer helped to transfer wounded to the SS *Medway Queen*, a paddle steamer, before he finally clambered on board. Lieutenant Harold Dibbens, the second-in-command of 102 Provost Company, spent about 100 hours on the Dunkirk beaches and in the town. Dibbens found his company commander, Captain J Spencer-Churchill, near La Panne Promenade. Together, they organised troops waiting to be evacuated into groups of 50 under an officer or senior rank, and ordered them to wait in the comparative safety of the dunes before calling them forward to embark. Dibbens and his men worked through the night of 29/30th May, frequently up to their waists in the sea, directing and helping men, exhausted and often wounded, into small boats which would ferry them to larger ships further out to sea. On Dibbens' instigation, a temporary jetty was constructed from abandoned 3 ton lorries by 250 Field Company RE. Dibbens' party was moved to I Corps Rear Headquarters near Dunkirk on 31 May. There the bulk of his men were embarked, but Dibbens and eight volunteers stayed behind for duty at General Alexander's headquarters. They finally embarked on a destroyer, HMS *Windsor*, at 0200 hours on 2 June, having completed over 100 hours of continuous duty. In Dibben's words, during this stint 'I witnessed and experienced total unselfishness; a strong sense of discipline; many outstanding acts of courage; and a high sense of loyalty by the British serviceman to his country and comrades. In short, "The Dunkirk Spirit".'[13]

The Middle East, 1940–43

The defeat in France and Belgium in May–June 1940 robbed Britain of her only major ally and forced her to concentrate her attention on the Middle East. Initially, her enemy was not Germany but Fascist Italy. Mussolini had entered the war on 10 June 1940, just as the Allied cause appeared on the point of collapse. The Italians delayed launching an offensive into Egypt from Libya until 10 September, when Graziani's Tenth Army advanced 70 miles across the border and halted at Sidi Barrani. Despite being heavily outnumbered, having 30,000 men to the enemy's 80,000, the British Western Desert Force (WDF) prepared to carry the war to Graziani. Under conditions of great secrecy, training for the offensive took place on 25–26 November, with provost policing the training areas. Having been told that the exercise was to be repeated, the military police assigned to the 7th Armoured and 4th Indian Divisions and WDF Headquarters once again took up positions, only to find that the 'exercise' was a mere cover for the beginning of the offensive, code-named Operation *Compass*. Beginning on 9 December, 1940, *Compass* was a classic example of mobile warfare. By 11 December, a great victory had been won. Almost 40,000 prisoners had been taken. The Italians were routed. The British pursued them into Libya, and in January 1941 first Bardia and then Tobruk fell, again with large numbers of prisoners falling into British hands. Finally, at the Battle of Beda Fomm, a further 20,000 POW were taken.

The sheer scale of the success of the British offensive placed a severe strain on provost resources. Their major role in the initial stages of the offensive was that of track marking. As the campaign progressed, two other roles came to prominence. The first was the handling of POW. After the fall of Bardia on 5 January 1941, the APM, WDF, Lieutenant P V Lovell-Payne was tasked to march a huge number of POW 16 miles from the advanced cages to Sollum. No more than five CMP NCOs could be allotted to each batch of 5,000 Italians, and 'the difficulties of getting such large bodies of utterly demoralised troops to march the distance need no vivid imagination to visualise' The 4th Indian Division's DAPM used captured enemy vehicles, complete with Italian drivers and fatigue parties, to collect rations for the POW. The presence of the CMP in the vanguard of the WDF enabled the infantry and armour to be relieved of such duties. Learning from the experience of Bardia, the military police followed close on the heels of the infantry when Tobruk fell on 21 January 1941. Fortunately, disciplinary patrols were carried out by the provost company of 6th Australian Division, leaving the CMP to cope with POW evacuation. On this occasion, the 'bag' included '19 Italian ladies of easy virtue'. Traffic control also became a major headache. The bulk of the WDF used the single coast road, which was in bad repair. Vehicles leaving the road frequently became bogged down in soft sand. As ever, thousands of route signs had to be erected.

Two sections of 7th Armoured Division provost arrived in Benghazi on 7 February, delayed by the necessity to make a diversion over difficult terrain, 'to find the usual state of chaos'. Not only was discipline among Allied troops poor, but in the absence of any form of authority the APM had to organise a civilian police service, and even run the fire service. The achievements of the CMP in Cyrenaica were considerable. They never exceeded a total of 3 officers and 80 NCOs, and 'not one of them was trained in anything but Town work'.

The campaign in Libya was just one of several fought in the Middle East in 1941. At the beginning of the year a two-pronged attack against Mussolini's East African empire was launched from the Sudan and Kenya. The 4th and 5th Indian Divisions advanced from Sudan to Eritrea over some very mountainous terrain. In these conditions, traffic control took on a particular significance. One stretch of the road leading to Keren was vulnerable to shellfire, so a detachment of provost under Captain Riall, DAPM 4th Indian Division, was stationed there to guide traffic. All vehicles escaped damage. By November 1941, Italian East Africa had been conquered by a force which had been greatly outnumbered by its defenders.[1]

* * * *

In the spring of 1941, the British were forced to mount a campaign in Iraq, where the forces of the pro-German government attacked the RAF base at Habbaniyah. Among the forces committed to the campaign was 10th Indian Division. By November of that year, the Divisional Provost Unit under Captain L F Richards had moved elements of the Division over very long distances in very difficult conditions, dealing with traffic control problems of an exceptional nature. Traffic signs were frequently stolen by the locals, so military policemen had to be placed to direct traffic at key junctions. The difficulty of the terrain ensured that a sizable part of provost duties involved 'rounding up stray vehicles and going to the assistance of men who had become separated from the vehicles'. Provost had to co-operate closely with field workshops and the RAMC, and each provost vehicle became 'a "mobile straggler post"' carrying spare food and water. With Iraq – and hence supplies of oil – secured, a major threat to Britain's position had been removed and the area, along with Persia (Iran) was occupied until the end of the war. Military police also participated in the invasion of Vichy-French controlled Syria and Lebanon in June 1941.[2]

* * * *

Greece was attacked by Germany on 6 April 1941 and Churchill ordered British troops to be diverted from their successful Western Desert campaign to support the Greeks. Greece was rapidly overrun and British military police once again had the thankless task of patrolling evacuation beaches. The debacle of the Greek campaign was followed by another defeat in Crete, which was invaded by German airborne troops on 20 May. Despite taking heavy casualties, the Germans succeeded in gaining a foothold in the Maleme/Canae/Suda Bay area. A 'Crete Provost Company' had been established on the island. Prior to the invasion, its main tasks were 'provost, security and dock duties', although on 18 May the company began to take 'security measures' against the threat of enemy parachutists. Once the invasion began, the military police were forced to carry out their duties under air attack, a number being killed and wounded as a result. On 25 May the company was manning defensive positions overlooking Canae, suffering from 'intensive bombing and machine gunning'. Three days later the position in the north-east of Crete had become untenable and the company moved off to Sphakia, on the southern coast. The unit moved in small sub-sections which were unable to maintain contact because of the attentions of the Luftwaffe. Reaching Sphakia, the company carried out security duties on ration dumps and, inevitably, embarkation duties. The remains of the company embarked in the early hours of 1 June on HMS *Jackal*, arriving in Alexandria at 1700 hours on the same day. They were among the last British troops to escape from Crete.[3]

On 12 February 1941, a new Axis general arrived at Tripoli: Erwin Rommel. Using German divisions, he took the offensive at the end of March. The British forces were thrown back. Rommel raced towards Egypt, cutting off the port of Tobruk, which was to besieged from April until December 1941. Operation *Battleaxe*, an attempt by the British to regain the initiative, was a failure. Although the Provost of the 4th Indian Division had handled about 400 German and Italian POW by 15 June, they then switched to the by-now familiar role of covering a British retreat. Men of 204 Provost Company manned an information post at Kilo 91 on the Sidi Barrani road from 18 until 27 June, when they were relieved by the 7th Armoured Division Provost Company.[4]

Eighth Army was formed in August 1941, and Major A R ('Freddy') Forbes was appointed DPM. He faced many difficulties. There was no Army provost company, and nearly all provost units were understrength. Gradually, as new units arrived, such as 105 Provost Company (which became the Eighth Army provost unit), the position improved, but it should not be forgotten that for most of 1941 the Desert campaign, Britain's major ground effort against the Axis, suffered from a chronic shortage of military police.

Many military police tasks were far from glamorous. Much provost work was routine, even tedious – virtually every entry in 202 Provost Company's war diary for the latter part of 1941 reads 'Provost, Traffic and Dock duties carried out' – but nonetheless vital. The desert itself was an enemy to be mastered. Members of 105 Provost Company 'were green and untried' on arrival in Egypt, 'ignorant of the ways of the desert; but quickly we learned and the traditional "brew" on a desert fire became a routine, together with communal washing and the eating of so much sand with every meal . . . [the work was] grim, monotonous and trying – alleviated only by the single-minded spirit of comradeship born in the trials and pains of a body of men living in a barren land'.[5]

The next British offensive was Operation *Crusader*, launched on 18 November 1941 by the new Commander in Chief, Middle East, General Auchinleck. Initially, the offensive brought startling success. By 24 December the British reached Benghazi, having relieved Tobruk *en route*. Naturally, supply lines were considerably lengthened. There were no provost companies dedicated to the lines of communication. 105 Provost Company assumed responsibility for Tobruk, where traffic control, theft of stores, and, not least, enemy air raids posed a triple-headed problem; Major Kirk, APM XIII Corps, was badly wounded in one air attack. Behind the main battlefront, sandstorms exacerbated the problems of traffic control. In poor visibility, drivers tended to drive too close to the kerb, knocking over traffic signs. Once halted, provost had to ensure that vehicles were properly dispersed and camouflaged as a precaution against air attack.

On 24 November 1941, at the peak of the confused fighting to relieve Tobruk, a convoy of 150 vehicles approached 204 Provost Company headquarters. The convoy, which included an armoured car, was halted by military policemen and consisted of unarmed and largely demoralised stragglers from the 1st South African Division. The convoy was directed towards a collecting post. This was one of many similar occurences of stragglers attempting to escape from the battlefield, although not all stragglers were as co-operative as these. In a fluid, mobile battle such as *Crusader*, provost units operating just behind the front line were placed at risk by an enemy breakthrough. On 25 November, a truck manned by two NCOs of 204 Provost Company, was chased by an enemy armoured fighting vehicle which had penetrated into the British rear. The two military policemen narrowly escaped by hiding in a wadi, but on the following day they reported back to headquarters together with a number of stragglers they had rounded up.[6]

In January 1942, the pendulum of the Desert War once again swung towards Rommel. On the 29th of the month Axis forces retook Benghazi. The DAPM, Captain Melville, left a note in provost headquarters asking the Germans to leave the building clean for when the British next returned. On 26 May 1942, Rommel attacked the Eighth Army on the Gazala Line and by 18 June the British were streaming back. In retreat, provost again proved their value, particularly in controlling the movement of XIII Corps through a narrow defile between Tobruk and the Knightsbridge position. At another place, Major Forbes, DPM Eighth Army, was forced to intervene in person to 'persuade' the driver of an extremely slow road-roller to pull over and allow a lengthy and frustrated queue of traffic to speed up. One positive result of the campaign was the much needed appointment of a DAPM (Traffic), Captain Wedlake–Lewis, to Forbes's staff. This retreat also saw the extensive use of straggler and information posts, manned by two or three military policemen. To ensure that the retreat ended at El Alamein, provost set up a post on the coastal road. Drivers were stopped and their *bona fides* checked. Those who failed to halt were fired on.[7]

The El Alamein position lay only 70 miles from Alexandria. There, in July 1942, Eighth Army personally commanded by Auchinleck fought a stubborn defensive battle known now as the First Battle of Alamein and halted Rommel. In August Lieutenant General B L Montgomery was appointed to command Eighth Army. Axis forces mounted an unsuccessful attack on British positions at Alam Halfa on 31 August. Among the formations which fought in this model defensive action, widely regarded as one of Montgomery's finest battles, was 44th (Home Counties) Division, which won its spurs in the defence of Ruweisat Ridge. The Divisional Provost Company carried out excellent work. Sections were deployed to man straggler posts, and at 1230 hours on 30 August the provost was ordered to establish information points at the west end of 133 Brigade's minefields and to sign the main axis of advance. These tasks were achieved by 1900 hours the same day. Before, during and after the battle the 'dusty and difficult job' of traffic control was carried out by 44th Division's military police, eliciting high praise from the Divisional commander, Major General I T P Hughes, in his Order of the Day.[8] Alam Halfa was Rommel's last throw. On 23 October, Montgomery took the offensive.

The second battle of El Alamein, in contrast to the flowing mobile engagements usually associated with the Desert campaigns, was a World War One-style battle. Since Rommel's flanks rested on the sea and the impassable Qattara Depression, Montgomery was forced to launch a frontal assault. The strength and depth of the enemy defences, and the weight of the Royal Artillery's preliminary bombardment, further reinforced the similarity with the Western Front. The fighting of a setpiece battle, in 1942, just as in 1917, made great demands on provost. In his eve-of-battle message, Lieutenant Colonel T Irvine (DPM Eighth Army) declared that the CMP were about to carry out 'both operationally and administratively a bigger job than Military Police have ever tackled before . . . In a nutshell . . . [this] is the biggest day in the life of the Military Police since formation'.[9]

The major task before the offensive was to move the assaulting troops and subsequent waves up and through the British lines, and then through the enemy positions. The problem was not simply one of avoiding confusion and ensuring that the right units arrived at the right place at the right time, but also of keeping the enemy guessing exactly which area would be attacked. Thus behind the chosen breakthrough sector in the north traffic was carefully controlled, but in the south there was continual (and obvious) movement of vehicles. Provost was allocated a major part in the operational plan, and responsibility for traffic control was divided up between Army, Corps and Divisional provost units.

The task of moving units forward was complicated by the need for secrecy. Much of the movement which took place between D–5 and D–1 through the Qattara Gap was carried out at night, without the benefit of lights. No less than two complete divisions (51st (Highland) and 4th Indian) were handled by provost during this period. This was in addition to the artillery of both X and XXX Corps, the 'B' Echelon of the latter, and rations, fuel and ammunition for the foregoing. However, this logistic feat was just the beginning of the provost achievement. During the night of 23/24 October, 1942 three major forces had to be moved up to the front line: the 2nd New Zealand Division, and the 9 Armoured Brigade, and the 1st Armoured and 10th Armoured Divisions. These troops had to be moved through a corridor 26 miles long but only four miles wide.

In order to handle this volume of traffic, six tracks had to be provided to supplement the coast road. They were code-named Sun, Moon, Star,

28 Malaya. A control point manned by 99 Gurkha Infantry Brigade Provost Unit RMP

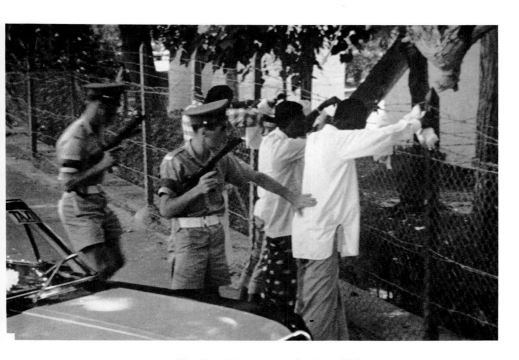

29 Searching suspects in Aden, 1968

30   On mobile patrol. Gibraltar, 1961

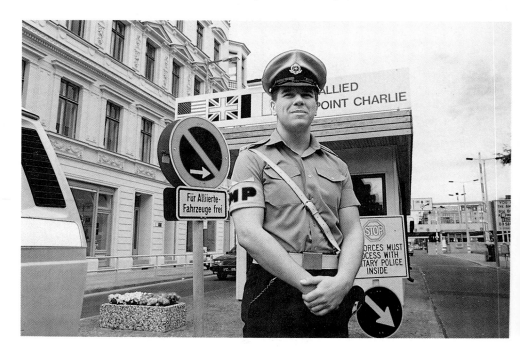

31   Check Point 'Charlie', West Berlin, 1987. Corporal Marriot RMP on duty at the
international crossing point from West to East Berlin

32 Inkerman Barracks, Woking. Home of the Royal Military Police Depot and Training Establishment from Spring 1947 – February 1964

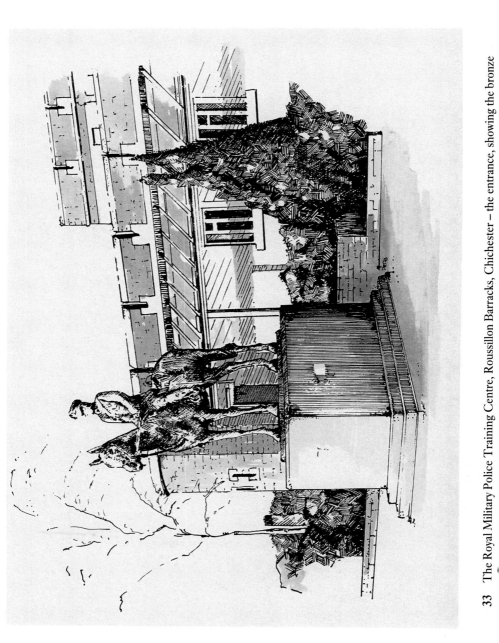

33   The Royal Military Police Training Centre, Roussillon Barracks, Chichester – the entrance, showing the bronze

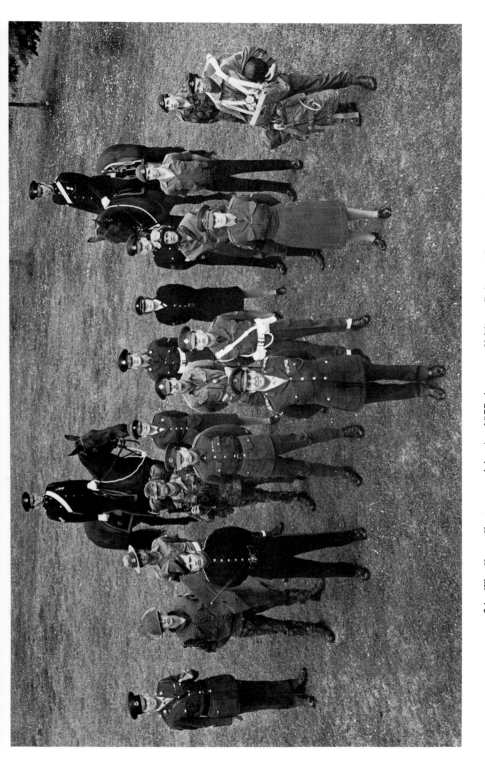

34 The Corps Centenary celebration 1977. An array of Military Police uniforms over the years. (Foreground: Brigadier M Matthews CBE, Provost Marshal (Army))

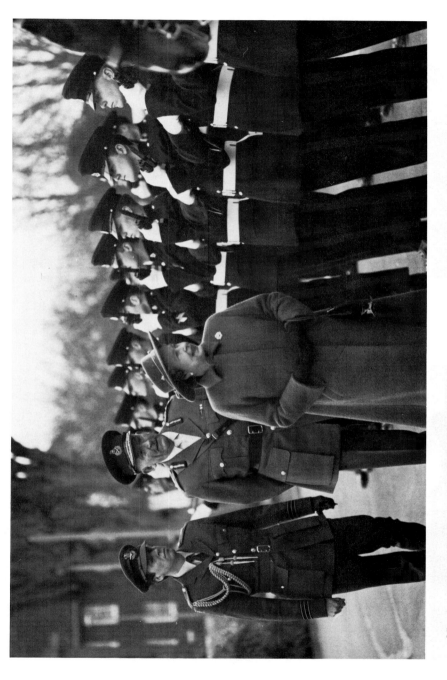

35   Accompanied by the Colonel Commandant, General Sir Peter Inge, Her Majesty Queen Elizabeth II visited the RMPTC as Colonel–in–Chief Royal Military Police in 1990. Her Majesty inspects the Guard of Honour

36 The Queen inspects the Mounted Troop

37 The Queen inspects a display by the RMP (TA)

38   Staff Sergeant KM Davies DCM RMP outside Buckingham Palace after receiving his award. Whilst commanding 3 Platoon, 203 Provost Company RMP during the Gulf conflict in 1991, Staff Sergeant Davies displayed exemplary personal courage and robust leadership in clearing mines from the path of an armoured brigade, thereby mirroring the act of Lance Corporal J Eeles CMP of 10th Armoured Division Provost Company, who cleared mines prior to the Battle of Alamein in 1942 and was also awarded the Distinguished Conduct Medal

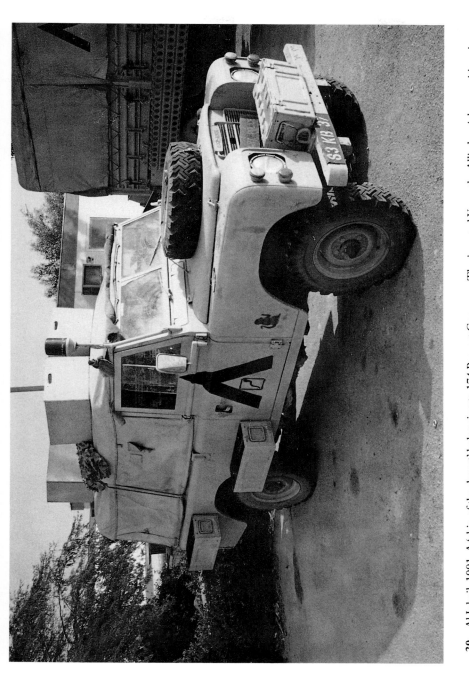

39 Al Jubail, 1991. A 'ship of the desert' belonging to 174 Provost Company. The inverted V was the Allied aerial recognition sign. Beneath it may be seen the Blackadder insignia of Headquarters Force Maintenance Area

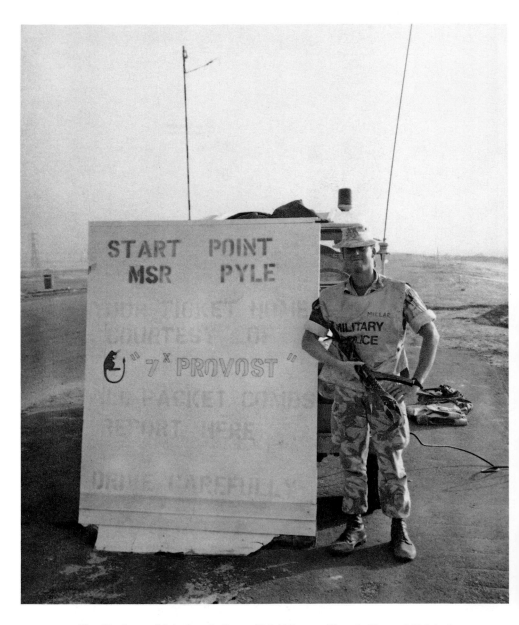

40   Signing on Main Supply Route 'Pyle' between Kuwait City and Al Jubail,
203 Provost Company RMP

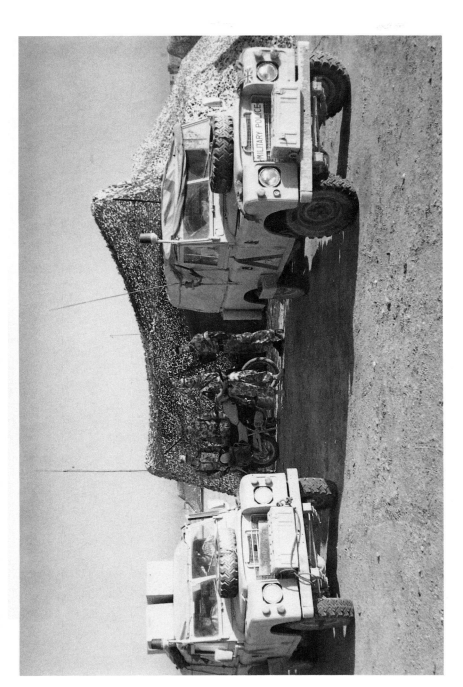

41   In the Gulf. 174 Provost Company prepares to deploy traffic patrols

42 Platoon base, 203 Provost Company RMP – with 4 Armoured Brigade

43 Inspecting a deserted Iraqi bunker

44   After the surrender. Searching Argentinian prisoners at Port Stanley, Falkland Islands, 1982
(*From a painting in the RMP Museum by Major Michael S Kitchen RMP*)

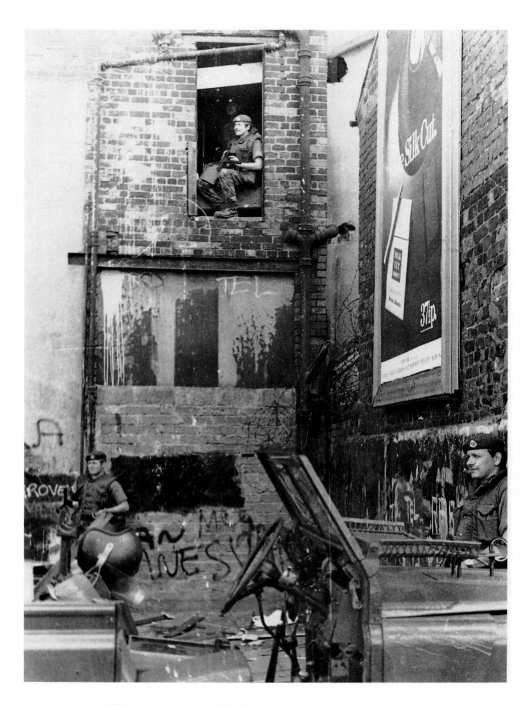

45 Northern Ireland, 1976. 180 Provost Company in Young's Row

46   A *Vehicle Check Point, Northern Ireland (From a painting in the RMP Museum by Major Michael S Kitchen RMP)*

47   An RMP patrol in Northern Ireland, 1993

48   Post Script: Operation Grapple, Bosnia/Herzegovina, 1993.
RMP on duty in bitter weather

Bottle, Boat and Hat. The tracks were marked by cairns of stones, the side facing the driver being painted white. Two provost sections policed each track; for instance, 501 Traffic Control Unit, which had been formed as recently as 7 October 1942, deployed three sections on the tracks, with a fourth manning a 24 hour Straggler Post on the Matruh–Alexandria road. One of the many duties thrown upon traffic police was the maintainence of improvised hurricane lamps. These had been produced by the CMP, and were placed inside petrol cans which had the appropriate shape – Moon, Bottle and so on – stamped out of it. Eighteen telephone posts were situated along the tracks, manned by officers attached to provost.

Considerable flexibility on the part of the military policeman had to be exercised when, very late in the day, it was decided that the New Zealanders and 9 Armoured Brigade would complete half their move on the night of 22/23 October. While this move went smoothly, it transpired that neither 1st nor 10th Armoured Divisions were in Irvine's words 'prepared to entrust themselves to Provost . . . and at the last moment [they] demanded that the provision of lights, stakes, etc., should be completed under Divisional arrangements'. Unfortunately this equipment was late in arriving and when it finally turned up, 'at 1800 hours on the evening of THE DAY' a number of defects come to light, including the fact that the hurricane lamps, some 1500 of them, had not been assembled, and that instructions had been issued to 'collect paraffin at Burg-el-Arab (200 miles there and back with four hours to complete the journey)'. Fortunately, provost's foresight in preparing for the move by manufacturing lamps and the like saved the move from becoming a fiasco. Instead, the move was completed in six hours, which was considerably ahead of schedule.

In the words of one desert veteran, 'it was the sappers, signals, and military police who led the armour into battle' at El Alamein. One significant advance on defences of the previous war was the widespread use of anti-tank and anti-personnel mines. In order to facilitate movement through both British and Axis minefields, special Minefield Task Forces were formed to create and mark gaps through which the assaulting infantry and armour could advance. This was where divisional provost companies came into their own. They were responsible for illuminating gaps in the British minefield to guide advancing troops, and, during the artillery bombardment, they went out in front of the British positions with their colleagues of the Royal Engineers and Royal Signals to mark the routes. On arrival at the enemy minefield, the Task Force would begin to sweep for mines, and in the breakthrough phase, provost would take on the vital task of Traffic Control.

These tasks were carried out under heavy shellfire, with the additional risk of stumbling upon enemy positions concealed within the minefield. After his fellow military policemen had been killed or wounded, Lance Corporal Eeles of 10th Armoured Division 'and two sappers, whose help he enlisted on his own initiative, completed their gap under heavy fire of all descriptions, thus providing the passage for the Armour to advance'. Eeles was awarded the DCM. One historian has referred to the role of provost in the minefields as 'one of the star performances of Alamein', and many soldiers who had previously had a low opinion of the Redcaps were fulsome in their praise for the manner in which the military police carried out their dangerous tasks.[10]

The Battle of El Alamein was an attritional slogging match. By 4 November 1942 the mobile elements of the Axis forces were in full retreat. Provost roles were those associated with the pursuit of a beaten enemy. Some 30,000 Italian POW had to be processed, routes had to be signed, captured towns had to be policed. Compared to the numbers of military policemen available in early 1941, provost resources at Alamein were lavish. But considering the sheer amount of work to be done, and the importance of the tasks undertaken, DPM Eighth Army did not exaggerate when he wrote that 'one can see that 73 officers and over 2,000 NCOs of Military Police were by no means excessive.'

* * * *

Eighth Army's advance after El Alamein brought them to Tunisia. There they united with the Anglo-American forces under the command of General Eisenhower who had landed in Vichy-French controlled North Africa on 8 November 1942. Despite meeting some resistance from Vichy forces, Algiers, Oran and Casablanca rapidly fell to Eisenhower's forces, First Army's thrust towards Tunis, some 400 miles away, came to within 10 miles of the city. On 30 November, the unit nearest to Tunis was 2nd Battalion, The Parachute Regiment, one platoon of which was commanded by Lieutenant D B Rendell, who, many years later, was to become Provost Marshal. On 17 November, contact was made with German troops. Hitler had taken the decision to pour troops into Tunisia. The Allied forces would have to fight another gruelling campaign before North Africa was finally cleared of Axis troops.

Provost operations had been an integral part of the planning of the North African landings. Provost companies had been placed under the command of assaulting formations, and allocated various roles in the initial landings included route-marking, establishment of traffic circuits, and straggler control. In the event, the landings were unopposed.

Some of the problems faced by provost during the early part of the campaign can be judged from the experience of IX Corps. In May 1943 it was noted that IX Corps had travelled 460 miles in 42 days, moved locations 17 times, and fought three major battles; in all, provost motor cyclists had covered 2,500 miles. In the mobile phase of the campaign, a typical day for the APM would begin by interviewing various staff officers to discover the route, and approximately how many miles would be covered that day. Then joint provost/sapper reconnaissance patrols were sent out, with provost having the all-important task of route signing. These tasks exposed deficiencies in the equipment and scale of transport available to the CMP. In particular, there was a serious shortage of lorries to transport the tins of paint, oil, lamps, notice boards and all the rest of the paraphernalia of route marking. 4th Division Provost Company was forced to rely on two lorries reluctantly loaned by the RASC, and many of the Norton motor cycle combinations on the strength of the Company were written off by the third day of operations (motor-cycles were later replaced by the ubiquitous jeep in many units). The lack of wireless trucks also became apparent.[11]

Traffic control on the lengthy Lines of Communication between the main bases on the coast and the battlefront was complicated by the lack of first class roads. Secondary roads had an alarming tendency to become quagmires after rain. Provost were not helped in their task by poor staff work. On 3 April 1943, for example, in an incident rather reminiscent of Loos in 1915, 103 Traffic Control (TC) Company CMP had to deal with a series of British and US convoys which had appeared 'out of the blue', causing unnecessary traffic congestion at Duvivier and Souk Arhas. This was not an uncommon experience, due in part to the confusion that arose from the division of responsibilities between different sections of the staff. Sometimes under air attack, military policemen carried out tasks which were 'bereft of glamour', but which materially aided the fighting troops. It is no exaggeration to say that without efficient control of traffic, offensive operations could not have been sustained.

Yet military policemen were also called upon to take a more active role in operations. Partly as a result of the success of the use of provost in mine clearing at El Alamein, in February 1943 it was decided that all First Army military police should be trained, not only in the control of traffic passing through gaps in minefields, but also of lifting mines and the detection of booby-traps. Before the assault of the veteran 50th Division of Eighth Army on the Mareth Line in March 1943, a provost detachment had reconnoitred the route to within 200 yards of the enemy positions, and, on the day of 69 Brigade's attack, military police braved heavy artillery fire to sign the route and establish straggler posts at the exit to the minefield.

Fighting against a cornered and still dangerous enemy, military police-men were sometimes propelled into the firing line. During Rommel's Kasserine Pass offensive Sergeant F R Hanagan of 78th Division Provost Company successfully commanded 12 military police in repelling a Ger-man fighting patrol at Tally Ho corner on the night of 24/25 February 1943. On the following day this small force was attacked by German infantry supported by four tanks. The military police conducted a fighting retreat and then succeeded in holding a position for four hours, whilst they covered the evacuation of a dressing station.[12]

Military policemen on the Lines of Communication could also become involved in fighting. On 16 January 1943, a small force of Italian para-troopers dropped in the vicinity of Beni Mansour. 77 Company CMP, a traffic control unit, dispatched patrols to investigate and prepared to defend the town, and patrols were sent out. In the event, it proved that the enemy force amounted to only 11 men who were swiftly captured, but not before they had caused some damage to a railway bridge and killed some French sentries. [13]

The liberation of large towns and cities posed particular problems for provost. In a report of May 1943 Lieutenant Colonel Paton-Walsh, DPM First Army, bluntly stated that 'the story of Algiers in the early days was a sorry one'. Allied troops entered the town and proceeded to get drunk, and the enforcement of discipline proved very difficult. SIB sections carried out anti-vice operations in the city. By the time that Tunis fell on 7 May, plans to avoid a repetition had been laid, but were not enforced, with the result that a city of 250,000 inhabitants was 'thrown open, without any preparation, to the troops as a place of amusement'. Once again, the provost struggled to maintain discipline, but eventually a Guards battalion had to be sent in to restore order. In the eyes of the inhabitants, the conduct of British troops compared unfavourably with that of the Americans. Military policemen were also powerless to prevent a different type of looting during the German collapse of 7–12 May 1943 as units simply helped themselves to equipment that had been abandoned by the enemy, leading to the loss of valuable spoils of war.[14]

Throughout the campaign, First Army's provost arrangements suffered from inexperience. Improvisation, and learning from mistakes, was the order of the day. The Kasserine Pass battle taught Paton-Walsh the hard way that straggler posts should either be situated close to the front or as far back as the railhead; anywhere in between interfered with the move-ment of traffic. The 6th Armoured Division formed a company-strength 'PRO FORCE' from Guards and RAC personnel which, reported the APM, proved to be of great value, but was cobbled together at short notice and needed to be more efficiently organised.[15]

The end of the campaign presented provost with a number of difficult and unpleasant tasks. Men of the 6th Armoured Division Provost Company assisted with the unloading of wounded men from ambulances. Lance Corporal R P Ratcliffe later recalled that this was 'a horrible experience. In some cases the bandages etc had slipped to reveal missing limbs, head wounds and abdominal wounds . . . I can still see some of those mutilated men, it brought a horrible aspect of war home to me'. The sudden collapse in Axis morale in May presented the provost with the problem of dealing with vast numbers of enemy prisoners. At Grombalia, IX Corps Provost received 20,000 POW of which 11,000 were evacuated on the following day, as yet others were arriving.[16] Approximately 275,000 German and Italian personnel surrendered in Tunisia in May 1943. This total was comparable with Axis casualties sustained at Stalingrad, which had fallen to the Red Army in February. The war in Africa was over, but the problems of the aftermath were legion, and cast a heavy burden on provost units at every level.

16

The Italian Campaign, 1943–45

After the victory in Tunisia, the eyes of the Allies turned across the Mediterranean to Sicily and Italy. Initial hopes of a swift and decisive victory were wildly over-optimistic. The Allied forces found themselves forced to wrest every inch of the Italian peninsula from the German Army, which enhanced its reputation as a skilful and determined opponent. Like El Alamein, many phases of the Italian campaign resembled the Western Front of 1914–18, with the added complication of mountainous terrain. For the CMP the campaign posed a set of challenges which were very different from those of the Desert. Major G W Jones, a provost officer, came uncomfortably close to the truth when he wrote that nowhere were 'so many apparently insurmountable traffic problems overcome' and that no other place 'has ever had . . . quite as much rain as fell in that so-called sunny land'.[1] Allied soldiers soon came to appreciate that Italy was not the 'soft underbelly' of Churchill's imagination.

Operation *Husky*, the invasion of Sicily, began on 10 July 1943 with the amphibious landing of seven Allied divisions. At an APM's conference held on 3 July, it was decided to issue all NCOs with handlamps and signs to avert the chaos which some feared would occur on the beaches. In the event, the landings were unopposed. The experiences of the 51st (Highland) Division Provost Company were typical. A section attached to 152 Brigade landed with the assault forces at 1420 hours. Once ashore, the military police set up a traffic control post. They then reconnoitred and signed routes from the brigade assembly area to the road, under a screen provided by 5 Camerons, coming under mortar fire in the process. That evening and night the CMP were at full stretch installing and policing a one-way traffic circuit, directing stray personnel to their units and generally keeping order.[2]

Provost history was made during the invasion of Sicily, when military police went into battle for the first time by parachute and glider. It was intended that on the night of 9/10 July elements of the 1st Airborne Division should seize objectives ahead of XIII Corps, which was to arrive by sea. In the event, while some objectives were taken, the airborne operations were not a great success. Personnel of the 1st Airborne Division Provost Company, in common with their fellow airborne troops, were

118

scattered all over Sicily and the seas surrounding the island. These airborne Redcaps had a number of adventures. Lance Corporal Peter Dale's glider was released too early and crash-landed in the sea. Fortunately, he was plucked out of the sea by an invasion barge and was eventually landed ending up at Suez, which was rather a long way from his original destination. Lance Corporal J Pummel, who was attached to 1 Parachute Brigade Headquarters for the attack on Primasole Bridge in the early hours of 14 July, landed squarely on the DZ but found himself separated from the rest of his party. He attached himself to 1 Para and fought alongside them in repelling German attacks, including one by a patrol of German armoured cars. Lance Corporal D Watson jumped with 3 Para in the same operation, and eventually ended up as a member of a 35 strong party, which moved by night and hid by day. In the early hours of 16 July this party, which had by this stage taken 15 POW, linked up with an advanced unit of Eighth Army. Others, including Lance Corporal 'Jimmie' James and Corporal Len Formoy had similarly hair-raising adventures.[3] Once the Allies were ashore, they completed the conquest of Sicily in five weeks. The campaign was relatively bloodless, although the CMP took some casualties. While carrying out traffic duties in Syracuse, for instance, one NCO of the 5th Division Provost Company was killed and a number of other military policemen, including Captain Danny Birrell, the unit commander, were wounded by shrapnel.[4]

Montgomery's Eighth Army landed on the coast of Calabria, the 'toe' of Italy, on 3 September. Mark Clark's US Fifth Army, which included the British X Corps, landed at Salerno, south of Naples, six days later. Eighth Army's landings were virtually unopposed. A total of eight provost companies were deployed in the first instance, with others arriving later. The Eighth Army's military police were faced with the problems produced by success. Montgomery's men advanced 300 miles in only 17 days, despite the fact that the retreating Germans had destroyed many bridges, which multiplied the problems of traffic control. Taranto, a major Italian naval base, posed particular problems, because, in the words of Colonel J R Archer-Burton, DPM Eighth Army, 'large numbers of unemployed naval ratings wandered around the town at all times of the day'. Several cases of knifing and assault had to be dealt with.

On 16 September, Eighth Army forces linked up with Fifth Army. One of the major reasons why Montgomery's advance had been so rapid was that the German forces had concentrated against the Salerno beachead. At Salerno the landing met with fierce resistance and the Germans came close to pushing Clark back into the sea. So dangerous did the situation appear on 14 September that the 56th (London) Division set up a 'Divisional defence scheme'. The DAPM, Captain C E Mercer was placed in command of provost and signals, and defensive positions were dug around the company location.[5] On 15 September, the Germans finally accepted that they were going to be unable to defeat Clark, and began to withdraw to the Winter Line to the north of Naples.

The Allies now held the southern part of the Italian peninsula, which once again posed problems for provost. The pressure under which the military police were working can be gauged from the problems that occurred when the move of a single company (200 Provost Company) from Sicily to the mainland was suddenly cancelled, causing a hasty juggling of resources. It is clear that the allocation of provost was insufficient. Army provost had to be retained on lines of communication duties, instead of being released to fulfil their correct function.

On 16 September 1943 provost at Salerno had to deal with the worst mutiny experienced by the British Army in the Second World War. For a variety of complex reasons, including the strong *esprit de corps* that had developed in their parent regiments, 700 replacements refused orders to join the units to which they had been assigned. Military police had the distasteful task of escorting a hard core of 192 mutineers who ignored the personal appeal of X Corps commander.[6]

From Foggia, which lay roughly parallel with Naples, Eighth Army's lines of communication ran along two axes of advance: the coastal road, and the central road. The poor state of the roads was aggravated by the weather. A stretch of road from Termoli to Foggia was an extreme example of the problem faced by provost. This route amounted to 30 miles of bottlenecks, including two miles of road on which only one way traffic was possible, and nine Bailey bridges, including the Trigno river crossing. The build-up of divisions in the south also caused problems. The 8th Indian Division's British provost sections were inexperienced and had only the scantiest of training, and a section of 105 Provost Company had to be attached for a brief period.

By the end of November, the campaign was effectively stalemated. Although the Allies continued to inch their way forward, the period of rapid movement was over. On 20 November, Montgomery attacked across the River Sangro in poor weather. V Corps provost handled the crossings in the main bridge area, while divisional provost concentrated on duties forward of the river. As with movement through minefields, traffic control was an essential element of effective river crossings. Military policemen co-operated closely with the sappers and carried out nightly reconnaissance to discover the most suitable fording places for tanks and other vehicles. During the actual crossings, routes were illuminated by hurricane lamps tended by military police. Once the operation began, strict road discipline was applied. Bunching had to be prevented, for the crossing points were under enemy artillery observation. Broken down vehicles were removed by towing them or simply pushing them out of the way.

The town of Ortona, just ten miles north of the Sangro and on the far side of yet another river, was not taken until 28 November. 505 Provost Company entered the town but were forced to pull out after five days because of enemy activity. The difficulties of moving men and vehicles over bad roads in heavy rain caused Army provost to be deployed up to the Sangro in support of Corps provost. Things were little better in the rear, as fresh formations were constantly being moved forward. On 24 December, a particularly horrendous snarl-up occurred on the coastal road, when a number of two-wheel drive lorries became stuck on the greasy road surface. Colonel Archer-Burton stated that in this period:

> it was essential for Provost officers and senior NCOs to be on the roads almost continually. Provost Company Commanders were averaging less that four hours sleep a night for over a fortnight. It was a period of intense activity for all ranks of Div, Corps and Army Coys.[7]

The bogging down of the Eighth Army brought a sharp increase in disciplinary problems. In the period December-January over 100 crimes, including many serious cases, were investigated by the SIB. By June 1944, thirteen SIB sections were operating in North Africa, Sicily and Italy. Much of the SIB's work was concerned with petty crime, so much so that in September 1944 it was decided that, as a 'general principle', the SIB would only become involved in cases of theft of goods worth more than £50. However, serious crime in the rear areas was always a problem. To take an example at random, in March 1944 an Italian civilian was shot dead by an Indian soldier near Lanciano, and No. 26 Section SIB had to carry out ballistic tests on a nearby Indian unit in an attempt to trace the weapon used. The SIB occasionally tangled with gangs of Italian criminals who used firearms, and even hand grenades.[8]

* * * *

By the beginning of 1944, all hopes of a swift victory in Italy had vanished. Nevertheless, the campaign had acquired its own momentum, illustrating the simple truth that it is easier to start military operations than it is to break them off, and planning began for a fresh offensive. The plans had to compete with the demands of the invasion of Normandy scheduled for the spring, and of a landing in the south of France, which caused some divisions to be withdrawn from Italy in the course of the year. The Fifth Army had battered its way up from Salerno to the Garigliano river line by the end of January 1944, at a cost of 40,000 casualties. The glittering prize of Rome was still 80 miles away. Fifth Army's military police had faced problems similar to those of their sister formation. The efficiency of the enemy's sappers in destroying bridges had created much work for provost in controlling diversions and carrying out various tasks. 'Since [the] present campaign has commenced', noted a Fifth Army provost officer in December 1943, 'the Coy appears to have combined RE and Sigs work with normal duties'.[9]

On the night of 17/18th January, McCreery's British X Corps of Fifth Army attacked across the Garigliano. Initially successful, this offensive rapidly degenerated into a painful, inch by inch advance. On 22 January, the second phase of the offensive began. This was Operation *Shingle*, an attempt to outflank the Gustav Line by the landing of an Anglo-American force (designated US VI Corps) at Anzio, which was only a few miles from Rome but some 60 miles behind the German positions. At 0300 hours on D–Day No. 2 Section of the 1st Division Provost Company disembarked from a Landing Craft, Tank. Once ashore, they quickly established a POW collection point, opened an information centre, and posted pointsmen. By 25 January, 98 POW had been dispatched to the cage. The 1st Division provost were to have an unpleasant time in the Anzio beachhead. Twelve casualties occurred in one incident when the Divisional HQ section was bombed.

The achievement of surprise is useless if it is not exploited. The force commander, US Major General John Lucas, had been sceptical about the plan from the beginning, writing in his diary in mid-January that 'this whole affair had a strong odour of Gallipoli'. This was a self-fulfilling prophecy. By failing to break out swiftly, he gave the Germans time to rush eight divisions to the area and thus condemned his men to trench warfare within a very cramped perimeter which was indeed reminiscent of Anzac or Helles. Road discipline was exceptionally important at Anzio, noted an officer of 56th (London) Division Provost Company, simply because of the large number of vehicles packed into a small, congested, coastal toehold, every inch of which was well within the range of enemy artillery. Traffic control in such conditions was extremely hazardous. The 'Flyover Bridge' sector was particularly notorious. The ferocity of the German assaults, and the conditions in the beachhead led numbers of men to go absent from their units. On 27 February, a special check was made on stragglers in an attempt to return men to their units. Two months later the military police were deployed, dressed as ordinary soldiers, in an 'intensive search for absentees still in the beachhead'.[10] The bad weather, the intensity of the fighting, and the constant shelling ensured that the harsh conditions at Anzio equalled any endured by

British soldiers in the Second World War.

February 1944 was a relatively quiet period for Eighth Army provost but the following month brought a major redeployment of Allied forces in Italy. General Sir Harold Alexander, the Allied ground forces commander, moved the bulk of the Eighth Army west of the Appenines, leaving the Adriatic coast lightly held by the V Corps. All British forces were placed under the Eighth Army's command, together with Indian, Dominion, and Polish divisions. Provost had to liaise closely with their American counterparts in the change-over period. This, and the need to familiarise themselves with the different conditions in their new sector – Highway 6, the Naples–Rome road, which was vastly superior to the Adriatic coastal road – ensured that Eighth Army provost (together with provost transferred from Fifth Army) were extremely busy immediately prior to the next Allied push, which was codenamed Operation *Diadem*.

The key to the Gustav Line, the main German defences south of Rome, was Monte Cassino. The mountain was crowned by a medieval abbey and had already been unsuccessfully attacked by Allied forces on three occasions. In March, the abbey had been destroyed by bombing. Prior to *Diadem*, the Eighth Army took over the Cassino sector. Of all the battles fought in Italy, Cassino has the most evil reputation. In 1989 one provost officer recalled:

> the completely flattened area of Cassino, [the] pock marked fields, with just the stumps of a few trees left standing and the crumbling monastery still dominating the scene.

Equally eloquent is a terse entry in the War Diary of the 78th Division Provost Company in late April 1944:

> Relief of Div by 2 Polish Corps. All Sects. in Cassino area engaged throughout night. Conditions of relief difficult – rain, no visibility, different language, shelling, all reliefs carried out, men very tired.

An infantry officer of the 78th Division left a vivid pen picture of provost work in the Cassino sector. He wrote that at each junction of the tracks that wound through the mountains, many of which were notorious shell-traps, a military policeman, complete with 'impeccable white belt and equipment' would be stationed. Scorning the protection of a steel helmet, the military policeman would wear the famous red cap:

> It is impossible to praise too highly the work of the Redcaps who are a part of every fighting division . . . They developed a tradition of courteous helpfulness which never broke down under the most adverse and dangerous conditions.[11]

One such Redcap was Lance Corporal Johnny Harris of the 78th Division Provost Company. He left a brief diary which is an unassuming and frequently moving testimony to the experience of a very ordinary military policeman in the Italian campaign. In February, while on duty, he had been approached by a battle-shocked soldier who confessed to having deserted. 'I could not take him in', Harris recorded. Harris gave the soldier tea and food, and then 'told him to go back and tell OC he missed patrol. Won't last long by look of him'. On 21 May 1944, Johnny Harris was himself killed by shellfire while on duty below the monastery, four miles from Route 6. Long after the war, one soldier recalled a military policeman directing traffic at a much-shelled crossroads near Cassino. On a nearby tree hung the red caps of his predecessors.[12]

* * * *

Operation *Didem* began on 11 May. Seven days later the II Polish Corps of the Eighth Army finally captured the monastery, and on the 14th, General Juin's highly effective French Corps began the assault that was to carry them through the Gustav Line. In the build-up to the offensive, an average of 11,000 vehicles per day were handled on Highway 6 by the CMP, who were ably assisted by Canadian provost. Mobile patrols, loudspeakers, and observation aircraft were all used to keep the traffic moving. At this stage, Eighth Army could call upon 24 Provost and Traffic Control companies, two SIB sections, and a Signals section. Included in this order of battle were British, New Zealand, Canadian, South African, Indian, and Polish military police.

On 23 May, the breakout from the Anzio beachhead began. From the point of view of provost, it was the same old story: 'Rapid advance by forward troops resulted in greater strain being thrown on our limited resources'.[13] The same could have been said of the breakout up the Liri Valley from Cassino.

Rome fell to the Fifth Army on 4 June, and early on the following day, Lieutenant J C ('Cliff') Atkinson, second-in-command of 77 Company CMP (TC) set off to sign a diversionary route to the east of the city. His task was complicated by the discovery, in an area 'under enemy observation and fire', of a staff car containing both Lieutenant General Sir Bernard Freyburg VC, commander of the 2nd New Zealand Division, and the Prime Minister of New Zealand. Once Eighth Army Tactical HQ had been located and the VIPs shepherded to their destination, Atkinson's party entered Rome itself where their jeep was 'mobbed by the crowds around the Coliseum' and they were 'garlanded with flowers and given bottles of wine'. Another provost officer, Lieutenant C H Butt, arrived in the Holy City on 12 June to find the 'streets very confused and full of excited Italians. Truckloads of American soldiers were everywhere'. His account of his time in Rome reveal something of the complexities of provost work in a newly occupied city. In addition to 'normal' disciplinary duties among Allied troops, the military police had many other roles which brought them into contact with Italian civilians. The curfew had to be enforced. Some curfew breakers were merely warned, in an attempt to frighten them, while others, of a more bumptious nature, were locked up for the night. Theft and black marketeering were so common that to leave a vehicle unattended was to risk having its wheels stolen for illegal disposal. Anti-vice measures sometimes called for military policemen to display considerable diplomatic skills, as in the case of the high ranking American naval officer who was discovered consorting with a VD-infected prostitute.[14]

After the fall of Rome, the Germans conducted a stubborn fighting retreat to the Gothic Line. Florence was entered by Allied forces on 6 August. An *ad hoc* 'Proforce' was formed mainly from 105 and 506 Provost Companies, and this entered the south of the city with tanks of the 6th South African Armoured Division. The city was under shellfire and sporadic fighting was still occurring but one member of 105 Provost Company recalled that the first visitor to their information centre was a long standing resident of Florence, an elderly English lady, who congratulated them on their smart appearance.[15]

To be immaculately dressed under the stressful conditions of the battlefield is never easy and yet the standards maintained by the CMP were very high. The smart turnout of the Redcap enhanced his authority as a guardian of the army's discipline, and as we have seen, earned the admiration of both soldiers and civilians.

Field Marshal Kesselring, the German commander in Italy, had promised Hitler that he would hold the Gothic Line at all costs. The Allied armies were painfully aware that they were fighting in a secondary theatre – a bitterly ironic song, the 'D–Day Dodgers' was doing the rounds of the Eighth Army – and numbers of troops, including the French, had been sent off to other theatres. Nonetheless, the Eighth Army moved back to the Adriatic coast and prepared for the attack on the Gothic Line. The move once again gave provost the difficult task of moving vehicles over 'roads' never intended to take anything heavier than a farm cart. The CMP responded to the challenge: a road census taken on Route 16 on 6 September revealed that 10,723 vehicles had passed a certain point within 24 hours, figures which bear comparison with Route 6 before the final Cassino battle. By this stage, considerable numbers of Italian personnel were being deployed on traffic control work. This accretion of strength was generally welcomed by British MP. Those attached to 101 Provost Company were described as 'very keen'. They freed British personnel for employment in 'a more mobile role and for fuller deployment in practical Police duties'. The Allied forces (now known as the 15th Army Group) attacked on 25 August. They forced the Germans back but failed to break cleanly through the Gothic Line. The weather continued to play an active role in operations. Heavy rain, for instance, on the night of 4/5 September led to many diversions being operated by 101 Provost Company, at a time when no less than three infantry divisions, an armoured division and an armoured brigade were moving through the V Corps area.[16] The offensive was closed down at the end of October, with the Allies still 50 miles short of the River Po.

The Eighth Army's last offensive began on 9 April 1945. Provost fulfilled the by now familiar tasks of traffic control and disciplinary work. Despite stiff German resistance – on 19 April the headquarters of the 78th Division was bombed, wounding the APM and the Traffic officer[17] – 15th Army Group forced the enemy out of the mountains. It was the end. With their forces in rout, the Germans surrendered on 2 May 1945. Six days later, Victory in Europe (VE) Day was declared. In Ancona, 200 Provost Company mobilised special riot squads and mobile patrols to prevent celebration dissolving into disorder. Similar precautions were being taken by anxious military policemen across Italy.[18]

The experience of the First World War had left a deep scar on the British pysche. British commanders in Italy sought to keep casualties to a minimum, which led to some criticism by the Americans for what appeared to be the excessive caution of British generals and troops; similar criticisms were to be made about the conduct of the war in North-West Europe. The British method of fighting placed a great deal of reliance on weight of fire power. This style of warfare required the logistic support to be first class. The CMP, who were an integral part of that logistic support, had played a frequently neglected but essential role in the eventual triumph of the British Army.

17

Defeat in the Far East, 1941–42

At 0410 hours on 8 December 1941, the men of Lines Communication Provost Unit, Malaya, raced for cover as Japanese planes swept in to bomb Singapore; enemy forces had already landed on the Malayan coast. The five year struggle between the forces of the British and Japanese Empires had begun. A little over two months later, the Malayan campaign had ended. 130,000 troops of the British Empire had surrendered to a much smaller force of supposedly racially inferior Japanese soldiers. Within a short time, Burma too was lost, and the eastern frontier of India was threatened. Yet British military power was to arise phoenix-like from the ashes: the war ended in 1945 with the reconquest of Burma and destruction of a Japanese army.

In this chapter the term 'British' is used as shorthand for all the forces of the British Empire engaged against the Japanese. Yet it should not be forgotten that Australians, Burmese, and East and West Africans also played a major role in the South-East Asian campaigns, alongside their American and Chinese allies. Furthermore, the 'British' campaigns were conducted by the Indian Army.

Indian divisions contained a mixture of British and Indian battalions. Indian units were officered by both Britons and Indians, with the latter usually in a subordinate role. Indian provost units contained Indian and British sections. The position of Indian military policemen provides an interesting insight into the relations of white and Indian soldiers in the paternalistic Indian Army. The general rule was that white men should not take orders from Indians. Thus British military police could arrest Indian soldiers, but Indian MP technically had 'no power of arrest' over BORs (British Other Ranks), although they could assist British military police in arresting BORs. This was obviously an unsatisfactory situation which posed a threat to discipline. A sensible compromise between notions of racial supremacy and the realities of military life was reached by the instruction that if 'no competent rank' was available, Indian military police 'will effect the arrest if it is essential for good order and discipline. They will be supported by the Provost authorities'.[1] In this case, ideology took a backseat in favour of pragmatism.

The problem of relations between white and Indian military police was compounded by the fact that 'Indian' soldiers were drawn from many different races, castes and religions, and spoke many different languages. In the words of Brigadier L F ('Dicky') Richards, 'racial prejudice and sectarian differences varied from mild intolerance to near hatred at times'. The need for separate cookhouses, latrines and the like caused some administrative difficulty, but the sharing of common discomforts and dangers brought increasing tolerance, and even 'real enduring comradeship' between men of different races.

As we have already seen, prior to 1939 provost functions in India were performed by Garrison Military Police and Regimental Police, not by the CMP, and the Indian formations that served in the First World War were policed by British personnel. The tardiness of mechanisation of the Indian Army in the interwar years meant that there was no great demand for traffic control personnel. The Indian Army was belatedly brought into line with its British counterpart at the end of 1938, when the need for divisional provost companies for overseas service was recognised. Accordingly, when 4th Indian Division departed from India in 1939, it took with it a 'Divisional Provost Unit' raised in Secunderabad in July and August of that year. This unit of 38 men was the forerunner of what was to become a considerable provost presence in India.

Most of the officers and men who joined the newly-created Indian provost units had no experience of military police work. 'Dicky' Richards, a subaltern of the 11th Sikhs, was appointed as officer commanding of 10th Indian Division Provost Unit on 17 April 1941. He had not even heard the word 'provost' mentioned during his training, and Richards was told by his divisional commander that he would have to 'police his division'; the rules could be found in King's Regulations, the Manual (India) of Military Law, and the pamphlet on Field Punishment. The rest, Richards was told, 'would simply be a matter of common sense; just to ensure that I did not lose too many of his men and vehicles' while the division was on the move. Richards, promoted to captain with only 17 days service, formed his unit with one-third British personnel, each from a different regiment, and two-thirds Sikhs from his own and the 4th/ 13th Frontier Force Regiment. On 16 May 1941, the new unit landed at Basra to take part in the suppression of the Iraqi rebellion (see Chapter 15); a case, as Richards commented, of 'jumping in at the deep end'. In later years Brigadier L F Richards became Provost Marshal of the British Army, while his divisional commander, Major General 'Bill' Slim, became a Field Marshal, a Viscount and Chief of the Imperial General Staff.

The size of the Indian Army in 1939 stood at 189,000. During the course of the 1939–45 war, the Indian Army expanded to 12 times this number, to a total of 2,500,000 in 1945. At the same time, the Indian Army was rapidly being mechanised. The disciplinary problems associated with these momentous changes, not to mention the alarming number of traffic accidents, led to the formation of static provost units, the first one being raised in Bombay in October 1940, and divisional provost units for service in India itself. The bitter experience of the retreat from Burma in 1942 gave added urgency to the development of a proper provost service in India. One of the lessons identified by a committee established to examine the Burma campaign was the need for a properly organised, well trained provost branch. This led to the formal authorisation of the Corps of Military Police (India) on 7 July 1942. To all intents and purposes, the CMP(I) came into being on the 20th of the same month with the appointment of Captain C L Carnes, KOSB, as the first adjutant. The new Corps still lacked a Provost Marshal. The Director of Personnel Services carried out the functions of the head of the military police until the appointment of Brigadier A R Forbes as the first Provost Marshal (India) in July 1943.[2]

Brigadier Forbes and his successor, Brigadier Mark Sykes (January 1945 – August 1946) worked hard to police India at a crucial time. Some 60 battalions were deployed in India to counter the civil unrest which exploded in August 1942. The work of the CMP(I) paralleled provost work in other parts of the globe. Joint patrols were mounted with US Military Police (many US troops were stationed in India from 1942) and CMP(I) co-operated closely with civilian police. The Vulnerable Points Protection Wing (VPP) was formed in July 1943, from older or unfit British and Gurkha soldiers who carried out static duties. This organisation was very similar to Vulnerable Points Wing raised in Britain, which is discussed in chapter 19.

Special Investigation Branch sections were also raised in 1943. Major J G Ellis was selected by Brigadier Forbes to be DPM SIB India. Ellis had been one of the original team of SIB detectives in France in early 1940, and shortly after his arrival talked to senior commanders about the role of the SIB and how senior officers could support them. 'Subsequent events', noted Forbes, 'showed what a worthwhile exercise this had been'. SIB sections, consisting of Indian and British soldiers, were eventually posted to most major centres in India. Sections began operating with Fourteenth Army in Burma in 1944, and on odd occasions individual SIB men were sent to formations in the field to investigate crimes. At its peak, the SIB in India numbered 37 officers and 277 other ranks. By 31 December 1945, they had dealt with 5,734 cases and effected 6,453 arrests. As a whole, CMP(I) consisted of 12,233 British and Indian officers and men on 1 January 1946.

Many other facets of the CMP(I) are worthy of mention. Beach Maintenance, Ports, military prison and detention barracks, field punishment centres, POW camps and airfield provost units were all raised. No less than 62 'mainstream' provost units (two Army, three Corps, one Divisional, 31 L of C, six Brigade, two base and 17 other) existed by mid-1944, not including VPP, SIB and other miscellaneous units. As in the UK, the HQ and Depot (located initially at Faizabad and, from November 1944, at Secunderabad) bore a heavy load of responsibility, particularly for training. Colonel Ganapathi, historian of the Indian Military Police Corps writes that 'It was indeed a formidable task to raise and nourish the infant corps, starting from scratch with inexperienced staff' and he pays tribute to Lieutenant Colonel N H R Dutton, the first Depot Commandant (August 1942 – April 1944) and Colonel R Pouncey, who succeeded Dutton in April 1944. One other senior officer should be mentioned in connection with the growth of CMP(I): General Sir Claude Auchinleck, the Commander-in-Chief in India. Forbes 'always had ready access' to Auchinleck, who took a 'personal interest' in provost matters. Indeed, only on one occasion did Forbes face any strong opposition from GHQ staff, when an Indian Civil Servant dragged his feet over the raising of two beach provost units for Slim's Fourteenth Army. The Provost Marshal 'asked "Whose side are you on?" The question achieved its objective'.[3]

* * * *

At the end of 1941, British forces were dangerously overstretched. Priority was given to fighting Italy and Germany in Europe and the Middle East, and few resources were available to defend Britain's possessions in the Far East from the growing power of Japan. In the Malayan campaign, both the RAF and the Royal Navy were outclassed in terms of quality and quantity by the Japanese. On land, British forces were largely tied to the roads, while the Japanese carried out a series of 'hooks' through the jungle and amphibious landings to outflank the British. The British forces were forced into a retreat which eventually ended in the 'fortress' of Singapore at the southern tip of Malaya. The British fought a series of unsuccessful delaying actions. Provost's role on the retreat was to carry out anti-looting patrols in towns such as Ipoh and Kuala Lumpur, operate straggler posts, and to push motorcycle patrols down the roads along the line of retreat.[4]

One of the saddest stories of the Malayan campaign was that of the 18th Division, an East Anglian Territorial formation which had been trained for desert rather than jungle warfare and sailed from England more-or-less straight into Japanese POW camps. The divisional military police carried out disciplinary duties on board ship, leaving little time for training in provost duties during the voyage to Malaya. On arrival in Singapore, on 13 January 1942, the provost company had to be given a crash course in provost duties. The sketchiness of the training can be gauged from the fact that senior provost NCOs had received a brief course in firing the Bren gun and the Thompson SMG. These newly qualified 'experts' then had to teach their junior colleagues to fire these weapons. The 18th Division soon became caught up in the last spasms of the campaign. On 19 January, Corporal Fairhead and two lance corporals began duties on the causeway between Singapore island and Johore, where they remained until it was destroyed. The withdrawal across the causeway was carried out during the night of 29/30 January 1942. Every available man of the 18th Division Provost Company was deployed on the causeway to carry out traffic control duties.[5]

Lieutenant General A E Percival (GOC Malaya) saw with his own eyes the problems of traffic control in the Malayan campaign. The road network of the peninsula and the circumstances of the retreat would have presented considerable difficulties to a highly sophisticated system of traffic control. 'Picture then the situation in our semi-trained army with drivers and traffic control personnel often speaking different languages, with all roads leading to one bottle-neck [at Segamat] and with nerves already on edge'. The memory of a traffic block on Singapore on 10 February prompted Percival to write that 'Our military police were pretty efficient, but I did not envy them their job'.

The Japanese assault on the island of Singapore began on 8 February 1942. Most units lost a number of stragglers but maintained their essential cohesion – Percival compared the straggler situation to that of March 1918. In Singapore itself, discipline began to break down. Gangs of looters and deserters roamed the streets, some deserters forcing their way on board ships at gunpoint, hoping (usually in vain) that the vessels would take them to safety. There were too few military policemen to make much difference to the situation. The population of Singapore had doubled to roughly 1,000,000 people as a result of the tides of refugees fleeing from the advancing enemy, while a maximum of 350 military policemen were available for the campaign. On 15 February, the situation appearing militarily hopeless, Percival surrendered to the Japanese.[6]

* * * *

Posterity has not been kind to the defenders of Malaya. Historians have discerned faults at all levels of command, racial arrogance and, in some cases at least, poor morale. Percival's less-than-dynamic operational handling of the campaign has been the subject of much criticism. The handling of provost was typical of the overall want of clarity of vision on the part of senior commanders. As Colonel Ganapathi points out, there was no overall plan for the use of the communications network or for traffic control. Some military policemen were used on irrelevant tasks, such as senior officer's orderlies, and in general the role of provost was simply not understood. A battalion commander complained that battalions were 'milked' of trained personnel for 'odd job[s]' such as provost. While one can understand the writer's annoyance at losing skilled men, he scarcely demonstrated an awareness of the importance of provost.[7] Properly used, provost could have contributed to the slowing of the Japanese advance, buying time for the marshalling of reserves to mount a counterstroke against outnumbered Japanese forces who were operating on the end of a long logistic chain.

There is a grim footnote to the story of provost in the Malayan campaign. The surrendered British, Australians and Indians were herded into POW camps to endure treatment at the hands of their captors which has become a by-word for callous brutality. A party of 80 military policemen was sent to work on the notorious Burma-Siam railway in April 1943, as a part of a larger body of 7,000 POW. The men covered 193 miles in 19 nights, and then carried out the heaviest kind of labouring tasks. Ill-nourishment, exhaustion, sickness and the brutality of the guards all took their toll. 57 of the military policemen died; overall, of the 7,000 POW, 3,000 survived. All POW were concentrated in Changi Gaol in Singapore in May 1944. Incarceration in Changi was, in the words of Lieutenant Colonel C Wilkinson, 'bliss to those who had spent many months, and in some cases years, in the stinking rotten filth of the prison camps on the Thailand Railway or in Java or Sumatra'.

In Changi, British officers carried on a shadow administration of the camp, issuing orders and maintaining discipline, and in general continuing to run the camp as a military formation. The CMP carried out a series of investigations within Changi and Selerang camps into racketeering and theft, set up check posts within the camp and carried out searches. It was vital to stamp out black marketeering if everyone was to have a fair share of the food available from Chinese contractors (which was needed to supplement the inadequate rations issued by the Japanese) without being priced out of the market. A remarkable series of documents in the RMP Archives at Chichester testifies to the functioning of provost in captivity. Statements about stolen property, reports on accidents, and even a record of 'Police Reports and Charges' were handwritten and sometimes typed on scraps of paper. To pick a couple of incidents at random, on 13 July 1943, an Australian corporal was found in possession of a microscope stolen from the hospital which he hoped to sell outside the camp. Exactly a year earlier a court of enquiry had been held under Brigadier R Curtis RA, into the activities of officers and men found in possession of food and alcohol. The achievement of the CMP in Changi was considerable. It preventing the situation from degenerating into a crude form of unfettered capitalism, in which the weak majority were trampled by a handful of racketeers.[8]

Malaya was just one target of the Japanese offensive. Hong Kong, where the garrison included a force of 18 military police, fell on Christmas Day 1941. The Philippines and the Netherlands East Indies were taken from the Americans and Dutch respectively. G W Pringle, a CMP motorcyclist, was part of the British force sent to the Dutch colony of Java. Arriving on 9 February 1942, he saw a provost officer checking the names and units of men who had escaped from Singapore as they disembarked from ships. They were then put into lorries and taken to a Dutch jail for reorganisation. The CMP's final duties after the Dutch capitulation in March 1942 were to enforce orders forbidding the sabotage of equipment, such as motorcycles, lest this should give the Japanese an excuse to reopen hostilities. Pringle spent the next three and a half years in a POW camp on Borneo. On his liberation by the 9th Australian Division on 11 September 1945, of the 2,000 original British POW, only 750 were still alive and a mere 50 were fit to work.[9]

In Burma the British had only the inexperienced 1st Burma Division and the 17th Indian Division to oppose the Japanese. The Japanese invaded on 13 December 1941 and the pattern of Malaya was repeated. The British fell back along the roads which were frequently cut by Japanese moving through the jungle. Fortunately, the British had some assets which were denied to the defenders of Malaya and Singapore. The most important was firm and resolute leadership, particularly that of Major-General 'Punch' Cowan, who assumed command of 17th Division after the disaster on the Sittang River on 23 February, and of Lieutenant-General 'Bill' Slim, commander of 'Burcorps'. A less obvious advantage was that provost troops were correctly handled.

The 17th Indian Division together with 7 Armoured Brigade, was the formation that bore the brunt of the fighting in the 1942 Burma campaign, conducting a fighting retreat. The divisional provost unit performed magnificently. Probably the most difficult problem was the crossing of the Sittang river, when the bridge was blown on the orders of Divisional Headquarters, leaving a substantial body of troops stranded on the wrong side of the river. On 22 February, before the bridge was blown, the military police coped with an appalling traffic block caused by a crashed lorry. After the disaster, the divisional provost unit manned straggler posts in an attempt to reform the division. The move of 13–14 March from Tharrawaddy to Okpo was fairly typical. On the 13th, the DAPM, Captain Weir, went ahead with two sections, one Indian and one British, while the company commander, Captain Healy, remained behind at Main Divisional Headquarters to establish traffic control in Tharra-waddy. Weir carried out a reconnaissance of the road along which the division would have to move, and arranged traffic control posts and stragglers posts in Okpo. The provost worked without a break, controlling refugees (a difficult and distressing task since it entailed turning Indian civilians off the roads to make way for troops) controlling traffic, collect-ing stragglers, even providing men for the defence of Divisional Head-quarters. On 27 March, the war diarist recorded that 'Provost Unit personnel have been working almost continually [for] the past 48 hours and have had little sleep'. This pattern continued, with the division in retreat, under frequent air attack, and with the enemy in hot pursuit, until they reached the safety of Imphal, across the Indian frontier, in late May. By this stage 61 (L of C) Provost Unit was controlling traffic in the Imphal area.[10]

Burma had been lost but Slim's command had escaped to fight another day. Provost's role in the success of the retreat was recognised by senior commanders. Both Lieutenant General Hutton, and his successor as C-in-C Burma, General Sir Harold Alexander, reflected the importance of provost in their dispatches, the former suggesting that much of the straggling in the early days of the retreat could have been checked had larger numbers of provost been available, and the latter paying tribute to the effectiveness of properly organised traffic control.[11]

Victory in Burma, 1943–45

The Allies had a fundamental difference of opinion over the objective of operations in Burma. The British saw its reconquest as the first stage in the liberation of its lost colonies. The Americans saw Burma as a base to supply what Churchill sourly described as 'their very overrated China'.[1] General 'Vinegar Joe' Stilwell, an American commanding a largely Chinese force, fought a more or less separate war in the north, building the Ledo Road to China and eventually capturing the key airfield at Myitkyina. Whatever the motive for fighting, campaigning in Burma was far from easy. Burma had few roads worthy of the name, much jungle, many hills and valleys, mountains on the peripheries, and a monsoon that lasts for five months from mid-May. The four great rivers that cross the country formed the major means of communication. The problems of campaigning in central and northern Burma, across the grain of the natural communication routes, made the idea of a strike against the Arakan peninsula attractive to commanders, if not to the men who actually had to fight in the difficult terrain and malarial climate. The airfields at Akyab were a tempting prize, offering the promise of aircover when an amphibious operation to retake the capital, Rangoon – an overland advance was widely regarded as an impossibility at this stage – was launched.

On 21 December 1942, a reinforced division (14th Indian) advanced into the Arakan. The officer commanding of the divisional provost unit, Captain G H D Williams, and his batman were wounded when they were strafed by an enemy fighter while reconnoitring a road by car. One of the more macabre tasks of the unit was the furnishing of a firing party to execute six civilians sentenced to death by the Military Administrator. By mid-March 1943, the campaign was in serious trouble, and the provost unit, based at Maungdaw, was forced to deploy roving straggler posts. In the month before their relief by 26th Indian Division Provost, the straggler posts had plenty of work as the British fell back before a determined Japanese counter-offensive.[2]

'First Arakan' was a failure. The main result was a further decline in the morale of the British forces in Burma. Fortunately, at exactly the right moment, British spirits were boosted by Operation *Longcloth*, the first

Chindit operation. 3,000 men under the messianic Brigadier Orde Wingate penetrated deep into the jungle to carry out guerrilla attacks against
the Japanese lines of communication. Militarily, the operation achieved
little but it was made excellent propaganda for the British. 23rd Indian
Division Provost Unit controlled the initial crossing of the River Chindwin by the Chindits. The 3rd Indian Division, the force that carried out
the second, much larger, Chindit operation of March 1944 was originally
intended to be accompanied by a provost unit, but the latter never saw
action, because the necessary increase in its establishment was never
sanctioned.

British morale in Burma was restored not by Wingate, but by Slim.
The latter was appointed on 14 April 1943 to command the forces in the
Arakan, when the campaign was beyond redemption, but Slim skilfully
averted a disaster. In the months that followed Slim (who became commander of Fourteenth Army in October 1943) set about rebuilding
morale, earning the affectionate soubriquet of 'Uncle Bill' in the process.
Slim's achievement was to transform a collection of individuals and units
who had become accustomed to defeat into a well-trained team that
believed that it could win. The force that went into battle in November
1943 was a very different one from the body of men that had been beaten
in the Arakan earlier that year. Two of Slim's messages, hammered home
time and time again to his men, was that every unit must be prepared to
fight Japanese parties who penetrated into British rear areas, and that
'There are no non-combatants in jungle warfare'.[3] In 'Second Arakan',
provost, among other units, were to demonstrate that they had taken these
lessons to heart.

The key engagement of the campaign was the battle of the 'Admin
Box'. On 4 February, the Japanese launched an attack which pushed into
the rear area of XV Indian Corps (5th and 7th Indian Divisions). In the
pouring rain, units of the 5th Indian Division slithered back along muddy
tracks through Ngakyedauk ('Okeydoke') Pass to the Corps Administrative Area, which was promptly besieged. At this stage, 5th Indian Division
Provost Unit set up rallying points and 'strove to bring order to the
disoriented soldiery' who 'wandered in all that day, soaked and weary,
many of them wounded and drooping, with a mixture of bewilderment,
fear and relief at escaping alive from the early morning ordeal . . .' Many
civilian refugees were also collected by provost at the western end of the
pass. The British were supplied by air. All troops fought stubbornly, with
military policemen taking their place in the firing line, as well as handling
stragglers and controlling traffic. Four members of 7th Indian Provost
were killed. By 24 February, the Japanese raised the siege and the British
passed onto the offensive. Just as provost had controlled the retreat

through the Ngakyedauk Pass, they now organised the advance through the same area. 119 (L of C) Provost Company controlled traffic in the pass itself, and 5th Indian Division Provost marshalled convoys at the western end. 'The Battle of the Admin Box' was a psychological as well as a physical victory. Slim's training régime had been totally vindicated: the Japanese 'March on Delhi' had been halted in its tracks and the myth of Japanese invincibility was destroyed forever.[4]

* * * *

Although thwarted in the Arakan, in March 1944 the Japanese struck into the Indian province of Assam. Slim was ready for this move. He planned to withdraw IV Corps, fight a defensive battle on ground of his own choosing, crippling the enemy in the process, and then take the offensive into Burma. The campaign, as Slim readily admitted, did not go entirely according to plan. The Japanese attack began much earlier than Slim had thought possible. On 14 March, Cowan's 17th Indian Division began to fall back along the Tiddum road towards Imphal, their retreat controlled by the divisional provost unit according to a pre-arranged traffic plan. 16,000 troops, 2,500 vehicles and 3,500 mules were on the move; provost 'were severely taxed to exert the traffic control required to prevent a chaotic bottleneck as the columns moved away'.[5] 17th Indian Division faced a stiff fight. The enemy's 33rd Division inserted roadblocks ahead of the division's line of retreat; in Slim's graphic phrase, the fighting on the Tiddim road resembled 'a Neapolitan ice of layers of our troops alternating with the Japanese'. Such conditions called for considerable efficiency and skill on the part of provost in controlling traffic, refugees and stragglers. At the end of March, the divisional provost unit participated in the defence of the Admin Box established at Milestone 82.[6]

The other two formations of IV Corps (the 20th and 23rd Indian Divisions) had similar experiences in the withdrawal. 20th Indian Division Provost had previously reconnoitred routes of the division's retreat, locating turning points and parking spots. In the words of the historian of the 23rd Indian Division, 'Drivers, mechanics, provost and medical staff all discharged their appointed functions and . . . some . . . prove[d] that they were good soldiers besides being efficient at their specialist tasks'.[7] With IV Corps in hastily prepared defensive positions, the twin battles of Imphal and Kohima began. An important delaying action was fought between 19 and 26 March by 50 Indian Parachute Brigade against elements of the 31st and 15th Japanese Divisions at the Naga village of Sangshak. Slim, in a Special Order of the Day paid full tribute to the achievements of this brigade in buying time for Fourteenth Army.

Communications between the battle zones and the rear areas were largely dependent on a long and hazardous road running from Imphal in the south, through Kohima, to the major railhead and supply at Dimapur. Much responsibility fell to the L of C provost units, under Major W H Stabback, DAPM. Supplies from outlying areas and non-essential personnel such as unarmed labourers had to be moved back along the road, and reinforcements brought up. L F Richards, by now Brigade Liaision Officer of 50 Indian Parachute Brigade, had made much use of the services of provost since their arrival at Kohima in February. Richards 'saw at close quarters the vital and heroic work [performed] under the most appalling conditions at times' of Bill Stabback and his men; 'without their help the Indian Para Brigade could not possibly have moved on to Imphal unhindered'.

Military policemen were among the first to be attacked when the Japanese cut the L of C north of Imphal at Milestone 118 at Kanglatongbi on 29 March, 'but not before the Provost TCP had warned Headquarters IV Corps at Imphal, and had been able to halt and turn back convoys converging from Kohima, thus saving many lives and valuable stores, desperately needed; an example underlining the need for good Provost communications to the forwardmost troops'. When Stabback heard that the TCP at Kanglatongbi was under mortar fire, he personally gave the order to 'stop all traffic at our various Police Posts on the L of C' and to evacuate the area. Stabback received a mention in despatches for his excellent work on the Dimapur road.[8] The cutting of the road signalled that the garrisons of Imphal and Kohima were now besieged.

Kohima was only 30 miles from Dimapur and defended by a mere 1500 men. Fortunately, the Japanese commander, Sato, who was operating at the end of a tenuous logistic chain, failed to by-pass Kohima and head straight for Dimapur. At Imphal, Slim's aim was to wait for the arrival of XXXIII Corps from India, while 'writing down' as many enemy units as possible and inflicting maximum damage on the Japanese. Once again, the British were dependent on air supply. Military police played a vital role in keeping the air life-line open. A sub-section was established at the airfield at Comilla, the headquarters of Fourteenth Army, and three NCOs were flown into Imphal itself. They controlled traffic, organised parking on the airstrip, and assisted in other duties, including evacuation of the wounded. The runways were always busy with vehicles, calling for nerves of steel and fast reflexes on the part of the military police. 'Indian drivers proved the biggest source of trouble; they usually took fright on seeing a plane approaching and stopped. Usually the military police had to take charge and remove them'.

Within Imphal, military police continued to control road-bound traffic, operate straggler and information posts, and carry out disciplinary duties. Four provost units (23rd, 20th and 17th Divisional, and IV Corps) participated in the siege. They operated traffic posts on roads leading into Imphal, where civil police and Field Security personnel checked persons entering the area, to prevent the infiltration of Japanese and 'Jifs' (members of the renegade Indian National Army).

Fourteenth Army emerged triumphant from the bitter battles of Imphal and Kohima. The arrival of XXXIII Corps forces enabled Slim to pass onto the offensive. On 5 July, the Japanese pulled back to the Chindwin. Provost learned many important lessons from these battles. The shortage of military policemen and the importance of having high quality personnel was emphasised. In relation to this second point, a post-action report was scathing about the quality of some of the BORs and IORs serving as military policemen. The problem was caused in part by the repatriation of significant numbers of experienced men and their replacement with whatever material was available. Provost's problems were exacerbated by the fact that some, although far from all, staff officers still did not understand the proper function of military police. Yet it was clearly recognised that, in spite of all their problems, provost had performed their role with considerable efficiency.[9]

Slim followed up the retreating Japanese to the River Chindwin. Once again, the L of C provost units proved their worth in terrible monsoon conditions. XXXIII Corps Provost Unit kept the traffic flowing on the Imphal–Tiddim road, which was extremely narrow with a greasy, dangerous surface. A contemporary report shows that road control here was 'was largely a matter of individual TCPs and NCOs working long hours in the rain by day and night to keep traffic flowing'. The military police on this road enjoyed a rare popularity 'as way-side hostels' where many stranded drivers were given food and accommodation. Deeper into Burma, the military police of the 5th Indian Division acquired an additional role. This formation was operating without a conventional, landbased line of communication, relying entirely on air supply. Provost held up traffic if a dropping zone (DZ) was located near a road, and mounted 'anti-pilfering' patrols around the DZ. The theft of dropped supplies was such a problem that a report concluded that no resupply drops should be made after 1700 hours, because the cloak of night gave too much of an advantage to pilferers.

L of C provost in Burma, like their counterparts in Europe, played an unglamorous yet demanding and vital role. In Assam the monsoon frequently caused roads to be closed through flooding and landslides, bringing provost into action to control traffic control while the sappers repaired the damage. During the 1945 offensive, TCPs often had Indian Electrical and Mechanical Engineer (IEME) recovery detachments attached to them. Even before the Japanese offensive of 1944, L of C units could not ignore the possibility of enemy parties – Chindits in reverse – penetrating into rear areas. In January 1943, 61 Indian (L of C) Provost Unit, based at Diampur, organised a mobile reserve to deal with enemy parachutists and sabotage parties.[10] L of C units had numerous crimes to investigate. Just one of many cases involved the recovery of a Bren gun from an Indian civilian in May 1944 through the investigations of Sergeant Skinner and Jemadar Mohd Niwas of 81 (L of C) Provost Unit. Another ever-present duty was the enforcement of strict anti-malarial orders. Nevertheless, many military police too succumbed to malaria, placing a further strain on an always difficult manpower situation. 82 (L of C) Provost Unit controlled traffic on Stilwell's Ledo-Burma road, and co-operated with both Chinese and American military police.

Forward units too had their ingenuity tested to the utmost by the demands of traffic control. Once a bridgehead had been established over the Chindwin in December 1944, the provost units of the 2nd British Division, 20th Indian Division and IV Indian Corps were responsible for controlling traffic over a one-way Bailey bridge, 900 yards long, which at that time was the longest in the world.[11]

* * * *

The victories in the Arakan and in Assam had gravely wounded the Japanese forces in Burma. In December 1944, Fourteenth Army launched the offensive which would prove decisive. When it became clear that the Japanese were not going to fight west of the Irrawaddy, Slim demonstrated the greatness of his generalship by successfully changing his plan in mid-campaign. Deception was the key. XXXIII Corps was to be used to convince the enemy that Fourteenth Army was heading straight for Mandalay. In reality, the main blow was to be directed further south, where IV Corps would be secretly redeployed to strike at the key communications centre of Meiktila.

IV Corps's move down the Myittha Valley to Pakokku was a logistic triumph that owed much to effective traffic control. The move was made along a one-way road which allowed no passing, running through moutainous terrain 'with steep gradients and acute bends, while the surface was rutted and deep in dust'. In his memoirs, Slim asked the reader to imagine a scene in which two tank transporters met head-on along 'the same one-way track above a precipice'. It was provost's responsibility to ensure that this did not happen. The effectiveness of IV Corps's traffic control, Slim went on to write, 'can be judged by the fact that there were no major hold-ups.' Provost cleared roads by pushing broken-down vehicles off the track – and often over a cliff. Military police travelled with convoys to enforce road discipline, and TCPs were established at harbour areas. In the absence of line communications, the usual method of controlling TCPs was by the dropping of instructions from light aircraft.

19th Indian Division, masquerading as IV Corps, attacked across the Irrawaddy on 14–15 January, followed by XXXIII Corps on 12 February. Both formations faced stiff resistance from the Japanese. The 'real' IV Corps crossed the Irrawaddy on 13 February, and met minimal opposition.

In these battles, provost had its usual vital task of traffic control. The divisional provost units of XXXIII Corps handled the traffic as each formation crossed the Irrawaddy, with Corps provost controlling the rear areas. IV Corps's traffic control was conducted by Corps and 7th Indian Division Provost together with the men of the 5th Anti-tank Regiment RA, the whole being placed under the control of the commanding officer of the latter unit. The ground was reconnoitred by a force of military policemen and sappers, and a detailed plan prepared. Separate routes were allocated to assault troops and the various other units that were to follow on. A large Forming Up Point (FUP) was established a mile from the main Corps Regulating HQ, not far from the Irrawaddy. This headquarters issued orders for moves forward from the FUP. Vehicles were given instructions from a control tower on the near beach, to move to various jetties for loading. A similar set-up was organised by the 7th Indian Division on the far bank of the river, when the 17th Indian Division Provost Unit took charge of its own troops. The shoestring crossing of the Irrawaddy can be profitably compared to Montgomery's assault across the Rhine one month later. 21st Army Group, backed up by a vast logistic infrastructure, was lavishly endowed with modern equipment, guns and troops. The Fourteenth Army, crossing a river which was wider and less predictable than the Rhine had none of these advantages, but the crossing was a superb achievement of great significance.[12]

While the Japanese remained rivetted to the battle for Mandalay, which XXXIII Corps wrested from the enemy street by street, the 17th Indian Division and 255 Tank Brigade drove on Meiktila, 80 miles away, in a classic example of Blitzkrieg – 'lightning war'. Meiktila fell on 4 March, with the APM and OC of 17th Indian Division Provost Unit and some sappers entering the town ahead of the division. They were greeted by scenes of destruction. 'Many streets were blocked with wreckage and bomb craters'. After lifting six anti-tank mines, the provost party then signed and policed routes to the divisional and brigade areas.[13]

A confused battle now developed as the Japanese desperately attempted to retake Meiktila. Slim fed in his reserves, provost controlling their traffic under exceptionally difficult circumstances. For the first time, Japanese prisoners became a common sight, and the tending of POW cages was added to provost duties. Military policemen, reported one provost officer, 'although disgusted with their filthy condition and habits', seemed to bear the POW no malice, although, given the shortage of cigarettes, a prisoner's request for a smoke was usually rudely rebuffed.[14]

A force of provost drawn from 19th Indian Division, XXXIII Corps and 254 Tank Brigade was deployed in the northern suburbs of Mandalay from 13 March onwards. Their patrols penetrated deeper and deeper into the town as more of Mandalay was captured. The military police attempted to prevent looting and were often actually ahead of the infantry – a reconnaissance of a possible traffic circuit on 11 March was 'curtailed by [the] halt of our troops advance' – and on at least one occasion they were the first to reach a police station and make contact with an important group of officials. When Fort Dufferin, the centre of Japanese resistance, was taken on 21 March, decisive action by provost prevented a repetition of the scenes that accompanied the collapse of Axis resistance in Tunisia. All available military police were swiftly moved into the fort 'to check looting and establish checkpoints at gates'. General Slim was conducted to the Fort on 21 March by Captain Nicklin, OC of 19th Indian Division Provost Unit, where the Union Jack was hoisted at the Old Secretariat. Nicklin was much in demand as an escort for 'top brass' at this period. Within days he had shown Slim (twice), General Leese, (GOC 11th Army Group) and Admiral Lord Louis Mountbatten, (Supreme Allied Commander South East Asia) around the city.[15]

By the end of March, the Meiktila-Mandalay operation had ended in a crushing victory for Fourteenth Army. Slim then rushed his columns south to Rangoon, with IV Corps in the van. They had to cover 340 miles in a month, before the monsoon began. At any one time there were more than 1000 vehicles moving south, with these numbers rising to over 3000 at times. Fourteenth Army moved so fast that a Japanese military policeman on point duty in Tongoo was flattened by a British tank who failed to heed his, no doubt frantic, signals.

To complicate matters, numbers of vehicles (empty transporters, maintenance convoys and the like) travelled north along a road which was almost entirely one-way. Initially, Corps provost controlled the road south up to the rear of the leading division, with a series of Sector Controls set up at intervals of 25–30 miles along the road. As the advance neared Rangoon, 19th Indian Division took over the rear Sector Controls to release military police who were needed further south. On several occasions serious traffic congestion occurred, most notably at the Swa Chaung watercourse near Tongoo, around 24 April, 'Heavy and unseasonable rains occurred' which made the crossing points impassable. The retreating enemy had destroyed the road bridge. The traffic built up while the sappers worked to provide a crossing. Finally, by 5 May, a Bailey bridge was in operation. Matters were not helped by the lack of communications available to provost and by poor road discipline; a report charitably attributed this to prolonged jungle fighting which caused drivers to forget the lessons of road movement. At one point, the traffic jam stretched back 30 miles, and half the Corps Headquarters was caught up in it.

The problems at Tongoo were an exception. Considering that IV Corps provost's problem in this campaign could be concisely summarised as the 'control of a force consisting of at times two motorised divisions, one standard division, one tank brigade, one independent brigade, Corps, Army and RAF troops on a single road axis over a distance of 700 miles', it is surprising that so little traffic congestion occurred.[16]

In the event, Rangoon was taken not by Fourteenth Army but by XV Corps (now separated administratively from Slim's Army) operating from the Arakan. In January, Akyab was at last taken from the sea. At Slim's request, preparations were put in hand for Operation *Dracula*, an air/amphibious assault on Rangoon. On 1 May, a composite battalion from 50 Indian Parachute Brigade landed near Rangoon. The Japanese had already abandoned the city. The 26th Indian Division entered Rangoon on 3 May to find a chaotic situation. Law and order had effectively broken down. Unfortunately, the divisional provost unit was not deployed until three days later. It struggled manfully to cope with policing the city, as well as with all its normal tasks, and received a welcome reinforcement in the shape of 94 Beach Maintenance Provost Unit on 9 May. Gradually, the looting was curbed, crimes were investigated and order restored.[17]

On 6 May 1945, the Fourteenth Army linked up with XV Corps just to the north of Rangoon. A great victory had been won. Some mopping-up operations remained, involving some bitter fighting, but attention now turned to Operation *Zipper*, the reconquest of Malaya. Before that campaign could be launched, Hiroshima and Nagasaki were destroyed by atomic bombs and the Japanese surrendered. The war against Japan was over.

Provost, in common with the rest of the 'Forgotten Army', suffered from a lack of equipment and trained men. During the advance on Meiktila, traffic signs had to be improvised from materials taken from buildings. The only standard traffic control equipment ever received by one unit was hurricane lamps, red and green flags and stencil brushes. In the final campaign entire gunner units had to be used for traffic control. Although they performed 'sterling work' they were inexperienced in a role for which they were totally untrained. Another handicap was that, in the opinion of some observers, IORs proved to be less effective than BORs at provost work. All military police, British and Indian alike, were liable to be mishandled by staff officers who did not understand their function. The lack of experience and relevant training of many provost officers, and the fact that until July 1943 there was no Provost Marshal in theatre to offer 'direction from above', exacerbated these problems. The lack of communication equipment on occasions caused severe problems: the list of problems goes on and on, and these difficulties were but a microcosm of the difficulties suffered by the Fourteenth Army as a whole.[18]

Yet in spite of all these difficulties, provost made a magnificent contribution to the defeat of the Japanese Army in Burma, which had once been thought of as invincible. As in the other major theatres of war, provost had been a key element in the success of every operation and had won the respect of members of the rest of the Fourteenth Army. Slim's victory was a remarkable achievement, which has not dimmed with the passing of the years, and military policemen played an essential role in that victory.

19

The Home Front, 1939–45

After Dunkirk, Britain resembled nothing so much as a huge armed camp. In 1940, the army feverishly prepared to repel a German invasion. However, by the spring of 1941, the Battle of Britain having been won, the prospect of an enemy assault on Britain had diminished, and the German attack on the Soviet Union in June 1941 caused the threat to recede even further. Following the entry of the United States into the war in December 1941, large numbers of American troops flooded into Britain, to add to numbers of Dominion personnel and fighting men from France, Poland, and many other occupied countries, who were determined to carry on the fight.

Some Allied troops were dispatched to fight in the Mediterranean and Far Eastern campaigns, but the majority remained in the British Isles, training for the day when an assault would be made on Nazi-occupied France. These vast hordes – there were over 1,500,000 US troops alone stationed in Britain on the eve of D–Day – placed a heavy strain on provost resources. As Crozier remarked, Major General Sir Percy Laurie, Provost Marshal (UK), in his three highly successful years of office (1940–43) 'presided over the fortunes of the provost service during a period of unprecedented expansion, during which over 32,000 suitable officers and other ranks had to be trained and absorbed into the provost service'. In July 1940, Traffic Control (TC) companies were formed, partly as a response to the problems of refugee control which had been experienced in France and Belgium. These companies became part of the CMP in October 1940. The men of the Traffic Control Wing were mostly infantrymen with no special training, although the TC companies had a leavening of 500 CMP Warrant Officers and NCOs. The problems inherent in moving large numbers of troops were exacerbated by the removal of road signs as an anti-invasion measure. Another new type of military police unit formed in this period was Vulnerable Points (VP) sections. The VP Wing was formed in February 1941 from men of lower physical categories and was used for patrol, guard and security duties, thus releasing valuable infantrymen for their correct role. One contemporary source estimated that each 'Bluecap' (as VP personnel became known) released at least three infantrymen from guard duties.

London District Provost Company was three officers and 116 men strong in 1939. It grew to be the size of a small battalion; a month after the war ended, it consisted of 598 men controlled by a DPM, five APMs, two DAPMs, one APM (VP) and one DAPM (VP). The duties of this unit were diverse. The apprehension of absentees and deserters was a constant task. This involved much routine checking and the occasional raid on places such as pubs, clubs, greyhound tracks and gypsy encampments, often in conjunction with civilian police. More routine tasks included the maintenance of 'discipline and bearing' among troops on leave in the capital. This has, above all others, earned for the CMP its unhappy reputation among the general mass of soldiery, but the good work done by the Redcaps in assisting soldiers adrift in the capital is often forgotten. The 'remarkable spirit of self-sacrifice and quiet initiative' displayed during the Blitz by London's Redcaps was praised in a postwar official history. They also did security duty, on occasion taking the place of the Household Cavalry at the gates in Whitehall, and carried out guard duty to the Commander-in-Chief Home Forces, General Sir Bernard Paget.[1]

Further additions to the CMP family were the Ports Provost Companies and female provost, both introduced in 1941. It had long been recognised that it was important to have military police available to supervise embarkation and disembarkation on the dockside, but the alarming levels of theft at ports and in transit led to a decision to create a specialised force with extended duties (which included security against pilfering and sabotage) and greater powers. By February 1942, 16 provost and 25 VP Sections were deployed in this role. By May 1945, the War Establishment of Ports Provost stood at 28 officers and 1,371 other ranks. Nine companies were formed for overseas service from Ports Provost personnel, and a further two were manned by surplus sergeants of other units. In January 1942, a Ports Section of the SIB was formed. Like much provost work, the activities of Ports Provost were distinctly unglamorous. They are, however, of vital importance. Major Crozier did not exaggerate when he wrote that unchecked pilfering of essential war supplies 'would have seriously crippled our war efforts'. This theft was chiefly the work of the dock labour force, not the troops.

The Auxiliary Territorial Service (ATS), the ancestor of the Women's Royal Army Corps (WRAC), was established in 1938. On 2 February 1942, 15 ATS Provost began working in London, and a further 12 in Edinburgh. ATS officers were appointed Staff Lieutenants and DAPMS. The appearance of ATS provost was accompanied by an improvement of dress and discipline of ATS personnel. ATS provost were a great success, and began a tradition of service which has been inherited by their modern-day successors.

The last remaining SIB section left France on 18 June 1940. There was a question mark over their future, but eventually it was decided to post the 18 remaining SIB members in sections to each of the six Home Commands. From this modest beginning, the SIB gradually expanded, so useful did it prove at recovering WD property, uncovering fraud, and countering the burgeoning black market. By January 1943, the SIB section establishments had been increased to one captain, two lieutenants, one RSM, two CSMs, 20 sergeants and two corporals. In 1942, a school for candidates who wished to transfer to the SIB was set up at the CMP Depot at Mychett.

SIB operatives had a varied war. A subaltern of Western Command SIB interviewed Rudolf Hess, after the Hitler's Deputy Fuehrer flew to Britain in 1941. Rather more typical, and mundane, were SIB investigations of a sapper who brought looted jewellery home on leave and a sordid racket involving REME officers, Ministry of Supply officials, and the log books of wrecked cars. The scale of the success of SIB investigations in the UK can be judged from some figures for the year 1945: 6,727 cases investigated, 4,277 arrests made, £68,698 worth of WD property recovered.[2]

The vast expansion of the CMP enhanced the importance of the training of recruits in provost work, for military police duties placed an almost unique level of responsibility on the shoulders of junior NCOs. The depots rose magnificently to the challenge. The growth of the Corps placed a severe strain on the resources of the pre-war depot at Mytchett – lacking a lecture theatre, would-be military policemen were lectured in their own barrack huts. In April 1940, a second depot was opened in the somewhat austere surroundings of Northallerton prison, in Yorkshire. This operated for about a year before the two depots were amalgamated. Paradoxically, recalled Sergeant Robin Belben who served at Northallerton, the troops preferred living in the cells of the prison to sleeping in a large barrack room.[3] Lieutenant Colonel Mark Sykes, who appeared earlier in these pages, commanded both Northallerton and Mychett in 1940–42. Much credit can be given to him and to his successor Lieutenant Colonel F Wright for the high standard of military policeman who reached operational units. Colonel Wright's slogan, repeated to intake after intake of trainees, was 'Guide the responsible, check the irresponsible, incarcerate the incorrigible!' – a fair description of provost duties.

20

Normandy, 1944

While great events were unfolding in Africa, Italy, the Far East, and not least, in the Soviet Union, Allied forces were building up and training in the United Kingdom, ready, in the words of one military policeman, 'for the inevitable day when all the resources of the Allied might were to be flung against the Hun sitting pretty behind the proverbially "Indestructible" West Wall'.[1] Provost had been recognised as a vital component of the invasion forces for the 'Second Front'. Two major exercises, *Tiger* (1942) and *Spartan* (1943) revealed grave deficiencies in the administration of traffic control. As ever, the responsibility for movement in the forward areas lay with the General Staff, but the executive responsibility for traffic control was transferred from Q (Movements) Staff to APMs and DAPMs solely concerned with traffic control. In May 1943, the 'Common Doctrine' for road movement was issued, which embodied many of the lessons that had been learned by trial and error. In addition, dedicated Beach Provost Companies were formed. Since the general introduction of radios into the field army, traffic control had normally been controlled by radio. On occasions, units which had mobility and plenty of radios, such as artillery units and reconnaissance regiments, were used in the traffic control role, and a traffic control unit was converted to a provost signals unit for the Normandy campaign. There is no doubt that the control of traffic in Normandy benefitted greatly from the experience gained over the previous four years.

Detailed planning for the invasion of Western Europe began in the spring of 1943, but from the beginning of 1944 the pace intensified. Major P Godfrey-Faussett, APM I Corps, recalled arriving at Planning Headquarters in January 1944, knowing nothing of the details of the invasion plan. Yet within the course of a 30 minute briefing 'virtually *all* the beans were spilt! . . . Such white-hot knowledge so suddenly gained seemed a terribly big load of responsibility!' Briefly, the plan was to land five divisions on the coast of Normandy, with three airborne divisions being dropped as flankguards. Once a foothold had been secured on the coast of France, the invaders would build up their forces to enable them to break out. The experience of operations such as the Salerno and Anzio landings, and exercises such as *Jantzen* in 1943 had shown that provost's principal responsibility would be for traffic control. The scale of the problems faced by provost planners is indicated by the following details of I Corps's operations. Two divisions (the 3rd Canadian and 3rd British) were to land side by side on an 11 miles strip of coastline. Eleven companies, totalling 59 provost sections were allocated to I Corps. Excluding the four divisional provost companies, these troops 'were split up into no fewer than 46 "craft-serials"', ranging in size from three sections to a handful of drivers. Once ashore, four Beach Provost Companies (241, 242, 244, 245) would be committed to beach duties and laying out and control of Beach Maintenance Areas and Assembly Areas. 102 Corps Provost Company was split between the assault divisions, Corps Headquarters and Provost Reserve. Two other units were to be landed on D–Day: 601 CMP (VP) Company (who were to be used for POW work and reconnaissance) and 73 CMP (TC) Company.[2]

The movement of 21st Army Group to the embarkation ports on the south coast was a triumph of administration. An officer of a Traffic Control unit left this contemporary account:

> At all critical points were the Traffic Control Police and their auxiliaries, working all hours, leading convoys; pointing the way; marshalling vehicles; . . . calming the agitated, stimulating the laggard, always alert; always present . . . By the end of July nearly 30,000 vehicles had passed through the marshalling area. Traffic Control had handled them all.[3]

In June 1944 the British Army returned to France. 6th Airborne Division Provost Company were the spearhead of the British military police in Operation *Overlord*. Emplaning in England at 2330 hours on 5 June 1944, Captain K G Wells and HQ Section landed near Ranville at 0330 hours on the morning of D–Day, 6 June. The hazards of mounting an airborne operation at night were considerable, and many men landed far from their designated drop zones. One of many units to suffer from the scattering of its men was No. 2 Section of the Provost Company, attached to 3 Para Brigade; only four military policemen arrived at the rendezvous. In spite of all its initial problems, 6th Airborne seized crossings over the River Orne and the Caen Canal, and by 0700 hours Traffic Control Posts were in operation over these vital crossing points. Soon, POW cages were erected. A valuable reinforcement, in the shape of No 4 Section, part of 6 Airlanding Brigade, came in by glider at 2145 hours on 6 June.[4]

The amphibious landings began on the morning of 6 June 1944 – D–Day. On Sword, Gold and Juno beaches, the Anglo–Canadian assault areas, troops came ashore with generally light casualties. The provost units of the assaulting divisions and the beach groups were the first military policemen ashore. By 0810 hours all personnel of the 3rd Divi-

sion Provost Company were safely ashore on Sword Beach. On D–Day
the 3rd Division's military policemen signed and controlled the move of
the division off the beaches along the roads to the crossing held by the
6th Airborne Division. The bridges were to prove vital traffic arteries.
After completing the signing, a group of 12 men under Sergeant Ward
was attached to 17 Field Company Royal Engineers at the bridges. For
72 hours, they had no sleep, were subjected to continuous mortar and
artillery fire, and were threatened by German counterattacks. Ward's
work was subsequently recognised by a Mention in Despatches.[5]

242 Provost Company of 7 Beach Group came ashore on the 3rd
Canadian Division's Juno Beach within half an hour of the initial assault.
Lance Corporal W E Lawson recalled that 'the battle for a foothold on
the beach was still raging. Machine guns were spitting death from pill-
boxes in the sandhills. Mines were exploding, blasting holes in landing
craft and blowing up tanks and vehicles as they rolled over the sand and
shingle. Jagged obstacles protruded everywhere'. A member of a sister
unit, 245 Company, recalled that as his section arrived on Sword Beach
they were met by the advance party 'and before we could say "Jack
Robinson" we were on duty, directing the traffic off the beaches. Signs
were erected and the whole stretch of beach soon looked like Paddington
station'. Military policemen found themselves carrying out many other
duties on D–Day, including rounding up and caging enemy prisoners,
organising mine detection and wire clearing details, and carrying in
wounded.[6]

By the end of D–Day, it was clear that the Allies had successfully
established a foothold on Hitler's Atlantic Wall. The invaders' logistic
plans, described by one historian as being of 'unparalleled scope and
thoroughness', in fact proved to be over-rigid.[7] During the first few days
of the campaign the beaches became clogged as clearance of the landing
areas proceeded much more slowly than had been intended, in part
because insufficient exit roads had been opened. In short, the situation
on the Normandy beaches provided a textbook example of what Clause-
witz described as 'friction' and what the British Army knows by a less
polite term. Major P Godfrey-Faussett, APM I Corps recalled the scene
on arriving on the beach on D+1: 'There we found no RMP [sic], no
signs, nothing'. Moving along the beach, he found 242 Beach Provost
Company busy with route signing, but the OC had been injured; lacking
leadership they had done little to man traffic posts on the inland lateral
road. 'Of the three sections of 73 CMP (TC) Company, who should have
been signing and controlling the assembly areas, or the two sections of
601 CMP (VP) Company and their prisoner-of-war cage there was no
sign at all'. The landing of men, supplies, equipment and vehicles had

fallen badly behind schedule, with the result that provost sections were still at sea when they were desperately needed on the beaches to control the increasing congestion. In Godfrey-Faussett's words, 'the whole of D+1 was a nightmare day of exertion and improvisation, with every military policeman working at top pressure'. By dint of this hard work, and as the logistic situation improved as plans were modified or jettisoned, I Corps provost were able to hand over control of the beaches to HQ L of C by D+5, with 102 Corps Provost Company retaining control of the lateral road. Initial provost plans had gone awry, rather more obviously in some areas than in others, but despite suffering casualties, the men on the spot – from Provost Marshal downwards – muddled through.[8]

With the Allies firmly ashore, the CMP were presented with a new set of problems. By a narrow margin, German reinforcements had reached Caen ahead of the 3rd Division on D–Day. This prevented the Allies from expanding the beachhead to the east. The close nature of much of the terrain and the skill of the German defenders ensured that the Allied lodgement would only be expanded slowly, by great expenditure of lives and ammunition. Thus the Normandy beachhead was to remain a relatively small area. The British launched a series of offensives around Caen. Tactically, the German forces were superior to the British and Americans, but this advantage was outweighed by the Allied superiority in airpower, logistics, numbers and firepower. The remorseless logic of the Allied way of warfare in Normandy was that vast numbers of men and vehicles had to be crammed into a restricted area. The British sector was roughly the size of the Isle of Wight. By D+50, at the time of the Allied breakout, 631,000 men, 153,000 vehicles, 639,000 tons of stores and 88,000 tons of fuel had been landed: Allied forces totalled some 1,500,000 men. These vast numbers had to use a grossly inadequate road system – on one occasion a traffic census revealed that 18,836 vehicles passed a particular point in one day, at a rate of one every four seconds. Only Allied air supremacy made it possible for traffic to move at that density. The job of ensuring that nose-to-tail traffic flowed smoothly was the responsibility of provost. By 25 July the build up of provost units was virtually complete.

The small market town of Bayeux was a traffic policeman's nightmare. It was a communications centre which at the beginning of the campaign simply could not be by-passed. Bayeux was blessed with narrow, angular, winding streets. Normally, a vehicle could drive across the town in about two minutes but in the summer of 1944 a similar journey could take two hours. Every available military policeman was drafted onto traffic control, and traffic posts were set up in key positions, connected by telephone with DAPM Bayeux, who was thus able to cope with traffic crises as they occurred. Despite these measures, and the later creation of a by-pass, Bayeux remained a traffic blackspot. It only needed one vehicle to break down, or one driver to flout the traffic regulations, for a long traffic jam to be created. Bayeux also caused the CMP headaches of a very different kind. The town had been captured, in the words of Lieutenant Colonel F C Drake (DPM Second Army), 'with literally not a bottle broken . . . [Bayeux was] a town full of attraction and enough drink to float a battleship'. Cases of drunkenness, looting, and even alleged murder and rape were dealt with by provost and SIB.

The SIB had began to arrive in Normandy on D+6. The forward troops were accompanied by SIB personnel in order that accurate statements could be taken when British troops were accused of misdemeanours before 'imagination could be given time to develop'. Often, SIB men found themselves operating under enemy fire. Once 70 Section SIB held an identification parade in a factory which came under mortar and artillery fire. The SIB also had to investigate occasional cases of Self Inflicted Wounds among frontline troops. Both the SIB and General Duties (GD) provost had to cope with the problem of illegal disposal of government property. Perhaps the most enterprising British soldier in Normandy was the one who sold a Bren carrier to a local farmer for £100. The farmer used the carrier to draw a plough until it was confiscated by DPM, L of C.[9]

Entering Bayeux in late July, an infantry officer went to an information bureau, hoping to find it staffed by a young French lady. He was disappointed to find that it was run by a military policeman. The CMP set up about 400 information posts in Normandy, which handled up to 2,000 inquiries per day. In November, five months after the invasion took place, the Main Information Post in Bayeux answered 2,628 enquiries.

A number of deserters were at large behind Allied lines, and provost became involved in operations to catch them. Over one weekend, a round-up operation netted 423 deserters in the Lines of Communication alone. Many other tasks were performed by the CMP. Improperly dressed soldiers, many from former Eighth Army formations, were apprehended in Bayeux.[10] Straggler Posts were deployed behind the fighting troops. A section was deployed at 21st Army Group Tactical Headquarters; three men rode in an all black jeep as escort to the GOC, General Sir Bernard Montgomery. 247 Provost Company helped unload stores and ammunition from Landing Craft and DUKWs, and sorted out bodies from the rubble of Caen, after the town had been devastated by Allied bombers. The variety of provost tasks seemed limitless.[11]

In the beach areas, military policemen worked tirelessly to ensure that the flow of men and vehicles arriving from England was deployed as swiftly as possible. The excellent work done by such base troops was praised by the commander of 'Moon' assembly area, south of Ouistreham, who wrote of a detachment of 73 Company (TC) in these terms:

> I have nothing but praise for the way in which Lieutenant Mulheir worked his men under very difficult circumstances. The men themselves had a very wearing time and stuck to their job well . . . The success of the Assembly Area was very largely due to the work of the Section.

However, it was traffic control that provided provost with about 80 per cent of their work. The Provost Marshal 21st Army Group stated that his 'chief operational function' was 'the co-ordination of the over-all – and ever-changing – traffic plan from the base to the forward areas'. The Common Doctrine, perfected in England, worked well in Normandy. The use of signs, produced by military policemen or civilians under supervision, was also important. Only the CMP were allowed to use black signs with white lettering, which truck drivers soon learned to rely upon to find their way. Nine thousand signs were erected in Bayeux alone, pointing the way to transit camps, depots, petrol dumps and the like. As in the Mediterranean theatre, military policemen took to wearing whitened equipment in order that they might be easily recognised, although a war correspondent in paying tribute to the CMP in a BBC broadcast, commented that it seemed if the dust-covered men on traffic duty had 'been sprayed with grey paint'.[12]

Close co-operation between the various levels of provost command was vital in the smooth running of the campaign. Divisional and Corps military police were at full stretch coping with traffic control, thus many other tasks were left to Army and Lines of Communication police. Until Colonel Drake, DPM Second Army, persuaded the staff to adopt a system of movement control, provost had 'to accept any vehicle on any road at any time in any direction and get it to its destination – if it knew it!' Eventually, operational moves were made at night, with use being made of specially built tank tracks, reconnoitred, signed and lit by military police.

One event which threatened the campaign with disaster paradoxically brought relief to the CMP. The 'Great Storm' of 19–22 June caused the rate at which the Allies could land supplies to drop by about two-thirds, giving the CMP a valuable breathing space. Nevertheless, the pressure on the ordinary military policeman was intense. On one occasion Corporal A Edge of 3rd Division Provost Company had been on point duty for 14 hours, when he was relieved by a brigadier who took pity on him, allowing Edge to rest for 20 minutes, after which he resumed his duties.

The workload was typical, even if the rank of the stand-in military policeman was not.[13]

Crises such as the sudden, unannounced, arrival in Normandy of King George VI, which prompted Montgomery's ADC to pose an apparently simple request to 'clear the roads', were dealt with by maintaining constant patrols by provost officers and military police. All the resources and improvisational skill of the CMP could not prevent Operation *Goodwood*, the largest British armoured offensive in history, from being bedevilled by traffic problems. On 18 July, three armoured divisions attacked German positions east of Caen. The offensive was launched from a restricted bridgehead over the Orne. Inevitably, congestion occurred at the Orne crossings, but this problem was compounded by the fact that a minefield had been laid by 51st (Highland) Division several days before, and shortage of time and the desire to maintain secrecy meant that only a limited number of lanes were cleared for the tanks. Three armoured divisions were shoe-horned into an area which normally would have been assigned to a single armoured brigade. The leading formation, 11th Armoured Division, successfully cleared the minefield but the advance of the second and third echelon divisions, Guards Armoured and 7th Armoured, led to a long queue of stationary armoured vehicles on both ends of the minefield. Traffic control in the minefields was hazardous. Three out of four CMP NCOs of 3rd Division deployed at gaps in the minefield were wounded by mortar fire, their places immediately being taken by other military policemen. The divisional APM was also wounded by a mortar bomb. The congestion ensured that 7th Armoured Division's progress was slowed so that it had a greatly reduced impact on the day's fighting. The *Goodwood* traffic jam, and indeed the slow moving traffic circuits in Normandy generally, would have presented perfect targets to the Luftwaffe. The absence of an effective enemy air force removed the one factor which could have made the job of traffic control impossible.[14]

The freedom from fear of air attack meant that, in comparison with the experiences of the infantry and armour, soldiers on the lines of communication (who amounted to about 44 per cent of the total) lived relatively, although not entirely, danger-free lives once the frontline moved away from the beaches. On landing on the beach on 27 June, 'instead of horrifying scenes of fire and slaughter' the men of the Guards Armoured Division Provost Company found a 'few men playing football and one in his pants, trying to direct the boat in, without getting too wet'. One member of the 11th Armoured Division Provost Company, who had arrived in Normandy a week earlier recalled 'the thrill that I received from being on French soil . . . [yet] It seemed to us that the routine was just the same as that in England – security duty, mobile patrols, speed patrols and the rest. Yes, we were very, very, green then'. The company was distributed by sections, one each to the infantry brigade, armoured brigade and Rear Divisional Headquarters, and three sections and company headquarters to Main Divisional HQ. 11th Armoured went into action on 26 June, and the Provost Company soon discovered that life in Normandy was very different from that in England. They 'guarded bridges, signed routes, handled prisoners, signed minefields' and rapidly 'became expert hole-diggers, [and] we learned when to get into them'.

On 25 July, the breakout began in the American sector. A month later, the Normandy campaign was over; 50,000 prisoners had been taken by Allied forces in the Falaise pocket. Some members of the 53rd (Welsh) Division Provost Company were up with the forward elements of the division, 53rd Reconnaissance Regiment, as they approached Falaise. Thus 'the whole view of the slaughter house was open to [provost]'. Provost were deployed to guide vehicles 'through the heaps of rubble which were once streets'. By the end of the campaign 8,724 British and Commonwealth military policemen had been landed in Normandy, some of whom were used (most unusually) as Regimental Policemen. Most CMP were used to control the traffic which enabled the men and weapons that defeated the German Army to be assembled and supplied. This job was unglamorous, but demanding and vital. In the words of Colonel Bassett Wilson, Provost Marshal 21st Army Group, 'The bridge-head usually looked like a misguided effort to put a quart into a pint pot, which as we all know, won't go. But, by the skin of its teeth, creaking, groaning and near chaos, the traffic went; *just* went'.[15]

21

The Battle for Germany, 1944–45

The collapse of German resistance in Normandy was followed by one of the swiftest advances in history. The Second British Army swept across the Seine and into Belgium where, on 3 September, the fifth anniversary of Britain's declaration of war, the Guards Armoured Division liberated Brussels. The other part of Montgomery's 21st Army Group, First Canadian Army (which included many British divisions), advanced along the Channel coast. By the middle of the month, logistic difficulties and stiffening German resistance reduced the Allied advance to a crawl. The Allies were still relying on the port of Cherbourg and the Normandy beaches as points of entry for their supplies. Although Antwerp was captured on 4 September, the failure to clear the mouth of the Scheldt meant that the port facilities could not be used until 28 November.

The advance after Falaise had once again placed a strain on provost resources. The crossing of the Seine, in particular, was a difficult task for traffic control, which produced the occasional grumble from some units. Matters were made no easier by such accidents as the damaging of a pontoon bridge by a Churchill tank of the 4th Coldstream Guards.[1]

The arrival of fresh troops in September, including VP companies, eased the problem somewhat, but CMP's commitments remained immense. At the end of that month, the CMP order of battle on the Lines of Communication was as follows: one unit (59 Provost Company) under the command of L of C, in Malines and Paris; two L of C Areas (No. 11, Amiens and No. 12, Caen); six Sub Areas; two Base Sub Areas (No. 7, Antwerp and No. 8, Ostend); one Garrison (Rennaix); three SIB Sections (71 and 72 in Amiens, 73 in Caen); three provost companies in Normandy, and another four in other parts of France and Belgium; three Ports Provost companies, situated in eight ports stretching from Arromanches in Normandy to Antwerp; eight VP companies and ten TC companies, deployed right across the Allied route of advance; and 2nd Canadian L of C Provost HQ and six sections. Yet more units were to join this vast force before the campaign ended in May 1945, including Allied units: No. 8 Compagnie de Circulation Routière, a French unit under British tutelage, took over traffic control in Caen and Bayeux as early as September 1944.

By mid-September, the lines of communication of 21st Army Group snaked back 300 miles to Normandy, and the CMP were responsible for controlling the traffic on four main supply routes totalling 1200 miles of road. 'The role of TC Coys [*sic*] on the L of C is rapidly reverting to a mobile one from the semi-static one which has been forced upon us since D–day [*sic*]', an order from 21st Army Group explained, '[so] constant patrolling is now essential . . . The use of a static pointsman is very limited, whereas a mobile man with intelligence is invaluable'. The use of military roads by civilian, mainly horse-drawn traffic presented problems, but traffic control personnel were ordered to be 'ruthless' in ensuring that military traffic was not impeded. On the whole, road discipline was good, although French and American drivers tended to be worse than the British. The latter had a habit of giving illegal lifts to civilians although as Major W G Steward, APM (TC), L of C, noted this was largely due to the sympathy of the British soldier for 'people who are "up against it"'.[2]

In some ways, 21st Army Group were more fortunate than the Americans in having somewhat shorter lines of communications and operating over more numerous roads. Some problems were experienced with US vehicles driving along roads allocated to the British. At one point, the US supply route from Le Havre intersected 'British' roads; American MPs co-operated with 101 TC Company under Captain Papworth in coping with this.

Not all L of C units were concerned with traffic control. 245 HQ Provost Company arrived in the recently liberated port of Dieppe on 3 September, where they undertook disciplinary and security patrols in the docks and in the town. Later this unit moved on to Boulogne and on 3 October they entered Calais, where they impounded captured enemy vehicles for which retention certificates had not been issued.[3]

Several problems faced provost troops as the Allies liberated towns and cities in France, Belgium and Holland. The reaction of the liberated peoples sometimes verged on the riotous; traffic control and policing duties were extremely difficult to perform in the early days of the liberation because the exuberance of the Belgians. In addition, patriots took the opportunity to settle old scores. On 4 September, for example, firing occurred at spasmodic intervals in many parts of Brussels as German troops and collaborators were flushed out from their hiding places. Later, in the Dutch town of Enschede, military police witnessed a sight that was often repeated in other towns – shaven-headed collaborators being marched through the streets, each bearing a placard announcing their crime. Pockets of enemy personnel were sometimes uncovered. Two NCOs of the Guards Armoured Division Provost Company captured 14 German soldiers hiding in a barn. Having been tipped off by a young boy, the MPs 'shouted to the Germans to surrender, and saw numerous heads appear from a heap of straw'.[4] In all cases, close liaison with the civilian police of the liberated territories was essential.

* * * *

Operation *Market Garden*, which began on 17 September, was a simple, bold and very risky plan by which Montgomery aimed to restore the momentum which had carried 21st Army Group from Normandy to the Netherlands. Three airborne divisions would be dropped to seize crossings over five strategic watercourses. Horrocks' British XXX Corps would then advance through a narrow corridor and link up with the airborne troops. If the plan succeeded, the Allies would have won a major prize: a bridgehead beyond the German-held bank of the Rhine and across the River Ijssel. The first two objectives were duly seized by the United States 82nd and 101st Airborne Divisions. These divisions were, as planned, relieved by XXX Corps. Major General R E Urquhart's British 1st Airborne Division dropped on the furthest objective, the bridge over the lower Rhine at Arnhem.

XXX Corps failed to relieve Urquhart's men. Stiff German resistance cut the road from Nijmegen and prevented Horrocks' tanks from reaching Arnhem. Although 1st Airborne Division landed safely, it soon found itself involved in heavy fighting, for elements of two SS panzer divisions were resting in the area. Within hours, the men of 1st Airborne were fighting for their lives against fierce counter-attacks, with the 2nd Parachute Battalion under Lieutenant Colonel John Frost doggedly holding the approaches to Arnhem bridge.

> It is impossible [stated the Provost Company's war diarist] to give a complete picture of the operation since contact was only made in the very early stages with Nos 1 & 2 Sections, and of these sections only one NCO from No 1 Section has so far returned. At Div HQ the Coy Comm [*sic*] and all airborne personnel landed safely, including the jeep.

Urquhart established Divisional Headquarters in an hotel in Oosterbeck and here a POW cage was established on the hard tennis court. By the morning of 21 September about 200 Germans were held in this makeshift cage, of whom about 60 per cent were members of the Waffen SS. Enemy strength grew almost by the hour, but 1st Airborne Division gallantly defended their positions, desperately hoping that XXX Corps would arrive to save the day.

After the fourth day, the weather closed in. Few supplies were dropped 'and still fewer landed in the right place'. As a consequence, for five days no rations were issued to the POW. The British troops were little better off. Urquhart himself visited the POW cage on 21 September. In his memoirs he recalled 'the Military Police and glider pilots with Stens under their arms; the prisoners, in shabby uniforms and with weary, bearded faces, st[anding] in sullen silence'. Other military policemen fought alongside the infantry. Sergeant A Roberts, who was 'usually quiet and reserved' was killed charging the enemy with a Sten gun, although he had already been wounded in the arm.

By 25 September it was clear that 1st Airborne could not hold on for much longer. 'Shelling and mortaring has become very heavy', noted the provost war diarist on that date, 'and snipers have infiltrated into our position. APM [Major O P Haig] and RSM [W Kibble] both wounded'. On the following day, the division gave up the unequal struggle and disengaged. Two military policemen, Corporal Peter Dale and Lance Corporal Ken Storey, volunteered to stay behind to prevent the prisoners from informing their comrades of the evacuation, in order to buy vital time for the remainder of the Division to escape. In the words of one of their comrades, this was an act of 'cool, calculating grit'; Dale received the Dutch Bronze Cross, and Storey a MID. The main body of the Provost Company set out, under the OC, Captain W B Gray, to escape. According to the War Diary,

> they ran into opposition on the way to the river and Captain Gray received wounds from which he subsequently died. Only one of the party succeeded in getting across the river. Out of a total of 5 officers and 66 ORs who took part in the operation 1 officer and 11 ORs returned.

The rest were killed, missing or taken prisoner.[5]

XXX Corps failed to reach Arnhem in part because it was attempting to drive along a single road against tough German resistance. 113 Provost Company was largely responsible for signing this and the rest of Club Route, the main axis of XXX Corps' advance. On 22 September, at 1430 hours Corporal H Wall was on duty on Club Route 'when a Dutch Maquis [resistance fighter] . . . informed me in an excited manner that a German tank and some infantry were within half a mile of the road'. 107 Panzer Brigade had succeeded in cutting the road three miles north of Veghel. After some adventures Corporal Wall managed to rejoin 113 Provost Company. On the afternoon of 23 September, the Germans were repulsed and the road was reopened, but XXX Corps had been further delayed and the congestion on the road had grown even greater.

British military policemen had plenty of evidence of the strength of the German resistance. At 0600 hours on 19 September, Sergeant V Fisher

of 113 Provost Company had led a CMP patrol which cleared St Oeder-
ode church of German snipers, while on the following day Lieutenant
Smith of the same unit was caught up in a German attack. He 'went off
in a tank [of Guards Armoured Division], as commander, and engaged
the enemy with success, inflicting casualties'. The Guards Armoured
Division Provost Company were also caught up in stiff fighting, recording
with a certain amount of understatement that they found controlling
traffic 'very difficult owing to enemy counter-attacks'. Also on the 20th
Lance Corporal Dorman of 113 Provost Company led a fighting patrol
of American troops in clearing a wood of German troops. When he had
pointed out to the American officer who ordered him to lead the patrol
that he (Dorman) had been placed in command of an officer and several
sergeants, Dorman was told 'That's OK, boy; they'll follow you'! The
officer was right. They did.[6]

Market Garden was a gamble that narrowly failed. Many fundamental
mistakes were made in operational planning, not least the choice of DZs
and LZs some eight miles from the objective of Arnhem bridge, and the
fact that the lift of 1st Airborne Division could only be completed on the
second day of the operation. On the ground, despite careful attention
given to traffic control, in which both static Traffic Control Posts (comprising Royal Artillery wireless vehicles and REME as well as provost)
and mobile CMP units were used, the difficulties involved in passing an
entire corps along such a narrow corridor contributed in no small measure to the failure. A member of the 53 Division Provost Company neatly
summed up the problems encountered on one, not untypical, section of
the route – Nijmegen bridge. The bridge was under continual enemy fire,
so the flow of traffic had to be spaced by provost. It then had to run the
gauntlet of shellfire. In addition, the roads 'were so narrow it necessitated
"one way" traffic circuits on roads that hardly existed, and those that did
could not stand the strain and collapsed at the edges. It was enough to
whiten the hair of any APM'.[7]

* * * *

The failure to seize the Rhine crossings condemned 21st Army Group
to inch through the Low Countries in accordance with General Eisenhower's 'Broad Front' strategy. Until November, the First Canadian
Army was engaged in a painful series of operations to clear the Scheldt
estuary. The Dutch town of 's Hertogenbosch was the scene of heavy
fighting in October, which was followed by an offensive to clear the west
bank of the River Maas which lasted until early December. Nijmegen
bridge continued to be of crucial importance in providing a logistic lifeline

to combat formations in the area west of the Rhine known as 'The Island' – a flat sodden piece of polderland in which life for the troops was pure misery. It was the lot of many MPs to control traffic on Nijmegen bridge, which was under frequent shell fire. 12 TC Company CMP signals did particularly valuable work in maintaining communications across the bridge. On 13 December, XII Corps took over from XXX Corps on the line of the Maas. XXX Corps moved into reserve. In order to maintain security, no signing of routes was allowed, so the men of 113 Provost Company were deployed along 100 miles of road to act as human signposts.[8]

Service on the lines of communication did not necessarily mean freedom from danger. As late as May 1945, men of 26 TC Company CMP were deployed to search the 's Hertogenbosch area for a party of enemy saboteurs who had succeeded in mining a railway line. Antwerp was a vital logistic base for 21st Army Group, a fact recognised by the enemy, who bombarded 'buzzbomb alley' with 7,000 V–1s and V–2s from November 1944 onwards. CMP casualties were frequent. In one incident, four men of 73 TC Company CMP were wounded when a traffic post was demolished by a V–1. Earlier, the headquarters of 185 Ports Provost Company had received a direct hit. Four men had been killed and the APM, Major Mason, badly wounded. 73 Company organised an incident squad, equipped with a jeep and trailer loaded with signs and other equipment. When the report of an explosion was heard, the whereabouts of the incident was roughly ascertained, from the column of smoke, plotted on a map, and then the squad was dispatched to control traffic and to help restore order. The traffic was never held up for more than ten minutes.[9]

Traffic control and crime remained the bread-and-butter of military policemen serving on the lines of communication. In December 1944, APM Brussels Garrison was one of the world's busiest car park attendants, with some 33,220 vehicles passing through the car parks in use. Crime was a growth industry in the winter of 1944–45. Some of the cases dealt with by provost and SIB were fairly unusual – 71 Section SIB investigated an interesting case of the death of three soldiers through alcohol poisoning in Amiens, and 81 Section SIB grappled with the 'Field Corps Police', an audacious band of deserters who masqueraded as senior NCOs and officers and stole vehicles. Most of the crimes were rather more mundane affairs of black market trading in military food, tyres and petrol, and illegal currency dealings. No less than 509 arrests were made, and £11,567 of property was recovered in Antwerp in the space of two months. Moderately successful operations were launched against illegal activities. Operation *Blanket*, carried out in Ghent in

February 1945 netted two stolen vehicles and 77 deserters. The alarmingly high level of absenteeism demanding constant patrolling and checking of passes in cities such as Brussels.

The CMP, in common with the rest of the British Army in the last 18 months of the war, suffered from a dwindling supply of manpower. As a result, the CMP became ridiculously overstretched. In Antwerp, in November 1944, only one Warrant Officer and four NCOs of 81 Section SIB could be used on operations in the port area, a number which was admitted to be 'totally inadequate' but which was 'as many as could be spared' from other duties. Likewise, in the Ghent area, the bulk of provost work had to be confined to the city where one or one-and-a-half sections was considered 'adequate'. The manpower situation in Ghent was eased a little in 1945 by the use of Allied provost, but shortly after the end of hostilities the SIB situation was described as 'acute', with a long queue of cases waiting to be dealt with by a sub-section of 83 Section.[10]

Much SIB time was taken up with investigating claims of looting lodged against British troops by civilians. The experience of 70 Section SIB led them to believe that the British forces were on the whole, well behaved:

> without attempting to whitewash the conduct of British troops in this respect, it is considered that civilians were responsible for the majority of looting which later became the subject of claims on the Allied governments.

The task of investigating such claims, on top of all their other duties, was never ending. In the course of their spell in the Low Countries, 70 Section 'was badly-overworked and had no relaxation whatsoever'.[11]

The first ATS Provost, 26 in number, arrived on the Continent on 10 August 1944 and were deployed to carry out normal provost duties around Bayeux. Inevitably dubbed 'Monty's Glamour Girls', they were commanded by Junior Commander Buckle, DAPM. In the Normandy bridgehead, they were frequently called upon to furnish guards and escorts for various females (including Russians, Poles and French) captured with enemy forces. Later in October they moved to Brussels where they took part in organised raids on cafés, theatres and the like, and participated in flying patrols to other areas and towns such as Ghent. A half section of ATS Provost was posted to Vilvorde POW camp in February 1945. On 23 April, a section was sent to Antwerp, where they were regularly used by a grateful APM to search female suspects in the docks. ATS Provost more than justified their despatch to the L of C and there were soon demands for more sections. Six extra sections were formed in April 1945 from women taken from disbanding AA units. A further four sections arrived from the United Kingdom in June 1945.[12]

* * * *

On the morning of 16 December 1944, the Germans sprang one of the greatest surprises of the war. Hitler threw most of his remaining reserves against lightly-held American positions in the Ardennes, to the south of 21st Army Group. The 'Battle of the Bulge', as it came to be known, was in retrospect doomed to failure but at the time the speed of the German blitzkrieg appeared very threatening. XXX Corps was hastily deployed to the south and British forces were moved up from reserve. This involved some very tricky traffic control, necessitating the erection of British axis signs in American areas. At one stage 113 Provost Company and the Guards Armoured Division Provost Company shared traffic control duties with US MPs in Namur. An added ingredient to the normal recipe was the activities of enemy soldiers dressed in American uniforms, which entailed much checking of passes. By the end of 1944 the crisis had passed. The German offensive had failed. Never again were they able to seize the initiative in the West.[13]

21st Army Group's advance towards the Reich was renewed with the launching of Operation *Veritable* in February 1945. This operation was designed to clear the area between the River Maas and the Rhine, leaving Montgomery in a position to cross the Rhine itself. The initial attack was carried out by Horrocks's XXX Corps, under the command of First Canadian Army. Horrocks had the unenviable task of mounting a frontal assault against the well fortified and heavily defended positions of the Siegfried Line. The key to the battle lay in breaking through a 5,000 yard wide bottleneck between the forest of the Reichswald and polderland southeast of Nijmegen. As a post-action report noted, 'It was appreciated that the successful execution of the operation would largely depend on efficient traffic control'. To this end, 1600 military policemen were deployed to control the 25,000 vehicles that brought 200,000 men and their supplies to the front line. To preserve secrecy, much of the movement was done at night.

Traffic control during *Veritable* was carefully organised. In the initial stages, a 'Regulating HQ' and nine Traffic Control Posts were provided by 53 Reconnaissance Regiment, each TCP having a sub-section of CMP attached. The whole organisation was under the orders of APM 53rd Division. In addition, divisional provost companies controlled 'tactical' traffic in their sectors. The assault opened on 8 February. Many roads had been turned into quagmires by the heavy rain. The main axis of advance, the road running parallel with the Waal, was up to four feet deep in water, as the Germans had blown some important dykes. As a result, many military policemen worked long hours up to their waists in icy water.

The traffic congestion created by the appalling state of the roads was exacerbated by what Horrocks described as 'one of the worst mistakes I made in the war', the decision to pass a reserve formation, 43rd (Wessex) Division, through one of the assaulting divisions, 15th (Scottish), on 9/10 February. This created an enormous traffic jam which would have been a perfect target for air attack. It was fortunate indeed that the Luftwaffe had virtually ceased to exist by this stage of the war. The following day had to be devoted to disentangling of the two divisions. Despite the traffic problem at the beginning of the offensive, provost emerged from the battle for the Reichswald with its reputation largely intact. The official postmortem on *Veritable* argued that this and other operations had witnessed a 'serious decline' in traffic discipline, and that the British were actually inferior to the Americans in this respect. 'Provost are generally first class', the report concluded, 'but they alone cannot cope with this problem.[14]

At the beginning of March 1945, Nazi Germany was being crushed like a nut in a vice, as the Red Army advanced from the east and the Anglo–Americans moved in from the west. Montgomery's 21st Army Group prepared for an assault crossing of the Rhine in a typically methodical fashion. The British 6th and US 17th Airborne Divisions were to be dropped east of the river, and Allied airforces were to 'soften up' enemy positions. The vast logistic effort involved in assembling the assaulting forces – sometimes under fire, mostly at night, without the benefit of lights, which meant that reconnaissance had to be carried out after dark – once again tested provost, and they were not found wanting. On 23 March the operation began.

Montgomery disposed of a greater number of guns, with more ammunition, than any other British general in history. The CQMS of 22 TC Company later recalled that by 1700 hours on 23 March the 'steady rumble of the artillery had become "an ear-splitting never ending roar"'. This was the signal for the men of the Company to work 'as they had never worked before under nightmare conditions'. The second in command, Lieutenant Morrison, was killed during that night, and a pointsman badly wounded. 101 TC Company signed and lighted the last section of the route down to the river at H Hour minus 60 minutes (on this section of the front, 0100 hours, 24 March 1945), coming under machine gun fire in the process. Half an hour after midnight traffic was halted to allow the assault 'Buffaloes' (amphibious vehicles) to move down to the river bank. CMP Traffic Control assault sections crossed with the infantry, as did sections of the 15th (Scottish) Division Provost, and other sections followed close behind. Once across the river, 22 TC Company sustained some casualties from mortar and machine gun fire while a pontoon bridge was thrown across the Rhine. For this unit, as for others, the crossing of the Rhine was 'nerve wracking . . . the men [got] very little rest, working around the clock without relief owing to the number of casualties'. The reward was great. 21st Army Group was across the Rhine in force.[15]

* * * *

From the Rhine, the First Canadian and Second British Armies moved rapidly through Germany, overrunning towns and cities devastated by Allied bombers. The power of the Wehrmacht had been all but broken, but some opposition remained, sporadic but occasionally fierce. Several months later, Sergeant H Mitchell of 11th Armoured Division Provost Company recalled this period of the war:

> We soon found that Provost work in an enemy and hostile country can be a very trying and nerve-wracking affair . . . [on point duty] the mainstay of any Provost Company, the humble L/Cpl . . . had a most unenviable role. Without any sort of cover, and without a readily accessible weapon, they were hand-made targets for the highly organised sniper-system employed by the Germans . . . one was never certain or not whether a gun was trained on one's back, and when one has a radius of about 2 yds (*sic*) to move, this can be quite uncomfortable.[16]

By early May, British forces had reached the Baltic coast. Provost duties still had to be performed; traffic had to be controlled over rivers such as the Aller, Weser and Elbe; POW camps had to be guarded by VP Companies (the oldest recorded prisoner handled by 603 VP Company was 78 years old, the youngest a Russian boy of 10): crimes had to be investigaged by the SIB. Some of the most heart-rending scenes that CMP men encountered were connected with concentration camps. Some victims of the camps passed through the POW cages run by 603 VP Company, 'many in a pitiable condition . . . arriving with little clothing, badly nourished and in some cases in such a condition that they could not eat the food offered to them'.[17]

The end, when it came, was almost an anti-climax. On 4 May 1945, the War Diary of 601 VP Company noted 'OC visited APM 30 Corps. Company remained overnight at 113 Pro Coy. Hostilities ceased in NW Europe'. On that day, MPs of Tactical HQ accompanied Montgomery to Luneburg Heath, where he received the surrender of German forces. Apart from two sergeants of the Intelligence Corps, the men of the CMP were the only other ranks present at this historic encounter. Four days later, the war in Europe was officially over. On VE Day, men of 26 TC Company 'took part in an amusing mock arrest, trial and punishment of the "Hitler Gang"'. It was as appropriate a way as any to mark the end of the régime which had brought about the most destructive war in history.[18]

Part Four:
The Postwar Era –
From 1945 to the Gulf War

The RMP in Europe, 1945–1991

The Allied forces advancing into Germany in 1945 found a country physically devastated by war. Germany surrendered unconditionally and was divided into four zones by the victorious powers: the Soviet Union, Britain, the United States and France. 21st Army Group was transformed on 25 August 1945 into the British Army of the Rhine (BAOR), organised into two Corps Districts (I and XXX Corps). Lieutenant Colonels P Godfrey-Faussett and D W L Melville, the Corps APMs, were upgraded to DPM in recognition of their heavier responsibilities. DPM I Corps had 11 APMs and 60 other officers under his control. In all, I Corps could field six provost companies, five traffic control companies, two VP companies, three SIB sections, two Belgian provost companies, and three German *Feldgendarmerie* companies.

The CMP was to play an important role in producing order from chaos. The Western Allies held 7.7 million military prisoners, who had to be processed. The 5th Division Provost Company received 11,000 prisoners into the company cage in one day. In addition there were 3,750,000 former slave workers now categorised as displaced persons (DPs) in the Western occupation sectors. These victims of Nazism caused considerable problems. 120 Provost Company, based at Bad Oeynhausen, carried out an active campaign to capture Polish DPs who lived by a form of banditry. German war criminals were also sought out. A former commandant of Auschwitz, Rudolf Hoess, was captured by British military policemen near Flensburg in March 1945. At his trial for War Crimes, held at Nuremburg in 1946, Hoess admitted that about 3,000,000 people had died in the camp during his period of office. A CMP section was sent to Nuremburg for duties during the trials, and later volunteers were sought to assist the hangman at the execution of the condemned prisoners.

Two military policemen, escorts to Major General L O Lyne, GOC 7th Armoured Division, were among the very first British troops to enter Berlin. One recalled 'demolished bridges and very stubborn Russian sentries' as being the principal hazards of the journey.[1] Berlin lay within the Soviet zone of occupation, but was divided into four allied zones of control and governed by an inter-allied *Kommandantura*. In Berlin British,

US and French troops provided a western military presence behind what was to become known as the Iron Curtain. In the years immediately following the war, much provost work involved policing of the civilian population. Initially, relations between the four wartime allies remained cordial and this was reflected in the situation in Berlin. An 'Incident Squad' was formed, to which Soviet military police were attached. However, by June 1948, the international situation had deteriorated and the Soviets imposed a blockade of Berlin. The Cold War was well and truly underway.

The RMP – the Royal prefix had been bestowed in 1946 (this landmark event is described in greater detail later in this chapter) – emerged from the Berlin Blockade with its reputation enhanced. In a situation fraught with danger the risk existed of a minor incident escalating into a military confrontation. As Major Lovell-Knight rightly pointed out, in Berlin military police were far better suited to dealing with an incident than infantry, whose appearance 'may well be interpreted as a display of force calling for countermeasures'. By contrast, the RMP were 'organised, trained and equipped' to intervene in the least provocative and most tactful fashion, ensuring that incidents can be 'kept down to the scale of a police matter instead of escalating into military action'. This was especially important during periods of heightened tension. The Western Allies mounted a massive airlift, the greatest in history, and rode out the blockade, which was called off in May 1949. Life returned to what, in the divided city of Berlin, passed for normality. 247 (Berlin) Provost Company and SIB continued to co-operate not only with US and French military policemen and German civil police, but also on occasion with their Soviet counterparts. As well as normal disciplinary duties, vital in this 'showcase' city, the RMP had an important role in controlling the autobahn which provided Berlin with a vital landbased lifeline to the west.

Austria, like Germany, was divided into zones of occupation at the end of the war. In May 1945, British forces moved forward from Italy to occupy their zone of Austria. One particularly distasteful task that fell to the 78th Division Provost Company at the end of the month was that of handing over Cossacks and other Soviet citizens to the Red Army. These people had been captured while serving with the Germans.[2] The British occupation forces in Austria were served by a DPM, APM, 105 Provost Company and 92 Section SIB. Vienna, like Berlin, lay within the Soviet Sector and was divided into occupation zones although unlike Berlin, the temporary arrangements in Vienna did not harden into permanent partition; throughout, the city centre remained under international control. All foreign troops withdrew from Austria in September 1955 as the result of an international agreement.

The situation faced by provost in Vienna in 1945 was fraught with difficulties. Some Soviet troops were poorly disciplined, with looting and rape commonplace in the badly-damaged city. Captain Mike Hawkins of 105 Provost Company recalled the delicate situation which arose when raids on brothels unearthed high-ranking officers of allied armies. Everyday dealings with the Soviets could prove difficult. When a Warrant Officer of 105 Provost Company was arrested by the Soviets for possessing a cricket bat (thought by the non-cricket playing Russians to be a dangerous weapon), it proved to be a delicate and long-drawn out process to liberate him from a Soviet jail. In order to increase co-operation between the military police of the four occupying powers, the US Provost Marshal in Vienna suggested, in August 1945, that an 'International Patrol' of military police should be formed. Initially, the Soviets were strongly opposed to the idea, but under pressure from the British, French and Americans, they changed their views and entered into the spirit of it.

The International Patrol consisted of four military policemen, one from each occupying power, patrolling an area in a jeep. Who exactly commanded the jeep depended on the sector that was being patrolled. Five patrols, one for each sector of the city, operated in a 24 hour period. The patrol undoubtedly smoothed the course of the occupation, avoiding the diplomatic complications that might have arisen if, for instance, a drunken Soviet soldier had been arrested by an RMP NCO instead of a Soviet military policeman. Although the suspicions and antagonisms of the Cold War occasionally surfaced – Soviet members of the Patrol were reluctant to accept hospitality in a British mess, however friendly they might have been while on duty, for fear of reprisals from their superiors – the military police International Patrol in Vienna stands as an example of low-level international co-operation which was sadly rare in the Europe of the Cold War era.[3]

* * * *

BAOR was a much smaller force than the wartime army that it replaced. 234 Provost Company was not untypical in that it contained elements of four wartime units. The Cold War brought major political and military changes. The status of BAOR changed from that of an army of occupation to that of an allied army stationed in a friendly state, the Federal Republic of Germany. In 1949 the North Atlantic Treaty Organisation (NATO) was born, and in 1951 I (BR) Corps was formed, with four divisions, 2nd and 4th Infantry and 6th and 7th Armoured. 59 Provost Company became the Corps company and was renamed accordingly. In May 1951, an RMP unit was deployed to Supreme Headquarters Allied

Powers in Europe (SHAPE), near Paris where they co-operated with the military police of their NATO allies. In 1960, the first WRAC Provost was integrated into the SHAPE Independent Provost Unit. In 1966, SHAPE moved to Mons in Belgium.

* * * *

In June 1953, serious rioting broke out in Soviet controlled East Berlin. The newly introduced Town Radio Net greatly eased the task of the RMP in patrolling sector borders.[4] From 1955 the RMP also co-operated with the military police of the newly created *Bundeswehr* (West German armed forces). Thirteen years after the first Berlin crisis, the city once again became the centre of another major crisis. In the early hours of Sunday 13 August 1961, an RMP border patrol discovered that East German and Soviet troops, including tanks, had concentrated around the border crossing railway station at Staaken. The patrol commander, Corp- oral M A Blakey, contacted the APM by radio-telephone. Berlin had been the cause of international tension for some months. Many citizens of the communist East German state had been fleeing to the West through West Berlin, threatening its very viability. The APM, Lieutenant Colonel L F Richards, arrived at Staaken to find 'the East Germans blocking the railway crossing with reinforced concrete blocks' and erect- ing 'Dannert wire fencing between concrete uprights along the border, just on their side of line'.

Richards and his men were among the first Westerners to witness the building of the Berlin Wall. Lieutenant Colonel Richards alerted GOC Berlin about the situation and the latter agreed that Richards should move up to the Soviet Sector border to try to ascertain the intentions of the communists, which were far from clear. The Soviet Sector proved to be packed with troops and military vehicles. Richards was able to obtain two pamphlets which contained proclamations by the East German authorities about restrictions on movement to West Berlin. This placed the communist operation in perspective; it was not the prelude to an invasion of West Berlin. Later, the then Foreign Secretary, Lord Home, congratulated the APM and the border patrols, for, in Richards' words, the RMP border patrol 'had certainly proved its value'. Its actions had ensured that the senior British commander and the British Government were receiving information long before the Americans. Without this intelligence, 'a false move . . . might have had very dire consequences'.[5]

From the 1950s until the late 1980s the British Army of the Rhine consisted of about 55,000 men. By the end of the 1960s about one third of the RMP were deployed in Germany. In the event of a Soviet invasion the RMP's operational role would have been an updated version of that of March 1918, the greatest defensive battle ever fought by the British Army. Elements of some of the Western Desert campaigns of 1941–2 would have been thrown in for good measure, as Soviet armoured and mechanised forces could have been expected to have penetrated deep behind NATO lines and headed for the Rhine. Perhaps the nearest that the RMP came to an operational role at this time was the maintenance of 'flag patrols' along the Inner German Border.

The mid-to-late 1960s were a testing time. Training for war in addition to ever increasing demands for disciplinary duties placed a heavy burden on manpower resources for both provost and SIB. An effective plan involving high-profile policing, intended to reduce road accidents caused by excessive speed, alcohol and poor driving conditions, was devised by a distinguished trio of RMP officers, Lieutenant Colonel Dennis Rendell (APM I (BR) Corps), Major Jack Thomas and Captain Norman Allen – all of whom were later to become Provost Marshal (Army) – working under the aegis of the Provost Marshal (Army), Brigadier L F Richards. By the end of the decade, the number of deaths had been substantially reduced. However, another menace was beginning to appear, as the drug habit, prevalent among US troops serving in Vietnam, was spreading to American forces in Europe. The RMP, and the SIB in particular, took measures to attack the drug threat to British forces, so that the problem was effectively contained during the troublesome decade which followed.[6]

Apart from training for war, the RMP's major function was and remains the policing of garrison towns and the roads linking them, in close co-operation with the German Police. The introduction of increasingly sophisticated communications technology from the mid-1960s onwards made truly mobile provost patrols a reality.

Inevitably, given the large British garrisons in Germany, the SIB were never short of work. BAOR undertook 1896 investigations in 1966 and property to the value of £8,000 was recovered. In the 1980s, the SIB were all too frequently called upon to carry out a new role, that of investigating terrorist attacks committed against British soldiers and their families on the continent. At the end of 1989, 74 Section RMP BAOR sadly recorded that they had been busy investigating the murder of Mrs Heide Hazell, the German wife of a British soldier, and the shooting of two soldiers at Munster. In addition, NCOs had been detached to 70 Section to assist with the investigation of a car bombing in Hanover. The 1980s saw the SIB continue to battle against drug abuse in BAOR. Currently, there are two DITs (Drug Intelligence Teams), located in Germany and Britain respectively, carrying out 'covert observation, surveillance and intelligence gathering operations' against drug users and dealers.[7]

* * * *

From 1947 until the early 1960s, much of the British Army was composed of conscripted 'National Servicemen'. According to one writer, the
image of the Redcap was at its worst during National Service years.
Certainly, Roger Jones, who transferred to the RMP in the early 1960s
felt that as an ex-infantryman he was more prepared to use his discretion
in the case of erring soldiers than lance corporals straight from the RMP
Depot.[8] However, it should not be forgotten that many National Servicemen served in the ranks of the RMP. Lance Corporal M W Morris's
experiences were typical of many. Called up into the 'Glosters' in 1950,
he volunteered for the RMP after a fortnight of basic training. He was
trained as a military policeman at Inkerman Barracks, Woking, and in
January 1951 was posted to BAOR, travelling via the Hook of Holland.
Morris was posted to the 11th Armoured Division Provost Company at
Brunswick. His duties in Germany mainly consisted of foot and jeep
patrols of towns and hard training for operations. One of the strangest
experiences of Morris's military career was that of mounting guard on
the Soviet war memorial in Berlin on May Day, while an angry crowd
protested and waved banners. 'We looked very impressive with Sten Guns
at the ready', he remembered, 'but not one of us had a round of ammunition . . . I was thinking what the hell would we have done if they had
decided to rush us. Luckily, everything went off without much incident
in our section, but it was a frightening experience . . .'

One temporary military policeman had conflicting memories of National Service. During training in 1951 at Inkerman Barracks, F J B Smith
endured 'endless bulling' and 'verbal abuse', polished, blancoed, 'stuffed
various parts of my clothing and webbing with cardboard and paper and
stood, terrified, as inspections took place. And yet I was proud to complete the course . . . What power! I had been in the Army for six months
and I really was a fully fledged redcap [lance corporal], hated by all and
sundry'. This mixture of emotions perhaps sums up the feelings of many
many other National Servicemen who served in the RMP. The end of
National Service was marked by some bizarre rituals: one of the last
National Service Redcap military policemen to be 'demobbed' in the early
1960s was taken to the ferry handcuffed to a jeep.[9]

Quite apart from the arrival and departure of National Service, the
years 1945 to 1991 saw a number of significant developments in the
history of the Corps. On 28 November 1946, King George VI bestowed
the 'Royal' prefix on the Corps of Military Police. As a consequence of

its service on battlefields in Europe, Africa and Asia, the Corps emerged from the Second World War widely admired for its steadfastness under all conditions and its tireless efforts in support of every aspect of the Army's multifarious activities. The granting of the 'Royal' title was an honour which the Corps richly deserved for its vital contribution to the part played by the British Army in bringing about final victory in the long and bitter struggle with Germany and Japan.

The name 'Royal Provost Corps' was regretfully discarded and 'Corps of Royal Military Police' was chosen (it was felt that 'Royal Corps of Military Police', in some ways a more obvious title, was unsuitable because its abbreviation would cause confusion with the Royal Canadian Mounted Police). However, the King made it known that he preferred the title of RMP, and the Corps has been known by this title ever since. On 23 July 1947, the Duke of Gloucester bestowed the Royal title on the Corps at a parade at Inkerman Barracks, which had become the Corps Depot only a few months earlier. The Depot and Regimental Headquarters (the latter formed in 1961) moved to their present location at Roussillon Barracks, Chichester in 1964, where a museum was opened. The museum was considerably modernised and reopened in 1985.[10]

One of the most far reaching postwar developments was the creation of a permanent cadre of officers for the RMP. On 3 March 1954, the commissioning of Regular officers directly into the Corps was authorised. 206 serving officers were formally transferred into the Corps in the 12 months from 15 May 1954 to 15 May 1955. On 29 July 1955, Officer Cadet M R Biggs became the first Regular officer to be commissioned into the RMP direct from Sandhurst. Several other 'firsts' are worthy of record: in 1962, Major P R Stock became the first RMP officer to enter Staff College in open competition, and Brigadier R Davenport became, on 16 April 1965, the first officer of the Corps to become Provost Marshal (Army). All of his successors have also been officers of the Corps.[11]

The postwar period was marked by the steady integration of female personnel into the RMP. In 1986 two out of the 16 members of the RMP Mounted Troop were women, and in the same year Major P M Simpson became the first WRAC officer to command an RMP unit, 160 Provost Company at Aldershot, an event which excited considerable interest in the media. The disbandment of the WRAC in 1992, which allowed women to be recruited directly into the RMP, was the logical conclusion of a process which began with the first use of female military police during the First World War.

* * * *

In 1989, Berlin once again became the focus of the world's attention. The era of *glasnost* initiated by President Gorbachev in the late 1980s loosened the Soviet Union's grip on Eastern Europe. Beginning in August 1989, a remarkable series of revolutions toppled the rulers of the communist satellite states. On 9 November 1989, at 1830 hours, the East German authorities bowed to 'people power' and lifted travel restrictions on its citizens. In Berlin, all patrols of 2nd Regiment RMP (2 RMP)* were ordered to 'Watch for anything unusual and report'. The 'unusual' events were nothing less than the breaching of the Wall itself. In the early hours of 10 November, West Berlin police, East German border guards and Corporal Earing RMP were trying, unsuccessfully, to control the traffic at Checkpoint Charlie as thousands of East Berliners poured across the border. Eventually, the crossing was closed to traffic and the scene became one giant party. Even East German border guards were spotted throwing their hats in the air and smiling. As in the 1961 Berlin crisis, the RMP acted as the 'eyes and ears' for the British Army in Berlin. The Wall patrol of Corporals Slater and Winter had reported the sighting of people on the Wall at the Brandenburg Gate, one of the most potent symbols of divided Berlin; at Staaken on the border between East Germany and the British Sector, Corporal Ford and Lance Corporal Finister witnessed similar events.

The next few days saw 2 RMP working at full stretch to control traffic and pedestrians. Two of the more unusual of the Regiment's duties were the provision of information for the press at the Incident Control Point and water for over-heated Trabant motor cars! After dawn on 10 November, with traffic 'blocking all West-bound lanes at Helmstedt', the withdrawal of East German frontier guards left 246 Provost Company as 'the only effective policing agency between the Soviet checkpoint and the West German Border'. The Brandenburg Gate was finally opened to pedestrians on 22 December. As one military policeman remarked, 'this was THE emotive opening to confirm that finally The Wall was down. The party started again, the RMP Police Post in the middle of it'. Some 400,000 people gathered on New Year's Eve around the Gate.

Shortly after the Wall came down, a fine tribute to the work of the Corps was paid by the Mayor of Berlin, Herr Walter Momper. In a letter of 8 February 1990 to the Colonel Commandant of the Corps, General Sir Peter Inge, he wrote

---

*2 RMP had been reformed in 1982 from 246 and 247 Provost Companies and 248 German Security Unit, following the earlier creation of RMP Regiments in Northern Ireland. Like Northern Ireland, Berlin was a special situation where it was particularly effective to have military police working as a formed unit under its own commanding officer.

The Berliners and I know that the Royal Military Police have provided patrols on the Sector boundaries for over 30 years.

Since 1961 these unbroken patrols, especially along the Wall, have been of great help in maintaining confidence in the Allied committment to the security of West Berlin. Since the 9th November 1989, the continued Royal Military Police presence in assisting the West Berlin Police and the City authorities with the massive movement associated with the historical opening of the boundaries, typifies the co-operation and friendship on which Berlin will progress in the future.

I thank you and the Royal Military Police for their valuable contribution to the British support for Berlin.[12]

The Far East since 1945

The abrupt cessation of hostilities against Japan in August 1945 left a power vacuum in South-East Asia. Malaya and Singapore were rapidly reoccupied by British forces, but neither France nor the Netherlands was in a position to send troops to their colonies in the region. Thus, it was British and Indian troops that occupied French Indo-China and the Netherlands East Indies (NEI). However, local nationalists were not prepared tamely to exchange Japanese for European domination, and the Anglo–Indian forces found themselves involved in fighting. In 14 months the British forces in NEI sustained over 2,000 casualties. Provost played a major role in the attempt to restore order, by carrying out civil police duties and active operations. In November 1945, for instance, an Indonesian police station was raided by 23rd Indian Division Provost Unit. This raid resulted in the recovery of three tons of arms and ammunition. Problems did not come only from the Indonesians. On two occasions military policemen were witnesses of attempts on the life of the moderate Indonesian Prime Minister, Mr Sjahir. British troops were replaced by Dutch troops in the course of 1946. British forces also reoccupied Siam, Hong Kong and provided a force for the occupation of Japan, for which six provost sections (three British and three Indian) were deployed, under an APM.[1]

* * * *

In India itself, although in some respects little had changed – a military policeman who arrived in India in late 1945 was shaved while he slept in the time-honoured fashion by a 'napee-wallah' – the days of British rule were numbered. The months leading up to Independence and Partition on 15 August 1947 were difficult ones, as Indian units mutinied and serious inter-communal strife took place. Major L F Richards, APM 2nd Indian Airborne Division organised patrols of the Divisional Provost Unit to patrol Quetta on Independence Day. By midnight, the Bazaar area was blazing, and civilian casualties were mounting. Provost were instrumental in 'holding the fort' until a larger force could be assembled. The Unit also had the distressing role of attempting to control crowds of Hindus

and Sikhs at the railway station, as they tried to flee from what had
overnight become Pakistan. The last British troops pulled out of India in
February 1948. Two centuries of service had come to an end.[2]

* * * *

In contrast to the situation in India, service in Malaya seemed an enviable
option in early 1948. To the military policemen serving in Malaya in June
of that year 'it appeared as if peace had come to stay. All military forces
had been reduced . . . there were only nine sections of RMP in three
small units for the whole of Far East Land Forces (FARELF)! However,
in the second half of 1948, fate and the Communists intervened . . .'
Beginning in June 1948, the communist Malayan Races' Liberation Army
(MRLA), launched attacks on officials, plantations and security forces
from its bases deep in the jungle. The aim was to win a revolutionary
guerrilla war. In the early months of what became known as the
Emergency the weak and overstretched security forces faced an uphill
struggle but the prospect of losing Britain's richest colony prompted
reinforcement of Malaya. By early 1950, the Provost Marshal and his two
APMs could call upon five companies. 200 Provost Company, which had
been attempting to police the whole of Malaya, was concentrated in
Singapore on the formation of 210 Provost Company. In 1954 they were
heavily involved in controlling rioting in the city.

Other units deployed included the 17th Gurkha Division Provost
Company (composed of both Gurkha and British personnel) and 91
Section SIB. In 1949, a Singapore Guard Unit (later Regiment) of two
companies was raised, mainly from Malays. This unit carried out duties
analagous to the Vulnerable Point companies of the Second World War.
The four British and Gurkha companies were mainly used for disciplinary duties in Singapore and eight towns on the Malaya Peninsula.[3] With
up to 35,000 troops deployed in Malaya, this was a mundane but important job. As Lance Corporal A C Dart, a military policeman who served
in Kuala Lumpur wrote, infantrymen

> after spending three weeks in jungle on patrol had one week's leave to rest
> and spend a month's pay before going back in again, needless to say fights,
> bar brawls and drunkenness were prevalent and RMP patrols (foot and
> mobile) were busy with arrests, charges, escorts etc . . .[4]

General Sir Gerald Templer, High Commissioner and Director of Operations from 1952 to 1954 declared that the key to victory lay in winning
'the hearts and minds of the Malayan people'. Since the sight of foreign
troops smashing up a city was not calculated to achieve this end, the

RMP's firm control of indisciplined behaviour can be justly said to have played an important part in Templer's strategy.

In the early days, the operational role of the RMP was fairly limited, with relatively little call for traffic control. This changed in September 1949 with the launching of Operation *Swallow* in Kuala Lumpur, a cordon-and-search operation. *Swallow* was an early example of the close co-operation between civil police and the Army; the actual checking and searching were carried out by civil policemen with knowledge of Chinese and Malay, 'but mobility and firepower [was] supplied by RMP'. On one typical night, two sections of 2 Guards Brigade Provost Unit (a unit later absorbed into 210 Provost Company) commanded by Captain A R Graham were deployed. Half the party, with some civil police, were used to man temporary road blocks, where the identities of passers-by were checked. Meanwhile, the others searched suspected houses, which were surrounded by military policemen armed with Sten sub-machine guns. With the operation completed, it was repeated elsewhere in the town, well away from the first raid.[5]

The RMP were also involved in some rural operations in the early stages of the Emergency. The Malay village of Jenderam was targeted in Operation *Alka Seltzer*. This village was a source of supplies for Malay insurgents operating on the borders of Selangor and Negri Sembilan, and the headquarters of Abdul Manan, a prominent guerrilla leader. The operation began with a cordon being thrown round the area at night. The aim was to remove the inhabitants in lorries. It was essential to carry out this phase of the operation as smoothly and as quickly as possible. 17th Gurkha Division Provost Unit were tasked with closing the roads to all extraneous traffic and operating a one-way traffic circuit. To complicate matters, no prior reconnaissance had been carried out. As far as possible silence was maintained during the hours of darkness, in order to achieve surprise. Six traffic posts were set up, complete with weapon pits, should the insurgents try to interfere with the operation. The soldiers manning these posts were ordered to arrest anyone attempting to break out of the cordon, and shoot those who attempted to escape from arrest. In the event, 1500 villagers were removed, resettled in areas where they could not be intimidated by the insurgents, and the village razed to the ground. A 'wasp's nest of banditry' had been destroyed.[6]

Slowly, the security forces gained the upper hand. Independence was promised to the Malayan people by 1957. Landless Chinese squatters, hitherto a major source of support for the insurgents, were resettled in protected model villages. These political initiatives went hand in hand with military reforms. Emphasis was now placed on the co-ordination of military police and civil authorities and the gathering of intelligence. But ultimately the insurgents had to be fought in the jungle that covered 80 per cent of the country and which provided sanctuary for the guerrillas.

From 1952 onwards, the RMP's role began to change, with increasing emphasis being placed on 'jungle bashing'. Already, in 1951, NCOs of the 17th Gurkha Division Provost Company had been attached, six at a time, to an infantry battalion for jungle training and patrolling. The escort to GOC Malaya was also provided by the Gurkha provost in the form of two armoured scout cars each fitted with twin Bren guns. In July 1952, 18 Infantry Brigade Provost Company (a fairly new addition to the RMP order of battle) participated in Operation *Churchman*, the hunt for a notorious guerrilla leader, Liew Kon Kim, in the jungles of South Selangor. The military policemen

> were on duty continuously between 3rd and 26th July with little rest and living under jungle warfare conditions. They were called on to cope with the movement of a large number of troops at night arriving at many [points]. This undertaking was of the greatest importance, and if not carried out with silence and efficiency could well have defeated the object of the operation.

Liew Kon Kim, the 'Bearded Terror', was found and eliminated by a patrol of the Suffolks, the body being removed to the nearest police station by the RMP. In addition, 30 terrorist camps and eight food dumps were destroyed.[7]

91 Section SIB were kept busy in Singapore and Malaya, a particularly important task being the prevention of stolen weapons from reaching the communists. In early 1952, the SIB were tipped off that an Ordnance Sub-Depot was about to be raided by insurgents. In the event, the raiders and the SIB team came face to face outside the Depot. The SIB men were taken aback by this confrontation, having assumed that the movements they had heard in the dark had been made by other members of their team. Nevertheless, they rapidly recovered from their surprise and made six arrests. SIB operations were rarely as dramatic as this but they were demanding, involving the investigation of much violent crime, including murder.

By 1955, the corner had been turned, although five more years were to pass before the Emergency was ended. The RMP continued to play their role. Provost patrolled roads on the Peninsula, sometimes attracting the attention of ambushing insurgents. The Cameron Highlands (a particulary sensitive area which was home to large numbers of whites) were reached by 33 miles of continuous bends. Armed military policemen patrolled the convoys to deal with break downs and road traffic accidents. Early in 1954, the 17th Gurkha Division Provost Company reported that their main operational role was 'food control', enforcing the regulations that prevented the carriage of food which could end up in the hands of the insurgents. This policy of food denial was to be a key factor in the defeat of the insurgency, which nevertheless was not declared to be at an end until 31 July 1960.[8]

* * * *

Victory in Malaya was rapidly followed by another jungle campaign. In December 1962, 99 Gurkha Infantry Brigade Group were rushed to Brunei and successfully put down a rebellion against the Sultan. This began an undeclared war against Indonesia, ultimately involving British, New Zealand, Australian and Malaysian forces. Indonesia's aim was to obstruct the incorporation of British territories in northern Borneo into the new Federation of Malaysia. In April 1963, Indonesian guerillas were sent across the border from Kalimantan (Indonesian Borneo). The 'Confrontation', as it became known, escalated in December of that year with the commitment of Indonesian regular troops to cross-border incursions, which remained the main threat, despite the existence of a 'Clandestine Communist Organisation' within Malaysian Borneo.

The RMP, in co-operation with Federation of Malaysia Police, Gurkha Military Police (disbanded on 1 January 1965) and the police of other services, had many tasks. The inevitable disciplinary duties in the towns and anti-vice duties were vital for much the same reason as they had been during the Malayan Emergency, for the sixth of the ingredients for success laid down by Major General Walter Walker (then commander in Borneo) was winning the hearts and minds of the people of Borneo.

Although there were few roads in Borneo, this did not mean that traffic control was unimportant. The one road connecting Kuching, the capital of Sarawak, with the border carried much military traffic, was extremely narrow, was vulnerable to enemy ambush and was often flooded.[9] 'Armed provost patrols were constantly out locating and giving warning of floods, escorting heavy loads, searching civilian vehicles and even operating speed traps . . .' In addition, VIP escort duties, 'concierge' work (security duties) and the occasional arrest of civilians under security regulations were performed by the RMP.[10]

The Confrontation was a very different type of operation from the Malayan Emergency. Nevertheless, many of the techniques learned in Malaya were also found to be effective in Borneo. In July 1965, 99 Gurkha Infantry Brigade Provost Unit participated in Operation *Hammer*, the evacuation and resettlement of Chinese civilians from along the Kuching–Serian road. The RMP performed much the same role as in Operation *Alka Seltzer* a decade-and-a-half earlier. Provost also had its share of jungle operations. 19 Infantry Brigade Provost Unit mounted patrols with the Sarawak Police Field Force for the purpose of gathering intelligence. RMP units also contributed to the campaign to win or maintain the allegiance of the indigenous peoples. One river patrol of 51 Gurkha Infantry Brigade Provost Unit, who were tasked with carrying out topographical patrols, arrived at an Iban longhouse in 1965 and was promptly

> besieged with patients clamouring with treatment for injuries ranging from a severe parang cut to the shinbone to vomiting and ringworm . . . [Later] we were entertained royally . . . whilst we watched a most graceful and skilful display of their dancing to the rhythm of their drum-like gongs. [In return, the patrol demonstrated] the Twist and Limbo (which) fitted admirably to the tempo of their gongs. We feel, we acquitted ourselves well and helped to cement the already strong bond of friendship between the Iban and British soldiers.[11]

In numbers, the SIB commitment to the Confrontation was small but this was not reflected in the size of their tasks. SIB Detachment, Borneo was not set up until June 1966. Prior to that date, an SIB NCO had had to be flown in from Singapore as the need arose. The majority of calls for the assistance of the SIB came from infantry units deployed in the jungle, with the result that SIB men found themselves whisked from the splendours of Singapore to 'a sandbagged entrenchment . . . three hundred yards from the border'. A successful investigation by the SIB resulted in the trial of five servicemen for the attempted murder of a local headman. The SIB investigator, who happened to be in Kuching at the time of the incident was flown to the scene in a series of helicopters. Operations were suspended and the area was sealed off until the SIB man had completed his enquiries.[12]

The Confrontation ended in August 1966 when the Indonesians came to an agreement with Malaysia. This was formal recognition of the success of the model British counter-insurgency campaign and 'Claret' cross-border raids into Kalimantan. Two Gurkha (51 and 99) and two British (5 and 19) Brigade Provost Units, plus, from January 1964, Borneo Provost Section, had taken part in the campaign which caused less than 100 Allied casualties. Not everything had gone smoothly – the lack of a senior provost officer permanently stationed on Borneo was particularly unfortunate – but the RMP and Gurkha Military Police had performed well under difficult conditions, playing their part to the full in what was described by the then Defence Secretary, Denis Healey, as 'one of the most efficient uses of military force in the history of the world'.

Retreat from Empire:
The Middle East, Cyprus and Kenya

The British Army's role in the quarter century that followed the Second World War was very largely one of disengagement from Empire. The numerous colonial campaigns of this period were fought not to retain overseas possessions at all costs, but rather to ensure that successor states would be stable, pro-British and anti-communist. The Army has enjoyed a fair measure of success in its postwar counter-insurgency campaigns. The first major operation in the Middle East following the end of the Second World War was, however, anything but successful.

Even before the Second World War, Palestine had been a thorn in the flesh of the British. From 1936 to 1939, the Arab population were in revolt against the British. The CMP presence in Palestine was reinforced by two provost companies and three provost sections. A major reason for the revolt was that the Arabs felt threatened by the influx of Jewish settlers into Palestine. After the defeat of Hitler, the British in Palestine were opposed principally by the Jews. From 1945 to 1948, the British forces were harried by Jewish guerrillas. Sergeant David Ashley Hall arrived in January 1947 to serve with the Palestine Command Provost Company. A few laconic jottings in his diary give a clear picture of the role of the RMP in his time, much of which was occupied with the small change of garrison policing, patrolling brothels in Tel Aviv and Jaffa, and dealing with British soldiers on disciplinary charges; but his diary is also punctuated with details of terrorist bombings and shootings.

1.3.47.	To Tel Aviv. Jerusalem Officers Club blown up.
14.5.47.	Sarafand cinema blown up.
20.5.47.	Threat to blow up CRMP HQ.
16.8.47.	Funeral of Colonel shot in Jerusalem last night.
1.9.47.	All company on stand by to (*sic*) rioting in Tel Aviv, not allowed to join in.[1]

Much of the work of riot control and cordon-and-search operations was undertaken by the Palestine Police, with the Army in support. Naturally, close co-operation developed between the Palestine Police and the RMP. In Jerusalem, a 'Flying Squad' of RMP jeep patrols, controlled by radio from RMP Headquarters, was formed to supplement foot and motorcycle patrols. In September 1947, a journalist published an account of a Flying Squad patrol which consisted of two jeeps, each containing three men:

> As we toured the city, sometimes cruising slowly, sometimes moving at high speed, the whole city came under our observation in a space of a few minutes. It was often a question of 'follow the leader', reappearing at odd street corners every few minutes and on all sides of the city . . . The presence of the Flying Squad in the streets of Jerusalem has greatly cut down the number of incidents involving troops, while their prompt arrival on the scene of alleged incidents has proved an enormous number of these reports to have been pure fabrications involving no troops at all.
>
> Every few minutes, as we combed the streets, the leading Jeep pulled up alongside either a Palestine Police armoured car, or one of the Military Police foot patrols to pass on information picked up – things they had seen in such and such a street, a message from headquarters.[2]

A RMP mounted patrol was used in the hills around Jerusalem, a Dog Section was used for mine detection, and the inevitable load of traffic control came the way of the RMP. The SIB section was based in Jerusalem with detachments at Haifa and Sarafand.

For military policemen service in Palestine was a dangerous, stressful business. Eight members of the RMP were killed. One RMP veteran of the campaign recalled that although regulations stated that service revolvers should be loaded with five rounds, leaving one chamber empty for safety reasons, most were loaded with a full six rounds: 'we wanted the gun to fire first time, as we always felt the blank chamber could mean a matter of life and death'. One particularly hazardous operation was mounted by the RMP in 1947. It was customary for British troops in Palestine to make a pilgrimage on Christmas Eve to church services in Bethlehem. The problem was the Jerusalem–Bethlehem road, which winds through groves and valleys for about seven miles. It was an obvious place for an ambush. APM East-Palestine Sub-District was tasked with shepherding the convoys which would be staged throughout the night, taking some 7,000 troops to Bethlehem. Three infantry battalions and the armoured cars of the Palestine Police were deployed along the road. 40 military police were available to cover Jerusalem, Bethlehem and the road in between. A section was deployed at each end of the road, and mobile patrols with wireless communications patrolled the road in between. In the event, no weapons were lost and no military casualties were incurred, although three Palestine Police were killed by mines. By the standards of the Palestine campaign, the operation was a success.[3]

* * * *

In 1948 the British cut their losses and gave up their mandate in Palestine, but they still had a role to play in the Middle East. By this stage the British were regarded by many Egyptians as unwanted guests who had overstayed their welcome. Five military policemen manning a CMP outpost in Alexandria were attacked by a mob in March 1946, and two were killed. One of the survivors, Lance Corporal A D Jump, was later awarded the BEM in recognition of his meritorious service during the riots in Alexandria. By 1947 British troops, by agreement with the Egyptian authorities, had withdrawn from Egypt proper to the Suez Canal Zone, an area 110 miles long by 50 miles wide. The Canal Zone became the principal British base in the Middle East. This did not satisfy the Egyptian nationalists. In October 1951, the Egyptians abrogated a treaty of 1936, undermining the British right to remain on Egyptian soil. This action was followed by what amounted to a guerrilla offensive against the Canal Zone, where 80,000 British troops, including 11 provost units, were virtually besieged.

203 Provost Company and the 1st Infantry Division Provost Company did good work during the riots in Ismailia in late 1951. During the first day of the riots, 16 October, they reported the first signs of hostile activity, and controlled refugees and traffic. RMP patrols were the only British troops who patrolled the town on a regular basis. There was little or no co-ordination with the civil Egyptian police, an often ill-disciplined body who made their opinions of the British in general and the RMP in particular crystal clear. The riots culminated in Operation *Font*, the withdrawal of British personnel (including families) from Ismailia and Arashia from 20–26 November. The major operational lesson of the riots was, in the words of the DAPM, that 'wireless is as essential to the RMP as petrol is to the MT [Motor Transport]'. An all female unit, 144 WRAC Provost Unit, also distinguished itself during the riots. RSM Harry Burden paid tribute to 'the most efficient way Control HQ and the wireless cars were handled by the Provost girls' during the riots.

The work of No. 2 Section SIB in the Canal Zone was mainly concerned with the recovery of WD property. The battle against the traffic in narcotic drugs was another aspect of SIB work in the Canal Zone. On one occasion a petrol tanker, which regularly crossed the Canal, was stopped and searched, but nothing was found. An SIB NCO 'of a persistent nature' had the vehicle stripped down and found a packet of hashish actually inside the fuel container, suspended by a thread from the roof. The violence reached a peak in January 1952 when both sides took the offensive. The confrontation in the Canal Zone saw the RMP undertake many roles, from protection of VIPs (senior officers of the rank of brigadier and above were escorted by an RMP Bren Gun team), to the use of guard dogs by No.1 Dog Company RMP for protection of depots and dumps. Eventually, a compromise was hammered out, by which British troops would withdraw from the Canal Zone with the right of re-entry should the security of the Suez Canal appear threatened.[4]

Barely eight months after the last British combat unit had pulled out of the Canal Zone, the British went to war with Egypt over the Suez Canal. Early in 1956, the United States had halted their financial support for the Aswan high dam project, on the grounds that the Egyptian leader, President Nasser, was misusing their funds by purchasing arms from the Soviet bloc. In retaliation, Nasser nationalised the Canal in July 1956. The British and French, seeing Nasser as an Arab Hitler, secretly prepared a military operation in collusion with the Israelis. The plan was for the Israelis to attack the Egyptians, allowing the British and French to occupy the Canal area to 'separate' the two sides.

An Anglo–French invasion force of nearly 80,000 men was gathered to execute Operation *Musketeer*, as the Suez operation was named. The taskforce was commanded by Lieutenant General Sir Hugh Stockwell. The RMP was represented by Lieutenant Colonel L F Richards, who was appointed APM II British Corps and also Force Provost Marshal, thus bringing the RAF and French military police also under his wing. RMP AER and 'Z' Reservists were called up. 22 Corps Provost Company was formed under the command of Major Harry Cooper, mainly from officers and NCOs from the AA who were highly experienced in traffic control and related matters. In addition, a Sub-Area Provost Company was formed under a DAPM, Major Robertson, and the 10th Division Provost Company in Tunisia was alerted to join the invasion force if required.

The Israelis struck into Sinai on 29 October 1956. In the early hours of 5 November, 3rd Battalion The Parachute Regiment (3 Para) began to drop onto Gamil airfield, near Port Said. At 0715 hours Captain E W T Mitchell and two NCOs of 16 Independent Parachute Brigade Provost Unit landed. Their task was to sign a route through to Port Said and in the town, and then to prepare to control the traffic of the main seaborne assault, which would land 24 hours later. 3 Para rapidly secured the airfield and then attempted to fight their way into Port Said against tough Egyptian resistance.

The success of the amphibious assault on the following day led to preparations for an advance by the Paras to the south of the town. Captain Mitchell and Corporal Taylor of the Brigade Provost Unit were helicoptered to the headquarters of 2 RCP (French 2nd Colonial Parachute Regiment), to carry out a reconnaissance of the site for Tactical Headquarters. Mitchell found on arrival 'that far from being a site outside the battle area, the new location was the scene of fierce fighting'! The RMP team were unable to return 'to bring forward the Main Headquarters, owing to the heavy fire in Port Said and had, therefore, to remain in the waterworks area until the arrival of the main force that evening.'[5]

Among the leading elements of the seaborne assault forces were a party of 13 NCOs of the 3rd Infantry Division Provost Company, commanded by Lieutenant Tebbutt. Major E G Lawton, the officer commanding, was also with the party, but he had been briefed to carry out a special task. After a series of adventures, having missed his ship at Malta, he 'arrived at Casino Palace Quay just in time to observe Lance-Corporal Collins, on point duty, taking swift evasive action from an enemy sniper'. The landing forces pushed inland and the 3rd Division Provost and 16 Para Brigade Provost established information posts, carried out traffic duties in conjunction with the French on the Raswa bridges, and put into operation the preplanned traffic scheme including route signing. As 22 Corps Provost Company, scattered across no less than seven different ships, headed for Port Said, the APM, Lieutenant Colonel Richards arrived ahead of them with his staff and one section. While travelling by sea from Cyprus, Richards had learned that although the operation had been militarily successful, the whole situation was about to change. Under heavy international, principally American, pressure, the British and French governments agreed to a ceasefire beginning at midnight, the time that Colonel Richards had arrived from Cyprus. He was to write that, as far as Provost was concerned,

> The general cease-fire meant that there would be no further movement forward and that subsequent unloading and disembarkation would be severely restricted to essential stores and administrative units and troops. Provost traffic control problems were thereby greatly diminished but the disciplinary problems vastly increased.

In co-ordination with RN shore patrols, RAF police, French military police and even Egyptian civil police, patrolling and other measures were put into operation. These successfully combatted looting, pilfering, the sale of drugs, prostitution and similar activities. All this was in addition to the normal requirements of military discipline and good order. The instruction to seal off the Arab quarter was, in Richards' words, 'a fairly tall order' involving the use of about 400 out-of-bounds signs, but it 'was a good one and coupled with the imposition of the night curfew was instrumental in maintaining a very successful degree of law and order throughout this exceedingly difficult period'.

Orders were issued that vehicles would never travel alone, and that drivers would be accompanied at all times; the abduction of an infantry subaltern in the bazaar area showed how necessary these precautions were. Provost, SIB and Field Security personnel were deployed on a fruitless search for this officer, who died, probably accidentally, while in captivity.

When the main body of 22 Corps Provost Company arrived in Port Said by air, they were in action within minutes. A Norwegian battalion of the United Nations Emergency Forces had arrived, provoking 'a near riot'. Colonel Richards placed at the head of the Norwegian column

> four Land-Rovers containing crews armed with truncheons, from 22 Corps and 3rd Division companies, travelling abreast. Ahead of the Land-Rovers, and covered by them, a semi-circular screen of military police on foot cleared the route, giving a perfect demonstration of what can be achieved by minimum force in crowd control. Firmness, good humour and flat hands were the only weapons used.

The RMP carried out many other roles during the six week occupation of Port Said. These included supervising two detention centres and a prisoner-of-war cage; helping in the evacuation of British subjects from Port Said; and manning the RMP Harbour Patrol launch.

The Suez Emergency was, for Britain, a traumatic event which demonstrated the comparative weakness of the country in a world dominated by the Superpowers. Although 'Suez' was a political disaster, the Corps of Royal Military Police, along with the British Army as a whole, could rightly claim that they had carried out an immensely difficult task with considerable skill. The last Anglo–French forces pulled out of Egypt on 23 December 1956. The Port Commander, APM and Corporals Willcox and Jay were the last to step off the dockside: thus provost were among the 'first in and last out' of operations.[6]

The Headquarters of Middle East Land Forces (MELF) was moved in 1956 to Cyprus, another troubled land. In the spring of 1955 a military policeman on the island reported that 'the dynamiting season has opened in typically violent fashion . . . This summer may prove to be a hot one in more ways than one!' This prediction was all too accurate. In June 1955, a bomb exploded at the RMP billet in Limassol, wounding an RMP NCO. The Greek Cypriot guerrilla army EOKA had began a terrorist campaign to bring about *Enosis* or union with Greece. The British, determined to retain control, responded with a counter-insurgency (COIN) campaign; the violence escalated as EOKA murdered British troops and Cypriots who they regarded as collaborators. As in Jerusalem and later in Ulster, the RMP had an important role in riot prevention and, because they were often the first troops to arrive at an affray, riot control. Thus, military policemen were frequent targets of terrorist attacks. On 17 September 1955, a hostile crowd gathered in Nicosia. All available RMP NCOs were deployed to the city's main square, keeping off-duty British troops away from the crowd. During the evening a RMP Land-Rover was overturned. A patrol went to the aid of the driver but was fired on, fortunately with no casualties.[7]

By 1955, the British Army had learned many lessons from their COIN campaign in Malaya. A twin-tracked approach was maintained, involving political negotiations with the Greek Cypriot leader, Archbishop Makarios, but also aggressive patrols, cordon-and-search operations, road blocks in the towns, and large scale sweeps through the countryside. The RMP expanded from a mere section to a considerable force, which included SIB and WRAC provost sections, 227 (GHQ) Provost Company (as the 3rd Infantry Division Provost Company was renamed), and 51 Brigade and 16 Parachute Brigade Provost Units. The weakness of the civil Cyprus Police in the early years of the campaign meant that much of the Army's work lay in the sphere of policework – for which, of course, the RMP were ideally suited. RMP Land-Rovers carried out daily 'Mobile Patrols' in the three chief towns, Famagusta, Nicosia and Limassol, very much on the lines of the Flying Squad in Jerusalem. Added to this were traffic control duties and the escorting of military and civilian VIPs.

On 3 October 1958, an RMP Mobile Patrol commanded by Second Lieutenant J Rosier was moving through Famagusta when he noticed 'that the shop keepers were quickly shutting up their shops and moving out of the street'. A little further on, he found two women lying beside a car, 'and, kneeling over one of them was a girl aged between 17 and 20 years screaming and crying in an hysterical manner'. Two wives of British servicemen had been shot, one fatally. The RMP patrol promptly searched the area and detained Cypriots on the streets. EOKA's tactic of hitting 'soft' targets naturally placed the discipline of the British troops under severe strain. Lieutenant Colonel N E Huber, APM Cyprus District wrote in 1956 that

> the utmost vigilance by Provost is required and the relatively small proportion of troops who do break bounds has to be dealt with and protected from the possibly grave results of their actions. Our nightly mobile patrols are really necessary and never unexciting.

They were also dangerous. On 21 March 1956, three bombs were thrown at an RMP vehicle travelling through Famagusta. Bryan Welsh, an 18 year old RMP lance corporal, was killed when he attempted to throw the bomb out of the vehicle instead of jumping clear. His action, which probably saved the life of his comrades, was recognised by the award of a posthumous Queen's Commendation for Gallantry.

'Searching', Colonel Huber wrote in 1956, 'is really the basic function of all the Security Forces'. The Cypriot staff and visitors to the prison at Nicosia were searched by a team under the command of an SIB NCO, and RMP and WRAC provost were used to search houses for wanted terrorists. The SIB dealt with any case involving the use of offensive weapons, which resulted in serious injury or damage to property, hence the skills of the SIB were much in demand for tracking down terrorists.[8]

The Cyprus Emergency, which cost the lives of 10 members of the RMP, was one of the most frustrating campaigns of the postwar period. It ended in 1959 with a compromise. Cyprus gained independence, but not *Enosis*. Britain retained Sovereign Base areas on the island. The unstable nature of the independent Cypriot state led to internal violence between the Greek and Turkish communities, and, ironically, British troops were committed to Cyprus proper in 1964 as part of a United Nations Peacekeeping Force. The RMP contributed to an integrated provost unit. Their duties included patrolling the 'Green Line', which separated the Greek and Turkish areas of Nicosia.

The RMP's role in the Kenyan Emergency (1952–60) was nothing less than that of 'providing Provost cover for an area the size of France and Germany combined'.[9] The campaign was complicated by the presence of a sizeable body of white settlers, but a compensatory factor was that the Mau Mau insurgents were drawn almost exclusively from the Kikuyu tribe. Mau Mau insurgents were bound by fearsome oaths. Although they were generally poorly armed, Mau Mau activists carried out a number of terrorist actions. Reinforcements were sent to Kenya, including 39 and 49 Independent Brigade provost sections, and by 1954 the security forces were sufficiently numerous to take the offensive.

A massive cordon and search operation, Operation *Anvil*, was mounted in April 1954. During this operation the RMP signed all the routes in the city for the operation, and then took over traffic control in Nairobi, all the civil police being deployed on the other duties. 618 SMPS (Special Mobile Provost Section) reported the *Anvil* period as being 'very busy . . . With so many troops in the streets, the RMP night patrols were fully occupied and our cells were seldom without an occupant of some sort'. The pains taken over *Anvil* were fully justified by events: 16,000 terrorist suspects were rounded up and the Mau Mau organisation in Nairobi was effectively broken. More routine duties also needed to be carried out. Brothels, as ever a hazard to health, needed frequent patrolling and raiding, and port duties were carried out in Mombasa. Disciplinary duties in the main leave centres of Nairobi and Mombasa placed a strain on limited provost resources (which never amounted to more than 60 all ranks) but the pressure was eased somewhat by close liaison with the RAF and Kenya police throughout the campaign.[10]

The operations against Mau Mau rural strongholds involved the RMP in controlling large scale troop movements. During Operation *Emma* in 1953, 39 Infantry Brigade Provost Section helped move 1 Black Watch on some appalling dirt and gravel roads. The motor-cyclists of the section covered 59,000 miles in seven months. 5 Section SIB also played an active role in the counter-insurgency war. One detachment was situated at Nyeri, a centre of Mau Mau activity. During the spring of 1954, they were reported as 'coping with anything from rhinoceros on the road to Mau Mau ambushes'. For the Section as a whole, 'going on a job is really a hunting safari followed by many hours in Unit transport'. Many SIB investigations were concerned with the trading of ammunition, often as a form of currency in exchange for the favours of prostitutes.

The Independent Dog Section was the first RMP unit in action in Kenya. Two dogs plus handlers were loaned to the Kenya Regiment in the early stages of the insurgency; one handler, Lance Corporal Douglas killed a terrorist escaping from a native hut. Some members of 618 SMPS saw much of Kenya from the vantagepoint of escort to the Commander-in-Chief, General Sir George Erskine, and other dignitaries. Customarily, six NCOs rode in two vehicles when on escort duty.[11]

In contrast to the campaigns in Palestine, Cyprus and, later, Aden, COIN operations in Kenya ended with a military, and, more importantly, political victory. The major difference beween Kenya and these other insurgencies was that the British succeeded in 'winning the hearts and minds' of much of the population. The attitudes and behaviour of some white Kenyans sometimes threatened to undo such progress as had been made, and the RMP played a part in enforcing discipline. While the conduct of British Army units was mostly good the RMP also had a role in preventing the alienation of black Kenyans by ill-disciplined behaviour. On at least one occasion, the SIB searched men of a battalion who had robbed suspected Mau Mau detainees of their personal possessions, which resulted in British soldiers being court-martialled and jailed.[12] Such scrupulous behaviour had its eventual reward. The Mau Mau had been effectively crushed by the end of 1956. In 1963 independence was granted to a stable Kenyan state which was generally friendly to Britain.

The British campaign in South Arabia (1964–67) had much in common with the Cyprus Emergency of a decade earlier. A largely urban counter-insurgency operation was fought against nationalist insurgents, drawn from a population that was unlikely to be reconciled to British rule. The destruction of the Aden Special Branch, and the demoralisation of the Aden Police, threw a heavy burden on the shoulders of the RMP.

The RMP's role was very familiar to veterans of Cyprus. RMP mobile patrols once again received the attentions of the grenade-throwing insurgent; military police escorts were provided for VIPs; and numerous patrols were carried out with the infantry. A member of the HQ Provost and Security Services (Army Element) wrote in the spring of 1967 that 'We are heavily involved in the processing of terrorists and suspects and at times there seem to be more Arabs sitting inside our cage than we have NCOs outside'. WRAC Provost were deployed in the vital role of searching women suspects. A Port Security Section RMP (Aden) was dispatched from Britain in January of that year as part of a Joint-Service Port Security Force which attempted to halt the flow of illegal weapons into Aden. The third RMP unit in Aden was 24 Infantry Brigade Provost Unit.

Terrorist violence escalated in 1967, even though the British were due to leave Aden in 1968. The role of the RMP during the last months of 'the depressing spectacle of the disintegration of the colony' was 'the normal run of IS [Internal Security] patrols, numerous escorts and guarding arrested dissidents'.[13] Corporal S Patterson left this pen picture of life in Aden:

> Nights were shattered by the crump of grenades, and the cough of machine guns. Days were disturbed by constant strikes and 'failures' of water and power supplies. The cordons grew tighter, and barbed wire grew from the desert like black flowers, tension heightened . . . Silent Valley cemetery displayed more and more wooden crosses.

Even in these last months, the RMP had some operational successes. In July, a RMP patrol pursued the perpetrators of a grenade attack, stopped the terrorists' car and arrested four armed guerrillas. The main body of the RMP pulled out on 30 September, the residual military police party coming under fire for the last time on 14 October. The last British troops were evacuated on 29 November 1967. Few were sorry to leave the 'barren rocks of Aden'. For the RMP, the one redeeming feature was that the Corps did not suffer any serious casualties.[14] In 1971, the last British garrisons were withdrawn from the Middle East. A major, and traumatic, phase of the Retreat from Empire was over.

25

The Korean War

In the words of one military policeman who served there, 'Korea, unlike some of the countries where the British Army has serrrved, is not one of the "plum stations"'.[1] The terrain is mountainous, and the climate ranges from the very hot to the bitterly cold. From 1950 to 1953 the British Army fought in a conventional, attritional campaign against a determined communist enemy. RMP contingents served in Korea from the arrival of the first British troops until September 1956.

The attack of Kim Il Sung's communist North Korean forces across the 38th Parallel on 25 June 1950 was seen by the West as a dangerous escalation of the Cold War. A largely American multinational force, operating under the banner of the United Nations, was sent to defend South Korea. The first phase of the war (June–September 1950) saw North Korean troops overrun almost all of the South, with the exception of the Pusan bridgehead. The initial British contribution to the UN force was the Hong Kong-based 27 Infantry Brigade, commanded by Brigadier B A Coad. The bulk of the Brigade landed at Pusan on 28 August. The RMP element, consisting of Sergeant R B Johnson and 14 volunteers of the 40th Infantry Division Provost Company, moved forward on 29 August to the area to be occupied by the Brigade. Their task was considerable; all routes had to be signed and the locations of all units in the area located and recorded. Hundreds of signs were hastily improvised out of combat ration boxes.

By early September, the UN forces were struggling to retain even the Pusan bridgehead. On the 5th, 27 Brigade were committed to battle. General MacArthur's bold and imaginative amphibious landings behind the North Korean lines at Inchon on 15 September 1950, however, turned the tide in favour of the United Nations forces. In the subsequent breakout from Pusan, Major Kenneth Muir of 1 Argyll and Sutherland Highlanders, who had previously served as a Provost officer, was awarded a posthumous VC. Provost's main role in the advance beyond the 38th Parallel was the familiar one of route signing, a task that was not without its dangers. 28 October 1950 'was a day not to be forgotten by Sergeant Johnson and Corporal Turner . . .' Busily engaged in route signing, the two military policemen ended up about six miles in front of the foremost positions of 1 Middlessex, 'innocently putting up "Nottingham Forward" Signs at the Entrance of Enemy Occupied "PAKCHON"'. Only when 'they were fired upon did they realise the danger they were in'.

The road conditions in Korea were unsuitable for the motor-cycles and other two-wheeled drive vehicles with which the Brigade was largely equipped. The frequent break-downs of such vehicles, not to mention the aged Universal carriers, made effective traffic control more important than ever.[2]

27 Brigade took many prisoners in the advance and these were evacuated by the RMP. The large numbers of refugees also presented provost with a major task, for they had to be kept from military routes and searched for weapons, in case the 'refugees' proved less innocent than they appeared. By late October, the end of the war appeared to be in sight. Pyongyang, the North Korean capital, fell to the advancing UN troops on 20 October. This event presented the RMP with a traffic nightmare which they controlled, in part at least, 'by force of personality and their well-known authoritative manner'.[3] Brigade Headquarters was set up at Chongju on 31 October, and the Brigade went into Divisional rest after a hectic eight weeks of advancing. They were now barely 40 miles from the frontier of communist China.

On reaching the Headquarters of the 1st US Cavalry Division on 1 November, Brigadier Coad found 'a lot of very excited people' and the Divisional Commander told him 'The Chinese are in. The Third World War has started!' A Chinese offensive now forced the United Nations forces into a difficult retreat in appalling weather conditions. 27 Brigade, its steadiness and fighting ability fully appreciated by the American commanders, acted as the rearguard. A British military policeman recalled this period as

> one big withdrawal from then on. The Brigade moved from one front to the other holding the line to enable the badly battered American units to withdraw South. [The] Section was forever on the go for the roads were forever crowded with traffic, and streams of refugees all trying to get South away from the advancing Chinese.[4]

The retreat took 27 Brigade to Uijongbu, just north of Seoul. On New Year's Day 1951, a fresh Chinese attack was mounted, and the Brigade again found itself retreating south, this time to Changhowon-Ni, 45 miles south-east of Seoul, where the line was stabilised. As the Chinese advance faltered, the UN forces went onto the offensive on 25 January. 27 Brigade was committed in the later stages of the battle, and the RMP did sterling work in the Chongan-Ni area. The 'road' at this point consisted of a track across paddy fields and it was necessary to lay down a strict order of priorities for traffic movement. The fluid phase of the war came to an end after the Chinese were pushed back across the 38th Parallel in March 1951. With the end of the mobile war, 27 Brigade left Korea to be replaced by 28 Brigade. Half of the provost section, under Corporal Turner, returned to Hong Kong, while the other half amalgamated with a half section of the 40th Division Provost Company under Sergeant Myers to form a section for 28 Brigade. 27 Brigade's record in Korea was an impressive one. The fact that in the first five months of the campaign, provost had had to deal with virtually no crime, and no stragglers at all, is testimony to the formation's discipline and efficiency. The expertise and morale of the provost section, like that of the Brigade as a whole, was outstanding.

* * * *

Another RMP unit, 249 Provost Company, consisting of four sections under Major A W Evans, had arrived at Pusan on 3 November 1950 just after the start of the Chinese offensive. The APM was Major R Davenport. Major Evans and two sections less one sub-section joined 29 Infantry Brigade Group which arrived in Korea in the same month. Their activities and duties mirrored those of 27 Brigade Provost.

In the first five days of December, 29 Brigade formed a bridgehead over the River Taedong, north of Pyongyang, covering the retreat of the UN forces. On 5 December, the Brigade withdrew from their position three miles north of Pyongyang. 249 Provost Company policed the North Korean capital – a job which entailed much refugee control – until 0800 hours. The unit then withdrew to Sinmak, 55 miles to the south. The retreat continued, with the company eventually withdrawing to the Seoul area, where 29 Brigade were attacked by the Chinese at the beginning of January. A brief diary of the company's doings preserved in the RMP archives tersely notes the type of duties carried out during this battle:

> 12.1.51   Heavy traffic on 29 Bde front . . . Roads and MSR [Main Supply Route] kept clear for military traffic.
> 3.1.51   Withdrawal 29 Bde commences. 249 Pro Coy employed on roads from KUPABAL-LI to YONGDONGPO . . .
> 4.1.51   249 Pro Coy employed on bridges over River HAN and duties in connection with stragglers, etc.[5]

This was the first time in the campaign that straggler posts had to be manned.

By late April, the United Nations forces had pushed the enemy back beyond the 38th Parallel. 29 Brigade stopped and dug in on a position along the line of the Imjin river, about 35 miles north of Seoul. On 17 April, two signing groups of No. 2 section accompanied an infantry patrol mounted on tanks and Oxford carriers. One group remained at the fording place, while the other went ahead to signpost enemy minefields. It became clear that the Chinese were prepared to assault these positions to attempt to force the UN troops into retreat. During the uneasy pause before the battle, 29 Brigade maintained patrols into enemy territory.

On 22 April 1951, Chinese troops crossed the Imjin River and one of the bitterest battles in the history of the British Army began. The Chinese Sixty Third Army threw in attack after attack in an attempt to smash through 29 Brigade's positions. On 24 April, 29 Brigade began to withdraw to fresh positions five miles in the rear. The RMP role in the battle began after the enemy had attacked the frontline positions of the UN forces at 2100 hours on 22 April, and refugees began to flood back. Provost mounted joint patrols with Korean police in an attempt to keep the MSR (main supply route) clear, to ensure that the flow of supplies to the front was unimpeded. The RMP war diary laconically recorded the destruction of 1 Glosters: 'Slight retrograde movement of the Bde HQ and supporting arms, forward Battalions cut off, heavy fighting continued'. The next day, 24 April 1950, saw the situation worsen. Numbers 1 and 3 Sections were sent forward to help with an attempt to extricate the forward troops, and a Straggler Post was set up near Brigade Headquarters. Faced with the threat of a Chinese breakthrough, a 'tight harbour' was formed by Brigade Headquarters into which Provost HQ and No. 2 Section withdrew. The situation appeared critical. Two Bren guns were sited and manned by military policemen. Fortunately, the major enemy attacks were contained, although some Chinese parties did succeed in penetrating as far as the Brigade Headquarters' positions.

On 25 April, the order was received for all the rear echelons of the Brigade to fall back, and the RMP were used in a variety of vital work connected with the withdrawal, all under enemy mortar and small arms fire.

> All day the RMP personnel continued to keep things moving, escorting ambulances with urgent cases, carrying wounded out on jeeps, collecting stragglers as they came out over the hills and getting them down to the groups where required . . . Time and time again the gauntlet was run . . .

By the end of 25 April, the crisis of the battle had passed. The stand of 29 Brigade, made at such heavy cost, inflicted such damage on the Sixty Third Army that the Chinese offensive was halted. However, 249 Provost Company's work was far from over. Maintaining straggler posts and carrying out the reconnaissance of roads and tracks in the Brigade area were just two of their tasks in the immediate aftermath of battle.[6]

For the Commonwealth forces, the months May to July 1951 were relatively calm. The Commander-in-Chief of the UN forces, Douglas MacArthur, had publically disagreed with President Truman over the latter's decision to refuse to allow the war to be extended beyond Korea. In consequence Truman had sacked MacArthur on 11 April 1951, signalling that the war would remain limited. Negotiations for a ceasefire were opened at Kaesong between the two sides on 10 July 1951. Meanwhile, the series of offensives begun at the end of July had the strictly limited aim of moving the UN positions forward to take up more favourable positions forward of the Imjin. The major action fought by the British in this phase was Operation *Commando* (2–15 October 1951). Once again, the RMP carried out its 'battlefield' role of controlling traffic, evacuating POW, and controlling refugees.

The line gained as a result of *Commando* was to be held by 1st Commonwealth Division, which was formed under the command of Major General A J H Cassels on 28 July 1951, for the remainder of the war. This division consisted of 25 Canadian Infantry Brigade, 28 British Commonwealth Infantry Brigade, which included an Australian battalion, and 29 British Brigade, as well as New Zealand and Indian troops. The Commonwealth Division also had an integrated provost company formed from Canadian and Australian as well as British military police. Company Standing Orders proudly proclaimed that '1 COMWEL Div Pro Coy is the only integrated unit of its kind in the Allied Forces'. The command of the company rotated between the various nationalities. The second-in command was British, and he also commanded the British element. In addition, Americans, Nationalist Chinese and South Koreans were attached to the company. One section was permanently attached to each brigade, with a further section at main Divisional Headquarters and Rear Headquarters, leaving three sections at Company Headquarters as reserve.

Attempts were made to rotate the location of sections every three months. This experiment in integration was a success. All ranks co-operated gladly and a considerable *esprit de corps* was developed within the unit. Regrettably, the level of integration within the Provost Company was not always appreciated by outsiders who insisted on contacting provost officers of their own nationality on disciplinary matters.[7]

It was made clear in standing orders that military policemen should deal with troops of their own nationality, but it was recognised that this would not always prove possible. Joint patrols proved desirable, for although NCOs were allocated to such routine duties as traffic control irrespective of their national origin, soldiers inevitably tended to show more respect for military police of their own army. This was not the full extent of provost integration, for British, Australian and New Zealand personnel also served together in the British Commonwealth Base Provost Company. A close-working relationship was also established with the US military police.

The static war which lasted until the armistice in July 1953 bore many resemblances to the Western Front of 1914–18. Just as in the earlier conflict, trench warfare increased the demand for military police, and the RMP were at full stretch attempting to cover all their duties, operational and disciplinary. 262 Base Area Provost Company was committed to the lines of communication in both Korea and Japan, despite having a strength of only three sections. An RMP presence was needed at Seoul, the Forward Maintenance Area; Inchon, LST Sea Head; Pusan Main Sea Head, Kure (Japan) Headquarters Commonwealth Forces and Main Base Installations; and General Headquarters in Tokyo. It was the same old story of demand for military police greatly exceeding the manpower available, although the arrival during 1952 of Australian and Canadian personnel helped to ease the manpower crisis.

In the Commonwealth Division's area various traffic control methods were evolved. One was the use of an Auster light aircraft, fitted with a loud hailer. Another was to erect permanent telephone booths, painted with the legend 'Police Telephone'. Yet another was to set up a wireless section of five jeeps. A more traditional method, patrolling by two NCOs, was employed on the road leading up to Point 355, perhaps the most heavily shelled section of the divisional front. Roads in Korea were few and far between, and were rarely metalled. Those in the Commonwealth Division's area were made out of a mixture of sand and crushed rock. During dry weather, the dust thrown up by vehicles forced military police to use torches to control the traffic. The rainy season brought further problems. Flash floods often washed out sections of roads, which usually had to be closed. An important provost duty was to carry out dawn patrols, so that by 0700 hours the Royal Engineers could be notified of the roads which had been washed out. One never-ending traffic control task in Korea was route signing; dust, rain, frost and vandalism took a heavy toll of signs. The unit paint shop had to produce as many as 500 signs a month.

Traffic control on the bridges over the Imjin was also of the utmost importance. The deployment of the Commonwealth Division was generally to have two brigades 'up', with the third in reserve two miles to the rear. All three brigades were deployed with their backs to the Imjin. Their lifeline depended on a mere two MSRs which passed over Teal and Pintail bridges. Both routes had a section permanently committed to traffic control. At one stage, these bridges were in danger of being washed away. On 30 July 1952, heavy rains caused the Imjin to rise by 49 feet, turning it into 'a tearing brown winged giant, filled with debris . . . Chinese wooden bridges, bits of houses, timber by the ton and the unpleasant produce of the many graves'. It washed away two spans of Teal bridge. A major effort to re-route traffic over Pintail had to be put into operation. On 1 January 1952 the Company had 12 permanent police posts at road junctions and at formation headquarters, and seven points at bridges. A subsidiary duty was to watch for North Korean infiltrators attempting to cross the Imjin by boat.[8]

In addition to the usual run of policing duties, rear area duties included escorts for an impressive number of visiting VIPs, providing airfield security and the inevitable operations against vice and the blackmarket. In early 1952, an average of 20 raids a month were being made in co-operation with I Corps US military police to crack down on prostitution, infiltrators, spies and out-of-bounds personnel. A typical anti-blackmarket raid was mounted on 17 October 1953, which resulted in 200 bottles of NAAFI beer being confiscated from a Korean national.

An advanced party of the SIB arrived in Korea as early as 3 November 1950. It consisted of only two men, WOII Botting and Sergeant Kearns, who were deployed to Taegu and Pusan respectively. This was the beginning of a period of much hard work for SIB, often under extremely difficult and dangerous conditions. At one stage, in March 1951, WOII Botting found himself taking a statement while under mortar fire.[9] A later arrival, Sergeant D Kinnear, was murdered by Filipino soldiers whilst investigating a crime. On 9 December, the main body of the SIB arrived under the command of Captain Bennett, and set up its headquarters at Taegu, moving to Pusan in September 1951. The volume of their work can be gauged from some statistics. During 1951, 1,402 cases were investigated, 1,711 arrests or reports were made, and £28,288 worth of property was recovered.

Korea has been overshadowed by subsequent conflicts. Yet for the RMP it was a war which contained many interesting lessons. It showed the continuing importance of basic provost duties – traffic control, straggler posts, maintenance of discipline – and demonstrated that they might have to be applied in totally unexpected situations. Few in Britain in early 1950 would have been bold enough to predict that the Army would shortly be fighting the Chinese in Korea, in a war which at times closely resembled the Western Front; and yet that is exactly what happened. Korea also showed the possibility of close co-operation with other English speaking armies. The Provost Company was, in fact, more closely integrated than any other unit of the Commonwealth Division. Above all,

Korea once again demonstrated the value to an army of large numbers of dedicated, well-trained military policeman. Writing of US Military Police in Korea, Brigadier General Francis E Howard, Provost Marshal US Forces Far East, wrote that

> in company with the Military Police of other members of United Nations Command, they have achieved a record which once and for all dispelled any doubts as to the value of a permanent officer and enlisted Military Police Corps.
>
> I have observed the British Commonwealth Military Police in Japan and Korea, and am proud of my relationship with these outstanding representatives of your service.[10]

26

Northern Ireland

Since 1969, the 'Troubles' in Northern Ireland have enabled the RMP to adopt a variety of new roles and techniques. 'Consequently', an RMP officer claimed in 1973, 'the RMP contribution is now far greater in proportion and effect than in any previous campaign or similar situation'.[1] Certainly, the RMP's profile has never been higher, and its contribution to peacekeeping more important, than in the first months of the 'Troubles'.

The division of Ireland in the 1920s had left a substantial minority of Roman Catholic Nationalists in Northern Ireland, who were economically and politically disadvantaged. A long legacy of distrust between Catholics and Protestants exploded into inter-communal rioting in the summer of 1969. Troops were ordered onto the streets of Londonderry on 14 August to reinforce the Royal Ulster Constabulary (RUC). On the following day, troops were deployed in Belfast to protect the Catholic community from Protestant mobs. Two weeks later, the RMP appeared in the Falls Road area of Belfast to carry out traffic control duties. The RMP performed a vitally important role in the second half of 1969, becoming the first representatives of the government to enter the 'No-Go' areas which had been created in both Belfast and Londonderry.

The RUC and its part-time auxiliary, the B-Specials, had largely forfeited the trust of the Catholic population. On 10 October the Hunt Report recommended sweeping reforms to the RUC. The RMP stepped into the policing vacuum which had been created. Redcaps were sent into Catholic areas as 'stop-gap policemen'. Military policing was acceptable to most Catholics, and the RMP won the trust of many of the local population in the process; on 10 October a newspaper in the Irish Republic bore banner headlines reading '"Let the Redcaps in" – Pleas For Military Police Patrols in Bogside'.

The SIB investigated break-ins on the Falls Road, and the Public Protection Authority (PPA), a body composed of RMP, WRAC Provost, RUC and civil servants, was set up on 9 September under the command of Captain A I Purton, WRAC Provost, to inquire into allegations of intimidation. On 8 October 1969, RMP foot patrols entered the Falls Road area, the first police to do so since the riots in August. On the same

day Sergeant D M Swaby and Captain J K Bonell had carried out an investigation in the Bogside area of Londonderry; an act which would have been unthinkable only a few weeks before and which would still have been impossible for the RUC to carry out. As a symbolic act of some importance, on 22 October an agreement was hammered out with Catholic representatives which allowed the RUC to patrol to West Belfast once more, albeit unarmed and on foot in daylight hours only; but only on the condition that each patrol had to be made jointly with the RMP. Since 16 October, all 999 calls in the Catholic Andersonstown area had been answered by the RMP. On 29 October, the 'Andersonstown formula' of joint RMP/RUC patrols by day, but the RMP being solely responsible for night patrols, mobile patrols and 999 calls, was introduced into other Catholic areas. Captain S G Edwards wrote at the time:

> The unarmed Military Policeman in his 'red top' and armband soon became a familiar sight, and the helpfulness and good nature of the NCOs were a great asset to both the Army and the civilian population in keeping the temperature down.[2]

In 1973, the RMP was to play a similar role in Protestant East Belfast, when 1,000 troops were pulled out and joint RMP/RUC patrols were put in.

As 1969 drew to a close, more responsibility was being handed to the RUC and it seemed as if peace of a sort might be restored to Ulster. The successful use of the RMP in the civil policing role (of which most Corps members had little prior experience) had played no small part in the improvement in the situation. A 'snapshot' of a joint RMP/RUC patrol in Ulster appears in a 1970 article in the Corps Journal. On the Ballymurphy Estate they found slogans such as 'This is Free Ballymurphy' painted on the walls. The patrol was:

> surrounded by a battalion of children, all aged from 18 months to five or six years old . . . Their eyes studied us so intently that you felt that all the eyes in the district were following your every move.
>   'Are you in the Army, mister?'
>   'Are you a policeman, mister?'
>   'Who are you going to see, mister?'
>   'Are you a Military Policeman, mister?' . . .
>   At the top of the hill, we crossed to the observation post set up by the Infantry, where we stopped for five minutes and a cigarette . . . [Arriving at Ballymurphy Parade] we saw four youths . . . shouting and punching one another. Around them were another crowd of youths who were also shouting. We were just in time, because one of them pulled out a knife. They said it was 'Just for fun'. We 'joined in', arrested them and conveyed them back to the Police Station.[3]

* * * *

In 1970 things changed for the worse. The 'honeymoon' between the Catholic community and the Army began to come under strain during the 1970 'Marching Season' and RMP vehicles began to be attacked. During 1969, 173 Provost Company, the only RMP unit based in the Province at the beginning of the Troubles, was reinforced by seven NCOs from the 3rd Division Provost Unit and 24 Infantry Brigade Provost Unit. The latter unit was replaced by 5 Infantry Brigade Provost Unit in January 1970. On 1 April, Lieutenant Colonel J F Thomas was appointed APM. The Irish Republican Army (IRA), almost defunct in 1969, had begun to gain support among some of the Catholic population. Serious rioting took place in Belfast from 26 to 28 June 1970 and IRA and Protestant paramilitaries claimed their first victims. At this time, an RMP patrol in the Ardoyne area came under fire, Lance Corporal G V Eastham later being awarded the BEM for gallantry on this and other occasions. The RMP sustained its first casualty of the campaign during this period when Staff Sergeant T Watt was hit on the head by a hurling stick while in support of the 1st Battalion The Royal Scots. Even worse rioting occurred in July. By the end of 1970, the alienation of the Catholic community from the British authorities was becoming alarmingly obvious.

In 1971, the nature of the Army's role in Northern Ireland underwent a fundamental change. In the spring of that year, the Provisional IRA (or PIRA – the more dangerous of the two IRA factions that had emerged in late 1969) went on to the offensive using the bomb and bullet. Increasingly, the Army was committed not merely to peacekeeping, but also to fighting a counter-insurgency campaign. One measure decided upon was internment without trial. This proved to be 'a political disaster'[4] which was not counterbalanced by any effects it might have had in military terms. In the early hours of 9 August 1971, a massive arrest operation was carried out. The RMP manned three holding centres and over 340 people were detained initially. Later, nearly 2,000 statements had to be taken from soldiers to be submitted to the subsequent Compton enquiry.

The organisation of the RMP changed during 1970–71. An Operations Centre was opened to co-ordinate the many provost activities in Belfast. The section devoted to investigating complaints against troops grew into a platoon under a staff sergeant of the SIB. Escort duties for military and civilian VIPs were carried out. On 5 November 1971, 1st Regiment RMP was formed in Northern Ireland – the first such formation in the history of the Corps. It initially consisted of four companies (174, 175, 176 and 177) under Lieutenant Colonel J F Thomas. Two more companies (178 and 179) were formed shortly after, 178 acting as the 'investigation resource' of 1st Regiment RMP, consisting of both provost and SIB personnel.[5]

In 1972, the violence in Northern Ireland reached a peak. On 'Bloody Sunday' (30 January 1972) 13 civilians were killed by troops in Londonderry after the troops had come under fire. Suspected terrorists were arrested and handed to an (unarmed) RMP arrest team by men of 1st Battalion The Parachute Regiment and, within hours, 178 Provost Company began an investigation. 'Swift and expert follow-up of major incidents by the military police not only discloses the truth but protects soldiers suffering from stress and shock from any subsequent misgivings about their actions'.[6]

'Bloody Sunday' was followed by 'Bloody Friday' on 21 July, when a number of bombs exploded in Belfast. The Army retaliated to the run of IRA successes by launching, on 31 July, the largest British military operation since Suez. 21,000 troops were involved in operations *Motorman* in Belfast and *Carcan* in Londonderry, when Catholic No-Go areas were re-entered. The RMP deployed 20 Arrest and Find teams and 20 investigation teams and set up a major VCP (vehicle check point) on the motorway which leads to Belfast. The operation met with little resistance and the RMP mounted policing patrols. Two NCOs of the newly formed 180 Provost Company were wounded while patrolling the Lower Falls area.[7] *Motorman* and *Carcan* were striking successes in both military and political terms. Building on these successes, in the next couple of years the Security Forces began to gain the upper hand.

On 1 July 1972, 2nd Regiment RMP was formed from 175 and 179 Provost Coompany and a reformed 180 Provost Company. Its first commander was Lieutenant Colonel B A Gait. In November 2 RMP was given South and East Belfast as its 'parish'. This was a largely Loyalist area, but increasingly the Army and government was faced with a Protestant backlash, culminating in the 1974 general strike against power-sharing in the Province. Earlier, for three days in February 1974, members of the RUC had refused to arrest, escort or interview terrorist suspects, leaving the RMP as the only body legally entitled to carry out these duties. Throughout this period the RMP continued in its role, taking casualties but also winning plaudits; in 1974 Lieutenant Colonel Gait became the first RMP officer to be awarded the DSO.

* * * *

In the mid-1970s, the Army began to develop operational methods which have been continued, with modifications, down to the present day. At this time, 176 Provost Company manned border checkpoints on three sides of the city of Londonderry, which served a secondary function in protecting the city from attack. The RMP also continued to co-operate closely with the RUC. In December 1972, 179 Provost Company was used in the formation of a Task Force drawn from the two bodies (RUC and RMP) to counter sectarian killings (70 Catholics and 37 Protestants had been murdered in that year). This company provided five platoons for integration with the RUC's Special Patrol Group (SPG) in September 1973.[8]

Body searches were an essential RMP duty. To meet the need for female personnel to carry out searches on women – in 1969, female provost strength in the Province had amounted to only two – 181 Provost Company WRAC (or the 'Coffeepots') was raised in September 1972, consisting of about 40 WRAC Provost and general duty searchers. As many as 250,000 women might be searched in a month. In December joint WRAC/RUC/RMP patrols began in Belfast. WRAC Provost have not been spared from danger. To pick just one incident, a female NCO was wounded by gunfire while serving in Londonderry in 1981, at the time of the deaths of the Republican hunger strikers in the Maze prison.

The COIN campaign was not purely an urban one. A provost section, subsequently expanded, was moved to Armagh to support 3 Infantry Brigade along the Border. In the mid-1970s, 174 Provost Company's vehicles were each covering some 5,000 miles per month in mobile rural patrols. Provost strength in Ulster was augmented, at this time, by the presence of RAF and Royal Marine police.

Since the mid-1970s, the RMP in Northern Ireland has proved a remarkably flexible force, adapting to tactical roles which might later, under different circumstances, disappear. One such role was POINTER, whereby RMP support teams of 3 or 4 NCOs were attached to units in Belfast. First deployed in July 1976, they were rapidly dispatched to bombings, shootings, and other incidents such as arms finds to collect evidence, question witnesses, and in general provide expert back-up to infantry units untrained in police work. POINTER also served a valuable role as the custodian of operational information, in an excellent position to brief newly-arrived infantry units on their areas of responsibility. The last POINTER platoon was disbanded in 1984. Another such role was 175 Provost Company's committment to RUC Divisional Mobile Support Units (DMSU, the successors of the SPG). During the run-up to Christmas 1983, 175 Company were temporarily taken off general duties and deployed along side DMSUs, but in 1985 the Company's commitment to this role came to an end.[9]

The campaign moved into a new phase in 1977. On 12 January, the policy of RUC Primacy was announced. The Army was henceforth to act in support of the RUC to establish and maintain law and order in Ulster. In the early days of RUC Primacy, the RMP provided support for the

RUC while it found its feet in its new role. The Army had been reducing its role and presence since 1975. The RMP's commitment to the Province reflected this general trend, belying the fears expressed by some Protestant leaders that the RMP would undermine the role of the RUC. In April 1978, 2nd Regiment RMP was disbanded, 180 Company having been disbanded in October 1977, and on 1 March 1985 1st Regiment RMP was 'mothballed', the position of DPM/Commander RMP having already been downgraded to APM, a post combined with that of Commander, 1st Regiment RMP. The RMP presence in Ulster in 1989 consisted of 175 and 176 Provost Companies, 177 (SP) Platoon, SIB detachments in Armagh, Belfast and Londonderry, a Legal Affairs Department, and 173 (Force Troops) Provost Company. The latter was formed in October 1987 from 173 Provost Company SIB, 177 (SP) Platoon, Legal Process Office and the Courts and Witnesses Section.

* * * *

The 1980s and early 1990s have never seen the level of violence return to that of 1972. Nevertheless, the RMP has been involved in most major incidents in the Province, whether conveying 'comfort and support to the regiments involved' in the aftermath of Warrenpoint, where 18 soldiers were killed on 27 August 1979, or taking on extra security duties during the unrest that followed the signing of the Anglo–Irish Agreement in 1985. In contrast to these headline-grabbing events, other less spectacular incidents have served as a reminder of the Corps's frontline role. On 10 May 1980, for example, an IRA team, situated just across the border, fired 90 rounds from an M60 machine gun at the Buncrana VCP near Londonderry. Naturally, the RMP has sustained its share of casualties. Some, such as Sergeant David Ross, of the SIB Detachment, 178 Provost Company, killed by a bomb on the Ballykelly–Londonderry road in March 1984, have been fatal. Danger is not confined to those actually serving in the Province. In 1989, Staff Sergeant Andy Mudd and his wife were injured in a car bomb explosion in England, Staff Sergeant Mudd losing both legs. A staff sergeant recounted the events after he received a gunshot wound while on foot patrol in the Province in 1986:

> the JNCOs sorted out everything very quickly. This included defending our location, picking up kit, clearing weapons, bringing the helicopters in and, most important of all, giving first-aid to the two of us who were wounded. The two minute period from the rounds going off until lift-off was teamwork at its best. It is reassuring to know just how professional today's JNCOs are, and that under pressure their reactions are quick and very effective.[10]

But even service in Northern Ireland has its lighter side. One RMP NCO recalled how an operation to check a pub in the Divis area of Belfast was punctuated by the arrival of a young lad, lolly in mouth, who looked at a soldier lying on the ground and asked, 'Soldier, what are you going to do when you grow up?'[11]

Twenty years after the Army was ordered onto the streets of Ulster's cities, the Corps was still on the front line. In 1989, for some military policemen and women this meant:

> many hours 'up front' manning PVCPs [Permanent Vehicle Check Point] patrolling, investigating serious incidents and offences . . . For others in offices around the Province . . . in the Courts, in producing evidence to fight claims against the Security Forces etc. the fight has been no less hard, important or effective. The outstanding successes of Corporal Armstrong of 175 Pro Coy in capturing a terrorist and a weapon, and of members of 176 Pro Coy who so successfully captured two terrorists and prevented a mortar attack in Londonderry, highlight the importance of work done by the Corps here, and rightly received considerable praise from senior officers and, perhaps more importantly, from fellow soldiers in other capbadges . . [12]

The Falklands War, 1982

On 2 April, 1982, Argentine forces invaded and occupied the Falkland Islands, a British colony lying in the South Atlantic Ocean, 480 miles from the mainland of South America. The British reaction was swift. Instead of accepting the invasion as a *fait accompli*, as the Argentine junta had hoped, the British government began an intense period of diplomatic activity and, even more importantly, prepared to dispatch a task force to the South Atlantic.

The RMP's role in the campaign began on 3 April, when 160 Provost Company, based at Aldershot, was placed on 24 hours notice to move. However, it was eventually decided to send them for a month of intensive training at Sennybridge in terrain which was not dissimilar to that of the Falklands. On 12 May 1982, the RMP Detachment Headquarters 5 Infantry Brigade, consisting of Captain A K Barley, 16 NCOs and two SIB investigators left Southampton on board the liner *Queen Elizabeth II (QEII)*. The RMP were kept busy, not only in training but also in their responsibilities for running an information desk onboard ship and maintaining discipline patrols around the liner.

By the time 5 Brigade set sail in its role as the follow-up formation to 3 Commando Brigade, hostilities had begun in earnest. From 27–30 May 5 Brigade was 'cross-decked' from *QEII* to other ships. The RMP detachment was transferred to the liner *Canberra*, where they saw the survivors of HMS *Ardent* played on board *QEII* by a Royal Marine band. *Ardent* had been sunk as a result of damage sustained during the British landings at San Carlos on 21 May – a sombre reminder, if any were needed, that the RMP were about to enter into a war zone.

The recapture of South Georgia on 25–26 April had a curious footnote. Among the prisoners taken on the island was Captain Alfredo Astiz, who had been accused of a number of crimes, including murder, torture and kidnapping, committed during the 'Dirty War' in the 1970s. Several foreign governments wanted to question Astiz about the disappearance of their nationals. He was sent back to Britain – the only POW to reach the UK – and held in the Keep of Roussillon Barracks, Chichester, the home of the RMP. Astiz was questioned about his role in the Dirty War, but on 10 June he was flown back to Argentina. By all accounts, he was a model prisoner during his time at Chichester.[1]

For the final stage of the voyage to the Falklands *Canberra* was escorted by warships including the aircraft carriers *Invincible* and *Hermes* through Force 10 gales. At last, in the early hours of 2 June, a cold and foggy day, 5 Brigade entered 'Bomb Alley': San Carlos Water. The Brigade was landed at the main Beach Support Area (BSA) at San Carlos settlement. By first light the RMP began to dig in. The digging of trenches was, quite literally, a matter of life or death, as the Argentinians launched numerous airstrikes against the beachhead. Some idea of the conditions endured by the RMP during their first five days at the BSA can be gauged from extracts from a letter written on 7 June by Captain Barley:

> The BSA . . . is, quite literally, a sea of mud . . . The weather is foul with a cold, biting wind, heavy rain . . . We were to spend five terrible days and nights in the trenches, being flooded out on two of those nights and frankly, I estimate that in another few days we would have had problems of exposure . . . The morale of the boys is pretty good, with especially the SIB duo accepting life very well . . . Since we have been in this location we have been attacked by two Mirage fighters, this while Lance Corporal Cooper was marshalling helicopters; this morning four Canberras came to bomb us but were unsuccessful because two were shot down by Sea Dart missiles fired from HMS *Ajax* which is part of our air defence cover. Being under attack leaves no room for slow movers, and our trenches are used frequently each day as we receive a Red Alert.[2]

By this stage, Major General Jeremy Moore, the British Land Forces commander, was preparing to assault the main Argentinian positions around Port Stanley. The RMP's main role at this time was assisting with the build up of supplies at the BSA. For this purpose they were attached to Beach Logistic Control, working with the Beachmaster and the RAOC company. The BSA might have been described as a scene of organised chaos, a situation which was not helped by the delay in deploying the RMP, with helicopters, landing craft and vehicles moving backwards and forwards from ship to shore, offloading men and equipment. The RMP were a valuable addition to the beachhead. They established an Information Post (IP) which was generally manned around-the-clock, which was able to direct and control personnel arriving on the islands. The success of this IP suggests that it would have been useful to have included a provost element in 3 Commando Brigade, which had made the initial landings on 21 May. Until the IP was set up, commanders were rather vague as to exactly which units were actually ashore and located around the BSA; similarly, the location of equipment had not been properly recorded. Another vital role was the 'marshalling of helicopters into their areas on which to drop their underslung loads of supplies;[3] the intensive training that 160 Provost Company had received in this skill during their training at Sennybridge proved to be invaluable.

The main British advance on Stanley was carried out by the Parachute Battalions and Royal Marine Commandos of 3 Commando Brigade in the north of West Falkland, but Moore decided to increase his options by using 5 Brigade to open up a route through the southern part of the island. On 9 June, an RMP reconnaissance party moved forward to Brigadier Tony Wilson's 5 Brigade Tactical Headquarters at Fitzroy. There they witnessed what Captain Barley described as the 'terrible scenes around Fitzroy/Bluff Cove settlements'. The previous day 51 servicemen, including 33 members of the Welsh Guards, had been killed by an airstrike on the landing ships *Sir Galahad* and *Sir Tristram*. Corporals Savage and Davies, carrying out Close Protection duties to Brigadier Wilson, were already in the Fitzroy area and all but three of the rest of the platoon arrived in the area on the 10th. While they were digging in they were attacked by Pucara aircraft, one of which was brought down by small arms fire.

Despite the disaster at what the public came to know as 'Bluff Cove', the British continued to prepare for the assault on the mountains surrounding Stanley. The RMP's role in this stage of the campaign was to be the control of prisoners of war. On 12 June, Captain Barley's men were joined by 20 members of the Royal Marine Police, who already had experience of handling POW after 2 Para's battle at Darwin/Goose Green. On the night of 11/12 June 3 Commando Brigade began the series of battles that would take them to Port Stanley. Provost initially handled some 80 Argentine POW, most of whom were filthy and poorly clad. The arrangements to receive the POW included the organisation of search teams and documentation teams to record prisoner details on next of kin and capture cards. Lacking much of their equipment, the RMP used P and O luggage labels to identify the prisoners. Provost also assisted a Tactical Questioning Team, which interrogated POW who were believed to have useful information.

The second phase of the battle to seize the high ground surrounding Stanley took place on the night of 13/14 June. Provost were engaged in the processing of another 350 prisoners at Bluff Cove when they heard of the Argentine surrender, which took place at 2100 hours on 14 June. Senior British commanders recognised that it was imperative that provost should take up policing duties in Stanley and, ten hours after the surrender, Captain Barley's platoon was flown into the capital of the Falkland Islands by Sea King and Wessex helicopters, where it came under the command of 3 Commando Brigade.

At 0942 hours on 15 June 1982, Sergeant J Burton became the first RMP NCO to set foot in Stanley. As Captain Barley later recorded, the situation that greeted the RMP on their arrival was, 'to say the least, somewhat hairy. Thousands of Argentine soldiers were wandering about with loaded weapons' with 'primed grenades' hanging from their waist belts. Port Stanley was 'in absolute disarray'. Several public buildings had been wrecked, and 'the streets were like a tip where rubbish had just been dumped'. Some buildings were on fire, and many had been booby-trapped. So hazardous was the situation that for the first 24 hours, Barley's men were often forced to patrol in 'bricks', as in Northern Ireland.[4] The next seven days were fully occupied with rounding up and processing Argentinian POW. At the end of this period, some 11,000 prisoners had been searched and loaded onto ships bound for Argentina. One enterprising prisoner was found clutching a colour TV set, while others had secreted about their persons knives, hacksaws and even a 9mm pistol.

The SIB were also busy in the immediate aftermath of victory. Co-operating closely with Stanley's sole civil policeman, they worked to re-establish the Police Station, which had been badly damaged in the fighting, and also catalogued all property recovered from POW. In the weeks after the end of the war, the task of dealing with civil complaints resulting from the Argentinian occupation proved to be a taxing process for the whole platoon. By 24 June, the RMP had settled into a General Police Duties role, dealing with breaches of discipline among British units and, having been sworn in as Special Constables by the local Magistrate, assisting the local policeman in a civilian capacity. The arrival at the end of July of Major A J Figg and some NCOs from Colchester allowed the detachment from 160 Provost Company, at long last, to return home. The Falklands War was over, but the task of protecting the islands from further attack had only just begun.

On 28 July 1982 the Falkland Islands Garrison Provost Unit (FIGPU) was established at the prompting of Lieutenant Colonel A R Bell, a future brigadier and Provost Marshal (Army), who at the time was stationed at Headquarters, C in C Fleet at Northwood. FIGPU consisted of 11 RMP, six RAF Provost and Security Section NCOs and three RN Regulators, under the command of an RMP major.[5] The happy coincidence of the initials of the provost unit and the name of Force Provost Marshal, Falkland Islands, gave rise to the verb to be 'Figged'. No less a person than HRH Prince Andrew was one of the first servicemen to be Figged in Stanley, for being improperly dressed.

As an epitaph for the RMP's role in the Falklands War, some comments of the then Provost Marshal (Army), Brigadier Jack Thomas, are difficult to better:

> Captain Alan Barley's men . . . did a great job in the face of the most daunting
> difficulties and after the fall of Port Stanley brought order and commonsense
> to a chaotic and potentially disastrous situation. Once again RMP were
> deployed too late and in insufficient numbers. Many of the problems encoun-
> tered during the build-up and after the Argentinians surrendered could have
> been avoided if greater use had been made of RMP resources.[6]

28

The Gulf War

Within 18 months of the collapse of European communism, the British Army had mounted its largest conventional operation since 1945 in an area far removed from the plains of northern Germany. On 2 August 1990, Iraq invaded the oil-rich state of Kuwait. Under American leadership, an international coalition, eventually to consist of some 35 nations, began to deploy forces to the Persian Gulf. Initially, as the name of the operation, *Desert Shield*, implied, their task was to defend Saudi Arabia. The British contribution was codenamed Operation *Granby*. On 14 September, it was announced that 7 Armoured Brigade Group would be sent to the Gulf. The British presence would be increased to divisional strength, it was announced on 22 November, by the deployment of 4 Armoured Brigade. The newly-formed 1st Armoured Division, commanded by Major General Rupert Smith, was declared operational on 31 January 1991.

The RMP involvement in Operation *Granby* began on 9 October 1990 when Major D J A Bergin, the Force Provost Marshal (FPM), arrived at the Saudi port of Al Jubail with a pre-advance party 15 strong. His first impressions of Saudi were similar to those of many other British soldiers: 'sand, sand, and yet more sand'. In addition, the heat, the impressive size of the port and, not least, the large number of Apache helicopters parked on the runway gave him food for thought. Major Bergin was deployed to Headquarters FMA (Force Maintenance Area).[1]

The first RMP unit to arrive in the Gulf was 203 Provost Company, commanded by Major N J Ridout. This was a composite unit formed from 114 Provost Company and attached personnel from RMP units throughout BAOR. The number was derived from the last RMP unit to leave the Middle East in the 1970s. 203 Provost Company had assembled at Werl in Germany on 18 September. They were given little time to acclimatise. A mere 11 hours after the first member of the Company arrived at Al Jubail on 14 October, the first routes had been signed, and the first joint patrol conducted with the United States Marine Corps (USMC) Military Police, with whom excellent relations were established. It was, of course, also vital to liaise closely with the Saudis, and much of this important work was initially undertaken by Majors Bergin and

Ridout. Captain P W Grecki, commander of 61 Section SIB, also played an important role in this respect. Captain J S MacGill (174 Provost Company), who became involved in this work after his arrival in November 1990, described the job as involving attendance at numerous barbeques and the consumption of endless cups of sweet tea.

As Captain P C House, second-in-command of 203 Provost Company, was later to comment, 'The period from October to December [1990] had an almost "phoney war" feel about it'. Paralleling the politicians' and diplomats' negotiations, which continued right up until 15 January 1991, when the deadline set by the United Nations Security Council for Iraq to withdraw from Kuwait expired, the Coalition forces were building up their military strength. 203 Provost Company continued to patrol the Al Jubail area, whilst two platoons under Captain J Petrie (Brigade Provost Officer) accompanied 7 Brigade into the desert on 30 October for 'work-up' training. In the last three months of 1990, the RMP learned much that was to be of subsequent value. No one had any experience of desert operations, nor was the equipment to deal with the harsh environment always available. Whilst the Tactical Support element were developing new, or in many cases, reviving long-forgotten methods of navigation and route signing in the desert, the administrative team, under Captain House, were using any legal means at their disposal to get their fair share of the limited resources available.

The men and women of the RMP gradually adjusted to life in an alien and hostile environment. The heat was an obvious problem and 'command drinking' had to be enforced. Troops also found out the hard way that it rains in the desert and conditions of Passchendaele-like mud resulted. A routine was developed whereby platoons at base rotated with those out in the desert, allowing all to undergo 'degunging' in the relative luxury of Camp 4, Al Jubail.

There were remarkably few disciplinary problems among British troops. The SIB, co-operating closely with the USMC's CID branch, eventually dealt with 194 enquiries, including 15 accidental deaths and one murder, investigators being deployed to the Forward Force Maintenance Area (FFMA) in early 1991. The fact that Saudi Arabia is a 'dry' Muslim state was important, for numbers of cases of assault and criminal damage tend to reflect the amount of alcohol that is available. There was some petty theft, and some troops tried to smuggle in alcohol, and even to brew their own. However, at the end of 1990 the SIB reported that their case-load had begun to 'increase' as soldiers 'realised that alcohol-free beer was nearly as good as the real thing'.

Given the fears that the Iraqis would mount a terrorist offensive against the Coalition forces, Close Protection took on particular significance.

The RMP provided Close Protection for a number of VIPs, including Lieutenant General Sir Peter de la Billiere, the Commander British Forces Middle East (BFME), HRH the Prince of Wales, General Sir Peter Inge, the Colonel Commandant, and Mr John Major, the Prime Minister. Brigadier Patrick Cordingley's Close Protection cover was provided by 203 Provost Company and was led by Sergeant P A Cassidy from the FPM's office. They went into action when a civilian car hit the side of Brigadier Cordingley's Range Rover, which overturned and slid down the street on its roof. The RMP team, following in a separate vehicle, immediately put into practice Close Protection drills, much to the alarm of the offending driver who had merely been driving in the local fashion by ignoring 'give way' signs. The SIB were involved in the security for President George Bush's visit on Thanksgiving Day in November 1990, Corporal L Phillips WRAC Provost being the recipient of a hug from the most powerful man in the world. Another VIP showed his appreciation of the RMP in a more formal fashion. In his memoirs, General da la Billiere paid tribute to his RMP Close Protection team commanded by Staff Sergeant C J Young, who, the General said, 'knew their business'.[2]

The creation of the 1st Armoured Division entailed the doubling of 203 Provost Company to six sections by the addition of a composite platoon from BAOR and two platoons from 158 Provost Company. 174 Provost Company was also added to the RMP's Middle Eastern order-of-battle. 174 Provost Company, commanded by Major R T M Bishop, moved from Tidworth to Al Jubail, arriving on 29 December following intensive training. 174 Provost Company were fortunate to be housed in Pearl Beach Camp, rather than 'Baldrick Lines*', a vast tented camp with primitive facilities. Lieutenant Colonel S C McLean also arrived in the theatre, becoming SO1 Provost BFME with Major Bergin as SO2 Provost. Headquarters 1st Armoured Division also arrived, complete with the DAPM, Major J R Blackford, who acted as Provost advisor to the Divisional Commander. The increase in provost strength was a tribute to the fact that the military authorities had clearly recognised the operational importance of military police.

174 Provost Company's role was to be FMA Provost Company. It took over responsibility for rear area security and policing of the Al Jubail area from 203 Provost Company. It also manned Traffic Posts (TPs) on the Main Supply Route (MSR). Other tasks performed by the RMP in the

---

* For the benefit of readers in the far-distant future, Private Baldrick was a dim-witted character in a popular television series set on the Western Front in 1917.

build-up to offensive operations include policing of the port area, escorting convoys, work in the Convoy Marshalling Area, the reception of troops, unloading of shipping, MSR signing, and duties in support of the Divisional and Brigade Headquarters. The RMP's experience in Northern Ireland proved invaluable in counter-terrorist operations, such as operating vehicle checkpoints, and their skill drew praise from both the Saudis and the Americans. In the event, Saddam's promised terrorist offensive did not materialise. Neither did his threat to use chemical and biological weapons, but their use was seen as a very real possibility. This gave Nuclear, Biological and Chemical (NBC) drill added importance, and one vital provost task was that of NBC warning and monitoring. Every Scud ballistic missile alert had to be met by donning of NBC kit. One Scud came down on Hafar Al Batin, narrowly missing Staff Sergeant Greenan and one of his sections from 203 Provost Company deployed on MSR Dodge. According to Staff Sergeant Greenan, after the 'bloody big bang' the RMP completed the fastest change into NBC State Black in recorded history.

Having handed over some of their responsibilities to their sister unit, 203 Provost Company headed off into the desert. There was no time for their reinforcements to be broken in gently. Indeed, the platoons from 158 Provost Company deployed to the Divisional Administration area with the paint on their vehicles still wet. There was much work for both 174 and 203 Provost Companies to do, for the Coalition forces were preparing to take the offensive: Operation *Desert Shield* was to be superceded by Operation *Desert Storm*. The plan of the Coalition forces commander, US General H Norman Schwarzkopf, was to persuade the Iraqis that the main threat was a frontal attack into Kuwait. In reality, Schwarzkopf shifted his main striking force of US XVIII Airborne and VII Corps (the latter formation including the British division) far out to the west, while maintaining the appearance of massing for a frontal assault. XVIII and VII Corps would launch a left hook into Iraq itself, a manoeuvre which would outflank Iraqi defences in Kuwait and attack them from the rear. Schwarzkopf himself commented that he could think of no other occasion in military history when a comparable number of forces 'have moved over this distance to put themselves in a position to be able to attack'. 250,000 men, 12,000 armoured fighting vehicles and one million tons of ammunition had been moved into place by the eve of the ground war.[3] The RMP played a vital role in both the planning and execution of this immense logistic effort.

By this time Major Bergin was occupying the key position of UK Movement Control Liaison Officer, at US Army Central Command Support Command, ably assisted by Corporal P W Moon RMP. The 1st

Armoured Division had to move to an assembly area near Hafr Al Batin, a town hundreds of miles from its training area. The 15,000 vehicles of the 1st Armoured Division was allocated one road – MSR Dodge – which it shared with XVIII Airborne and VII Corps. In the finest traditions of the Normandy campaign, the quart was duly fitted into the pint-pot. The arrival of Lieutenant Colonel McLean and Corporal Meredith from Al Jubail made the provision of 24 hour cover in the liaison cell possible. A very welcome reinforcement was a two-strong detachment of Royal Signals, which provided a much-needed communications facility.

On the ground, RMP personnel quickly came to appreciate why MSR Dodge was nicknamed MSR 'Dodgy'. Although the Iraqis never seriously attempted to interdict these routes, the speed of the traffic, the long hours endured by drivers of many different nationalities and the varying degrees of traffic discipline made the MSRs dangerous places. The RMP's only fatality of the campaign occurred when Staff Sergeant D C Tite of 203 Provost Company was killed on MSR Dodge, while conducting forward reconnaissance. This tragedy was compounded by the wounding of Corporal P E Jarvis when a grenade fuse exploded while he was gathering Staff Sergeant Tite's personal effects. 203 Provost Company manned TPs along the route until the deployment of the 1st Armoured Division into its Northern Assembly Area was completed. Thereafter, 174 Provost Company assumed responsibility for manning the TPs and the control of FFMA, which was established at the northern end of MSR Dodge. 203 Provost Company provided support in the divisional area; in the next few weeks all movement was across the desert, with no roads used at all.

Some members of 174 Provost Company spent more than nine weeks manning TPs 'in the same lonely and desolate desert locations . . . processing convoys around the clock, maintaining their own defence, cooking, washing, and keeping their spirits up'.[4] The NCOs manning TP3 were among the British troops located furthest forward into the desert, about 35 kilometres south of the Iraqi border. Their nearest neighbours were some Egyptian and Syrian special forces. Also nearby were US military police, who behaved with great generosity to their British counterparts, providing things which made their sojurn in the desert bearable. A typical TP would consist of a sergeant and eight men, who were split into groups of four, working 24 hours on, 24 hours off. High technology not withstanding, on some occasions TPs were reliant on motor cyclists for communication purposes.

At 0336 hours, local time, 17 January 1991, the Coalition air offensive began and preparations for the ground war intensified. On 31 January, the move of HQ 1st Armoured Division was completed. RMP sections had by this stage been issued with satellite navigation aids in the form of

Ground Positioning Sensors which were invaluable for the reconnaissance parties who, more often than not, had to traverse virgin desert.
Many problems with route marking emerged and had to be resolved. For
40 years, the RMP had planned for a defensive battle in Germany. By
contrast, *Desert Storm* called for swift forward movement, in which routes
would have to be rapidly extended. 203 Provost Company were faced
with a never-ending task of trying to obtain additional signing equipment.
In conditions of poor visibility, small bitumen signs could not be seen
and bardic lamps could not be recovered. For the deployment up to the
breach in the Iraqi lines, six foot high signs were produced by the Royal
Engineers; each signing team were allocated an 8 ton vehicle for trans-
porting these monsters. The forward platoons used American cyalumes
– plastic piping which contained a chemical which glowed when activated
– with great success.

The Coalition plan called for 1st Armoured Division to exploit the gap
in the enemy defences which was to be created by US 1st Infantry
Division. 203 Provost Company, with an attached section of 174 Provost
Company, provided a forward platoon to each of the Brigades, with a
primary responsibility for the movement of the brigade administrative
area immediately behind the Battle Groups. The remaining four platoons
had responsibility in the initial stages of the battle for signing and manning each of the four British staging areas leading to the breach in the
Iraqi defences. They would then form a joint RMP/Sapper task force
with 32 Armoured Engineer Regiment RE – the Route Development
Battle Group (RDBG) – for clearing minefields, the reconnoitring and
signing of routes, and the control of traffic. This task force was going to
be in the vanguard of 1st Armoured Division's advance, and on moving
through the breach the armour of 4 and 7 Brigades was to be met by
RMP who had moved with the US forces and directed to the start line
for the break out. Just as at Alamein, 49 years before, military policemen
and sappers were to lead British armour into a desert offensive.

On the eve of battle, 287 men and women of the RMP were deployed
in Saudi Arabia. The main assault in the ground war began at 0400 hours
on 24 February 1991. The leading formations sliced into the Iraqi
defences to discover that six weeks of carpet bombing, culminating in a
massive artillery bombardment, had had a literally devastating effect on
the Iraqi defenders. Encouraged by initial success of the assault,
Schwarzkopf decided to bring forward the time when the heavy armour
of VII Corps, which included the British division, would be unleashed
upon the Iraqis. 1st Armoured Division's operations commenced at 1500
hours. The fact that the timetable had been brought forward by 15 hours
posed obvious problems, but the RMP rose to the occasion. The forward

Brigade Platoons of 203 Provost Company quickly proved their worth in signing the Brigade routes and leading the Battle Groups. The swift rate of advance and the need to maintain momentum led the military police-men to take risks which would not have been considered in normal circumstances. Captain House later commented on the 'amazing' number of routes 'that had to be signed right up behind the leading battlegroups. Many times units had to lead through areas of scattered bomblets and mines'. 4 Armoured Brigade followed her sister brigade into action. 4 Brigade Provost Platoon, commanded by Captain R West, who had arrived with 174 Provost Company in December 1990, carried out excel-lent work in the advance. In short, the Brigade Provost Platoons 'were always to the fore . . . [and] the rapid and efficient movement of the Brigades was due in no small way to their efforts and bravery'.[5]

Staff Sergeant K M Davies, commander of the RMP platoon support-ing 7 Brigade, was awarded a Distinguished Conduct Medal (DCM) – the highest award for bravery given to a soldier in the Gulf conflict – for his role in clearing away bomblets with a shovel. This showed leader-ship of a high calibre, for three soldiers had been wounded, and one killed, at the forming up point before he led the clear-up operation. 'As one soldier said, "RMPs had never been so popular"'.[6] Staff Sergeant Davies earned his DCM in circumstances that were strikingly reminis-cent of those in which Lance Corporal Eeles earned his DCM in another desert campaign, nearly 50 years earlier. Much had changed in the intervening years, but the qualities of courage and leadership had not.

The commander of 203 Provost Company, Major Ridout, graphically described the operations of 1st Armoured Division, in which 290 kilo-metres had been covered in 66 hours, as a 'mad dash across the desert'. The Division moved on a frontage of six miles but had to be prepared to close up to a mile and a half while in action. The RMP platoons of the RDBG had plenty of work in route signing, in areas that were liberally scattered with unexploded munitions. Captain House later reported that 'Most of the Division seemed to find their way on our routes and the sight of an RMP Traffic post was a welcome relief to the troops. 203 Provost Company proved that the RMP are still an essential requirement on the modern battlefield'.[7]

174 Provost Company also had an important role to play during the ground offensive. As 1st Armoured Division advanced, 174 Provost Company had responsibility for the vital logistic loop from Al Jubail to the FFMA and forward to the Division. On the second day of the operation, Major Bishop with his Operations Officer and a small escort carried out a reconnaissance through the breach, for 174 Provost Com-pany had the task of maintaining and improving the route in this area:

there was no room for error. By the end of hostilities the unit had eight TPs spread out over 700 kilometres in three different countries, Saudi Arabia, Iraq and Kuwait. During a 'fast and furious campaign, 174 kept up the pace and ensured the lines of communication were kept open and free of Iraqi troops'.[8]

At 0800 hours (local time) on 28 February 1991 the Coalition announced a ceasefire. Iraqi forces had been smashed and Kuwait had been freed. The end of hostilities found 1st Armoured Division situated to the north of newly-liberated Kuwait City which was, like Port Stanley after its surrender in 1982, a highly dangerous and volatile place. The city was placed out of bounds to British troops. 4 Platoon of 203 Provost Company under Staff Sergeant Gratton established checkpoints to enforce this regulation. The remaining platoons regrouped and began discipline patrols to prevent looting. A Land-Rover from 174 Provost Company commanded by Corporal Meredith led the first convoy of emergency vehicles on a nine hour journey to the beleagured British Embassy in Kuwait City.

The Basra road running north from Kuwait City was signed by 174 Provost Company up to the British Divisional area. Here an Iraqi convoy had been destroyed by Coalition aircraft and destroyed, leading to the road being dubbed 'Carnage Alley'; indeed the scenes of war witnessed by the RMP personnel in Kuwait will forever remain etched on their minds.

Huge numbers of Iraqi prisoners were captured by the Coalition forces. Major Bergin ended the campaign as UK Prisoner of War Liaison Officer with 800 US Military Police Brigade, which resulted in the award of the US Army Commendation Medal. WRAC Provost, in the shape of Corporals Chessington and Carrington were also represented in the British POW Guard Force. Corporal Carrington, attached to 1 Cold-stream Guards, recalled that she 'was shocked by what I saw. The prisoners were scared stiff . . . malnourished and dehydrated, many of them would not have survived another night in the desert . . .'[9] Operating on 12 hour shifts, the British POW Guard Force processed some 4,000 prisoners in a week.

With the fighting over, the RMP had not only to keep the old MSR running smoothly but also open a new route directly from Kuwait to Saudi Arabia, to allow the Division to be supplied with its everyday needs. Attention also turned to reversing the logistic process. Men and material had to be transferred from Kuwait and Iraq back to Al Jubail, and equipment and ammunition of troops arriving back at the Saudi port had to be disposed of.

Operation *Desert Storm* was one of the most complete military victories in history. An American phrase much quoted in the build-up to the ground war was 'good logistics is combat power'. The RMP, as a constituent element of this 'combat power', were much in demand. Many old lessons were re-learned, usually the hard way, and the demands of provost operations stretched everyone to the limit. The RMP were a small but significant cog in a huge machine. If that cog had malfunctioned, logistic support, and therefore the entire operation, would have been seriously impaired. This, of course, was not a new lesson. The battle of Loos in 1915 had demonstrated what could happen if Provost fell down on its task. The Gulf War of 1991 confirmed what had been discovered long before at Amiens, Alamein and Mandalay–Meiktila: that effective military police are an essential element of offensive operations.

Epilogue:

The Adjutant General's Corps

The collapse of European communism in 1989 was followed by the self-destruction of the Soviet Union itself in 1991. These historic events brought an end to an era in world history. The repercussions for the British Army were far-reaching. For the previous 40 years, its soldiers had trained to meet a Soviet offensive against Western Europe. Now that that threat had all but vanished, the roles, size, structure and deploy-ment of the British Armed Forces were reviewed in 1990–91 under the 'Options for Change' process. The major change as far as the Corps of Royal Military Police was concerned was the federation of RMP into the Adjutant General's Corps (AGC) on 6 April 1992. This new body is an 'umbrella' organisation. The RMP lost its status as a Corps, becoming the Provost Branch (Royal Military Police) of the AGC. In practice, the title of RMP was retained, along with the cap badge, red cap, and the position of Provost Marshal (Army). Brigadier Ray Bell, the last holder of that position under the old system, wrote in 1991 that 'RMP will . . . retain its functional independence as the army's police force . . . although lines of responsibility will alter, our Role and Functions and the way we deliver them to the Army will be unaffected'.[1]

APPENDIX 1

RMP and Close Protection

In the last two decades the RMP have developed expertise in 'Close Protection' (CP), that is the provision of bodyguards, variously nicknamed 'Plastic SAS', 'Hitmen for Mothercare' and 'Cowboys', for VIPs. The Corps has long provided bodyguards for senior military and other personnel but the modern, highly specialised, role evolved as a consequence of the campaign in Northern Ireland. Senior military personnel were obvious terrorist targets, and in the 1970s military policemen were trained in CP duties. This lead to the establishment of an RMP CP course in West Germany. Training is rigorous and stressful, with the failure rate resting at about 40 per cent. 177 Provost Company, the only unit of the RMP formed entirely of volunteers for a specific type of work, became the Corps CP experts in Ulster, having two platoons dedicated to the role. In 1984, 177 was downgraded to 177 (Support) Platoon of 175 Provost Company, although continuing to carry out the same CP duties.[1]

A useful insight into the nature of CP work was given in an article written by an RMP officer in 1982. The 'well-trained, motivated and equipped attacker', he wrote,

> possessed of limitless patience and prepared to observe a VIP over a period of time, will eventually find a loophole [in the VIP's security screen]. However, therein lies the reason for CP. It lessens the chance of kidnaps or assassination by excluding the opportunist and by making it prohibitively expensive, in every sense, to mount an attack. When an attack occurs, the CP operator can prevent it developing successfully, as was amply demonstrated in the attack on President Reagan [in 1981].
>
> CP is generally mundane and boring. A great deal of time is spent planning and training, and only a short time actually protecting. The CP team has to ensure the VIP's life is disturbed as little as possible . . . [but] they must ensure that all the protective measures possible are taken, balancing the ideal against the practical. Preparation before a given task may take as long as a week for only a day's task. The operation is generally the easiest part![2]

The years 1979–80 were crucial in the evolution of the CP role of the RMP. The assassination of Airey Neave MP in 1979 symbolised the extent to which public figures had become vulnerable. The RMP, with a proven record of CP work in Northern Ireland, were the only realistic choice to taken on CP work from KMS, a private security firm. CP teams not only operated in the United Kingdom and Germany, but increasingly, RMP men were assigned to protect British diplomats in such trouble spots as Beirut. In 1984, the then Provost Marshal (Army), Brigadier Brian Thomas, wrote of two recent actions:

> Our Close Protection Team in Beirut acquitted themselves splendidly during the car bomb incident at the American Embassy in September. By their individual and team actions, they prevented a much greater loss of life in that tragic incident . . . In Kampala [Uganda], our team has twice come under night attack by bandits in recent months. They drove off the attackers but not without a miraculous escape by one member of the team whose neck was grazed by a bullet. The actions of both teams have received unstinted and well-deserved praise from the Foreign Office and the Army Board.[3]

In fact, in the Beirut incident, an RMP corporal had shot and killed the driver of a van packed with 2,000 pounds of high explosive, which exploded outside the Embassy. As it was, nine people were killed. If it had reached the underground car park, the death toll could have run into the hundreds. An award of the Queen's Gallantry Medal to an RMP staff sergeant for his work in an African city in 1986 pays testimony to the continuing role of RMP CP teams, which was formally recognised by the Foreign and Commonwealth Office (FCO) in July 1987. In October 1987 an RMP FCO CP Operations Wing was formed. It took over responsibility for all RMP CP duties from 174 Provost Company in 1988.[4]

Brigadier Norman Allen, the then Provost Marshal (Army), noted in 1987 that 'Close Protection has become a very important function for the Corps but it rarely attracts public "bouquets"[5], and even within the RMP the CP role was initially by no means universally popular. However, in some circles at least, CP has wrought a change in the image of the Corps. The jacket of a recent work on CP contained the inaccurate but nonetheless revealing comment that

> The RMP, once a team of men with uniforms pressed into straight lines and minds to match, are now – in the words of one observer – the undercover 'gunslingers of the Foreign Office'.[6]

Minor Stations, 1939–91

Belize

In 1975, Guatemalan forces massed on the frontier with Belize (formerly British Honduras), at that time a British colony. The British reinforced the garrison, which remained in place as a deterrent even after Belize gained independence in 1981. An RMP platoon plus a one man SIB detachment provided police for the garrison. Communications were poor, so much use was made of the helicopter for transport.

British Element Trieste Force (BETFOR)

The disputed city of Trieste, claimed by both Italy and Yugoslavia, had a British presence from 1945 to 1954 in the shape of 24 Infantry Brigade. The RMP was represented by 227 Provost Company and 93 Section, SIB, which co-operated closely with US military police. Provost had an important role in keeping order in the highly-charged atmosphere which sometimes spilled over into disturbances.

Gibraltar

227 GHQ Provost Company provided policing for Gibraltar garrison until 1963, when the RMP on the Rock was reduced to one SIB warrant officer. In 1991, the RMP presence consisted of an SIB detachment.

Hong Kong

The first Provost presence in Hong Kong after the Second World War was the Provost Unit of the 26th Indian Division, which became the British Independent Provost Company. The threat posed to Hong Kong by the Communist victory in the Chinese civil war (1949) led to the arrival in the colony of the 40th Division, complete with a Provost Company. In 1957, a new unit, the Hong Kong Provost Company, replaced its predecessors and later a Dog Company and a Provost Unit serving with 48 Gurkha Brigade were added. From 1976 onwards, only the Hong Kong Provost Company remained. In 1991 it had detachments on the island, in Kowloon, and at Sek Kong, plus SIB detachments. Hong Kong is due to revert to Chinese rule in 1997.

Libya

British forces remained in Cyrenaica and Tripolitania, conquered from the Italians in 1942, until 1967. By the time of the British withdrawal, the postwar provost garrison of Tripolitania, which had consisted of the 10th Armoured Division Provost Company, two Tripoli District sections and an SIB section had been reduced to one section and an SIB detachment under a DAPM. Cyrenaica District, which stretched for some 800 miles by the coastal route, was policed by two sections and an SIB detachment under a DAPM.

Malta

The Corps had provost and SIB personnel on Malta until 1971. They played an important role during the siege of the island during the Second World War, policing the garrison, which rose to 75,000 in 1943, helping to ensure that convoys could be turned around as quickly as possible, and ensuring the safety of stores once they had been disembarked.

Rhodesia

In December 1979, a Commonwealth Monitoring Force was sent to Rhodesia to oversee the ceasefire between the armies of the Patriotic Front and the Rhodesian Security Forces. 19 NCOs of London District Provost Company were deployed on security duties at Government House in Salisbury, duties that were similar to those that had been performed at Lancaster House during the negotiations in London. In addition, a platoon plus an SIB investigator was tasked with providing normal provost support. Duties included a 24 hour mobile patrol of Salisbury. The RMP enjoyed a good relationship with both their Rhodesian counterparts and the British South African Police.

The Commonwealth Monitoring Force's primary role was to man points at which guerrillas would assemble. The guerrillas were invariably more heavily armed than the Commonwealth troops; indeed, the latter's role was defined by the Chief of the Defence Staff as 'to get the hell out of it' if a shooting war restarted. The Corps played a vital role in bringing a difficult and dangerous operation to a conspicuously successful conclusion. On 17 April 1980, Rhodesia became independent under the name of Zimbabwe.[1]

Vietnam

The RMP's involvement in the Vietnam War is a little-known but fascinating episode. The Viet Cong's Tet offensive in 1968 prompted a party of three RMP NCOs to be sent to guard the British Embassy in Saigon. They also had internal security and escort duties. Although the RMP were not involved in the fighting, they witnessed the aftermath of the assault on the US Embassy, 'during which our own Embassy lost a large number of windows and suffered a few bullet holes'.[2]

Other Theatres: Second World War

CMP units and sub-units served in the Faeroes Islands, Iceland, Madagascar, South Africa, West Africa and Greece (1944–47). (For more details see Crozier, pp.154–168).

Appendix 3

RMP Territorial and Reserve Forces

Although the Territorial Force (later the Territorial Army) was formed in 1907, the first TA Provost Companies were raised in 1939. The wartime history of many of these units is discussed in the main body of the text*.

In March 1947, the TA was reconstituted. As National Servicemen had to spend a period of time in the TA following their service with the colours, the TA grew to a considerable size. In 1958 there were nine TA RMP units. In 1950 the Supplementary Reserve or SR (later re-titled the Army Emergence Reserve or AER) was reformed. This included 14 companies as well as SIB sections. (For the original SR of 1938 see page 100). The Reserve forces underwent a considerable reorganisation in the 1960s, with numbers of units being progressively reduced. In 1967, the AER and TA were merged into the Territorial Army and Volunteer Reserve. By 1969 there were only four RMP TAVR companies. The 1970s and 1980s saw something of a revival in the fortunes of the auxiliary forces, and in 1991 the RMP's Territorial Army (a title revived in 1982) element consisted of 163 (Ports) Provost Company (V), 116 (V), 164 (V), 243 (V), 252 (V), 253 (V), 254 (V), Provost Companies, plus RMP Territorial detachments of 150, 156, 158, 160, and 170 Provost Companies administered by CVHQ RMPTA at Chichester.

The TA is being reorganised under *Options for Change*. In 1992, it was proposed that the RMP's Territorial formations would consist of 116, 152, 163, 164, 165, 243, 251, 252, 253, Provost Companies (V), and 83 Section SIB RMP(V).

---

*Territorial Divisions of 1939–45 included those numbered 12, 15, 18, 23, 38, 42 to 59 inclusive, 61 and 66.

Appendix 4

Key Dates in the Evolution of the Royal Military Police

1511   First known mention of Provost Marshal.

1813–14   Staff Corps of Cavalry formed for the Peninsular War.

1815–18   Staff Corps of Cavalry reformed for the Waterloo campaign and occupation of France.

1854–55   Mounted Staff Corps formed for Crimean War.

1855   Military Mounted Police (MMP) formed at Aldershot.

1877   Military Mounted Police established as a permanent Corps.

1882   Military Foot Police (MFP) formed in Egypt.

1885   Military Foot Police established as a permanent Corps.

1926   Corps of Military Police (CMP) formed by amalgamation of Military Mounted Police and Military Foot Police. (NB the two Corps tended to be referred to as the CMP long before this date).

1940   Special Investigation Branch formed (SIB). A previous SIB existed during the First World War and the 1920s.

1946   Royal Prefix granted to Corps, now entitled the Corps of Royal Military Police (RMP).

1992   Corps of Royal Military Police became federated within the newly-formed Adjutant General's Corps as part of the Provost Branch, continuing to be known as the RMP.

APPENDIX 5

Provost Marshals from 16th century to 1994

England (1511–1707), Great Britain (1707–1800), United Kingdom (1800–1945). United Kingdom and all Overseas Theatres and Commands (21 December, 1945 onwards).

1511	Henry Guylford (or Guildford)	1597	William Bredyman
1540	Osborne Itchingham	1598	Captain John Owen Tudor
1544	Thomas Audley	1600	George Newcomen (or Newgent)
1547	Sir James Wylford	1643	William Smith
1549	Sir Anthony Kingston	1663	Richard Thompson
1557	Sir Gyles Poole	1719	John Martyn
1569	Sir George Bowes	1723	Joseph Garton
1582	Barnaby Googe	1726	James Howard
1588	Peter Crisp	1727	William Heath
1589	G. Acres	1727	John Martyn
1589	Humphrey Coningesby	1734	John Amyott
1590	Thomas Nevinson	1747	Christopher Predham
1595	Sir Thomas Wylford	1796	John Hicks

1829   Death of John Hicks and end of the office of Provost Marshal-General. Provost Marshals were then appointed locally and no records are available until:

1861	Major T Trout	1898	Major JWM Wood, MVO
1881	Captain W Silk	1910	Major RJA Terry, DSO, MVO
1885	Major C Broackes		
1894	Major JL Emerson	1914	Colonel F Darling

16 September, 1916–20 July, 1918	Brigadier General ER Fitzpatrick, CBE, DSO
4 November, 1918–4 November, 1919	Brigadier General AHC James, DSO, MVO
5 November, 1919–31 December, 1920	Brigadier General HS Rogers, CMG, DSO
1 January, 1921–1924	Colonel HS Rogers, CMG, DSO
1924–1928	Colonel CV Edwards, CMG, DSO
1928–1930	Colonel GT Brierley, CMG, DSO
1930–1934	Colonel J de V Bowles, DSO
19 March, 1934–18 March, 1938	Colonel WB Hayley, DSO
19 March, 1938–1 September, 1939	Colonel SV Kennedy, MC

2 September, 1939–16 July, 1940	Colonel WB Hayley, DSO (Re-employed)
17 July, 1940–25 July, 1943	Brigadier (then Major General) Sir Percy R. Laurie, KCVO, CBE, DSO
26 July, 1943–30 June, 1945	Major General J Seymour Mellor, CBE, MC
1 July, 1945–15 December, 1948	Major General ID Erskine, CB, CBE, DSO (UK only until 21 December, 1945)
16 December, 1948–7 January, 1952	Brigadier LFE Wieler, CB, CBE
8 January, 1952–20 January, 1955	Brigadier RH Maxwell, CB, ADC
21 January, 1955–22 January, 1958	Brigadier RHL Oulton, CBE
23 January, 1958–16 December, 1960	Brigadier PH Richardson, DSO, OBE
17 December, 1960–9 September, 1962	Brigadier GF Upjohn, CBE
10 September, 1962–15 April, 1965	Brigadier CG Buttenshaw, DSO, OBE

From this date all Provost Marshal (Army) appointments were from officers of RMP.

16 April, 1965–19 March, 1968	Brigadier R Davenport, OBE
20 March, 1968–13 March, 1971	Brigadier LF Richards, CBE
14 March, 1971–27 March, 1974	Brigadier PN Davis, CBE
28 March, 1974–27 February, 1977	Brigadier DB Rendell, CBE MC, ADC
28 February, 1977–25 March, 1980	Brigadier M Matthews, CBE
26 March, 1980–2 June, 1983	Brigadier JF Thomas, CBE
3 June, 1983–2 June, 1986	Brigadier B Thomas, CBE
3 June, 1986–3 June, 1990	Brigadier NC Allen, CBE
4 June, 1990–13 May, 1992	Brigadier AR Bell, MBE
14 May, 1992–	Brigadier I Cameron

Chapter Notes

All books are published in London unless otherwise stated.

Prologue: The most ancient military officer under the Crown?

For the medieval period, see H Bullock, *A History of the Provost Marshal and The Provost Services* (Aberdeen, Milne and Hutchison, 1929) pp.1–7; AV Lovell-Knight, *The History of the Office of the Provost Marshal and the Corps of Military Police* (Aldershot, Gale and Polden, 1945) pp.1–4; and RAJ Tyler, *Bloody Provost* (Chichester, Phillimore, 1980) pp.1–19.

1. RC Smail, *Crusading Warfare 1097–1193* (Cambridge, CUP, 1972 edn) pp.120–30.
2. See MH Keen, *The Laws of War in the Late Middle Ages* (Routledge Kegan Paul, 1965) *passim.*
3. BJH Rowe, 'Discipline in the Norman Garrisons under Bedford, 1422–35', *EHR*, XLVI, (1931), pp.194–201
4. JW Fortescue, *A History of the British Army*, I, (Macmillan, 1910 edn) pp.56–7; Sir H Nicolas, *History of the Battle of Agincourt and of the Expedition of Henry V into France in 1415* (1974 edn) Appendix VIII and IX; C Hibbert, *Agincourt* (Batsford, 1964) pp.166–74.
5. Tyler, p.8.
6. J Keegan, *The Face of Battle* (Harmondsworth, 1978 edn) pp.108–12.
7. P Godfrey-Faussett, 'The Provost Service: Its History and Achievements', part 1 *AQ*, LIII, 1947, pp.250–1. AV Lovell-Knight, *The Story of the Royal Military Police* (Leo Cooper, 1977) p.4.

Part One: The Antecedents, 1511–1902

Chapter 1: The Emergence of the Provost Marshal, 1511–1660

For this period see Tyler, chapters III to VIII inclusive; pp.35–50 contains much on 'civilian' provost marshals.

1. Lovell-Knight, *History* pp.4–5.
2. C Falls, *Elizabeth's Irish Wars* (Methuen, 1950) pp.45–6.
3. See CG Cruickshank, *Army Royal* (Oxford, OUP, 1969) esp. pp.61–7 and 94–104.
4. F Grose, *Military Antiquities of the English Army* I, (Hooper, 1786) pp.249–51; H Bullock, 'The Provost Marshal 1513–87', *JSAHR*, VII, 27, (1928) p.67.
5. Bullock, *History*, p.13–14.
6. W Bunbury, 'A Treatise on the Art of War by Thomas Audley', *JSAHR*, VI, 24 (1927) p.73.
7. CG Cruickshank, *Elizabeth's Army* (Oxford, OUP, 1968 edn) pp.159–73; L Boynton, 'The Tudor Provost-Marshal', *EHR*, 77, (1962) pp.437–55.

8. Lovell-Knight, *History* pp.18–20.
9. C Walton, *History of the British Standing Army AD 1660 to 1700* (Harrison, 1894) pp.199, 554–574.
10. CM Clode, *The Military Forces of the Crown: Their Administration and Government*, I, p.23; C Firth, *Cromwell's Army* (Methuen, 1962) pp.184, 281–3, 85–91, 402, 411–12; P Young and W Embleton, *The Cavalier Army* (Allen and Unwin, 1974) pp.62, 65; DH Pennington and IA Roots, *The Committee at Stafford 1643–1645* (Manchester, MUP, 1957) pp.145–6; CV Wedgewood, *The King's War* (Collins, 1959 edn) p.293, Bullock, *History* p.47.
11. Tyler, p.86, Walton, p.553, Young and Embleton, p.63.
12. I Roy, 'The English Civil War and English Society' in B Bond and I Roy, (eds) *War and Society*, I (Croom Helm, 1975) p.28, 35–42.

Chapter 2: Standing Army, 1660–1800

1. J Childs, *The Army of Charles II* (Routledge Kegan Paul, 1976) p.84; T Simes, *The Military Guide for Young Officers*, I, (Humphreys, Bell and Aitken, 1776) p.322; T Hayter, (ed) *An Eighteenth Century Secretary At War* (Bodley Head, 1988) p.31.
2. R Latham, (ed) *The Shorter Pepys* (Bell and Hyman, 1985) p.750; Hayter, p.213.
3. J Childs, *The British Army of William III, 1689–1702* (Manchester, MUP, 1987) pp.111–13.
4. M Maurer, 'Military Justice Under General Washington' in *Military Analysis of the Revolutionary War* (Milwood, NY, KTO, 1977) pp.57–58.
5. K Thomasson and F Buist, *Battles of the '45* (Batsford, 1962) p.126.
6. Walton, p.553; Childs, *William III* pp.125–6.
7. RE Scouller, *The Armies of Queen Anne* (Oxford, OUP, 1966) p.90, 62–3, 104–5, 265; R Savory, *His Brittanic Majesty's Army in Germany During the Seven Years War* (Oxford, OUP, 1966) p.310, 462; Simes, p.11, 14, 53–6; D Chandler, (ed) *The Marlborough Wars; Robert Parker and Comte de Merode-Westerloo* (Longman, 1968) p.121; PE Koppermann, 'The British High Command and Soldier's Wives in America, 1755–1783', *JSAHR*, LXI (1982) pp.24–5, 29.
8. MM Boatner, (ed) *Cassell's Biographical Dictionary of the American War of Independence 1763–1783* (Cassell, 1973) pp.312, 894–5; *Standing Orders and Regulations for the Army in Ireland* [1794] (Muller, 1969) p.109.
9. Lovell-Knight, *History* pp.14, 28–29; P Guedalla, *The Duke* (Reprint Society, 1940) p.88. For Ireland, see Tyler, pp.50–76.
10. *Army Lists* for 1778 and 1786; 'The Adventures of Serjeant Benjamin Miller', *JSAHR*, VII, (1929) p.22.

Chapter 3: Wellington's Army

1. C Hibbert, *Corunna* (Pan, 1967) pp.121–2; B Brownrigg, *The Life and Letters of Sir John Moore* (Oxford, Blackwells, 1923) pp.251–2. H Curling, (ed) *The Recollections of Rifleman Harris* (Davies, 1929) p.138.
2. G Simmons, (ed. W Werner) *A British Rifle Man* (Black, 1899) pp. 26–7; J Kincaid, *Adventures in the Rifle Brigade* (Maclaren, nd) p.9; J Selby, *Thomas Morris* (Longmans, 1967) p.94; GO 3, 5 May 1809, 30 Oct. 1810, 14 Oct. 1811.
3. G Davies, *Wellington and his Army* (Oxford, 1954) p.83; GO 9 Apr 1812; BH Liddell Hart, (ed) *The Letters of Private Wheeler 1809–1828* (M Joseph, 1951) p.68; Kincaid, p.60; GC Moore-Smith, (ed) *The Autobiography of Lieutenant-General Sir Harry Smith* (J Murray, 1903) p.59–60.

4.   GO 1 Nov. 1811, J Gurwood, *The Dispatches of Field Marshal the Duke of Wellington* X, (J Murray, 1838) pp.38, 424; 'An Officer in the Staff Corps Regiment of Cavalry', *Adventures in the Peninsula* (Murray, 1827) p.302.
5.   Gurwood, IV, pp. 404–7, IX, p.403 (See also A Brett-James, *Wellington at War 1794–1815* (Macmillan, 1961) pp.163–4; GO 7 Apr. 1812; I Fletcher, *In Hell Before Daylight* (Tunbridge Wells, Baton Press, 1984) p.106–7.
6.   G Bell, *Rough Notes by an Old Soldier* (Day, 1867), I, pp.74–5; C Esdaile, *The Duke of Wellington and the Command of the Spanish Army, 1812–14* (Macmillan, 1990) p.23; C Oman, *Wellington's Army* (E Arnold, 1912) pp.158–9; *General Regulations and Orders for the Army* (Adjutant-General's Office, 1811) p.124; SPG Ward, *Wellington's Headquarters* (OUP, 1957) pp.28–9, 125–6.
7.   GO 13 Mar. 1813, notes in 'Napoleonic Wars' file, RMPA; Ward, p.161; WY Carman, 'The Cavalry Staff Corps', *JSAHR*, 47, No.89, (1969) pp.33–34.
8.   GO, 5 Dec. 1813, Sir G Larpent, *The Private Journal of F.S. Larpent*, III, (Bentley, 1853) p.84.
9.   M Glover, *Wellington's Army* (Newton Abbot, 1977) p.71; RN Buckley (ed) *The Napoleonic War Journal of Captain Thomas Henry Browne 1807–1816* (Bodley Head, 1987) p.256.
10. GO 4 Feb, 15 Apr, 8 May, 20, 21 Jun, 11 Aug, 27 Sep 1815; Gurwood, XII, p.563, 579.
11. A Brett-James. (ed) *Edward Costello* (Longmans, 1967) pp.157–8; Moore-Smith, p.82.
12. See Chapter 4, footnote 2.
13. Gurwood, X, pp.140–1, XI pp.328–30; Tyler, p.166.

Chapter 4: The Crimean War, 1854–55

1.   Sir W Napier, *The Life and Opinions of General Sir Charles James Napier*, II, (Murray, 1857) pp.292, 379–80.
2.   Document in NAM 8202–65; J. Sweetman, '"Ad Hoc" Support Services during the Crimean War, 1854–6: Temporary, III-Planned and Largely Unsuccessful', *MA* 52, No.3, (1988) p.135.
3.   OB, MSC 1854, 29 Sep, 19 Dec 1854, NAM 6807–354; Bell, *Rough Notes* II, p.246; WH Russell, *The War: From the Death of Lord Raglan to the Evacuation of the Crimea* [II] (Routledge, 1856) p.221.
4.   OB MSC 6, 14 Dec 1854, 3 Jan, 29 Mar, 2 Jul 1855.
5.   *The Times* 4 Jan 1855. See also OB MSC 15 Jan, 4 Feb 1855.
6.   WH Russell, *The War: From the Landing at Gallipoli to the Death of Lord Raglan* [I] (Routledge, 1855) p.347; OB MSC 29 Dec 1854; Russell, Vol. II p.221.
7.   NAM 8202–65; P Warner, *The Fields of War* (Murray, 1977) p.39; Russell, I, p.335, 337, 366, 502; T Coleman, *The Railway Navvies* (Hutchinson, 1965) pp.188–9.
8.   Russell, II, p.221, I p.370; Tyler, pp.181, 188; Sweetman, pp.135–6.

Chapter 5: Military Mounted and Military Foot Police, 1855–1914

Generally, see Lovell-Knight, *History* pp.42–65; Tyler, pp.102–30, 198–207.

1.   COB, 13 June 1855, Exhibit 500, RMPA; NAM 8202–65; D. Anderson, 'The English Militia in the Mid-Nineteenth Century' (D. Phil. Univ. of Oxford, 1982) pp.380–7.
2.   SN Sen, *Eighteen Fifty-Seven* (Govt. of India, Calcutta, 1957) pp.414–6; Tyler, p.110.

3. JW Kaye, *A History of the Sepoy War in India 1857–8*, III, (Allen, 1877) p.439; JJ McLeod Innes, *Lucknow and the Oude in the Mutiny* (Innes, 1895) p.83. Lady Inglis, *The Siege of Lucknow* (Osgood, McIlvaine, 1892) pp.40–3; [JA Harris], *A Lady's Diary of the Siege of Lucknow* (J Murray, 1858) pp.198–99.
4. Kaye, II (1888), 399–400; W Gordon-Alexander, *Recollections of a Highland Subaltern* (Arnold, 1898) pp.209, 214, 352.
5. JF Maurice, *Military History of the Campaign of 1882 in Egypt* (HMSO, 1857) p.6; notes in EPS file, RMPA; J Lehmann, *The Model Major-General* (Boston, MA, Houghton Mifflin, 1964) p.332.
6. SH Shadbolt, *The Afghan Campaigns of 1878–80, Historical Division* (Sampson Low, 1882) p.119; L James, *The Indian Frontier War* (Heinemann, 1898) pp.290–300.
7. L/MIL/3/135, IOL (I owe this reference to Tim Moreman); ATQ Stewart, *The Pagoda War* (Faber, 1972) pp.126–131.
8. NAM 8201–13, pp.18–21.
9. Lovell-Knight, *Story* pp.9–10; GA Furse, *The Lines of Communications* (Clowes, 1883) pp.33–4.
10. WO32/8922, PRO; SF Crozier, *The Corps of Royal Military Police* (Aldershot, Gale and Polden, 1951) pp.xiv, 18.

Chapter 6: The Boer War

1. WO 108/268, PRO.
2. COB Oct–Nov 1899; Tyler, pp.208–11; WO 108/259, 'Report . . .' by Major RM Poore, 15 July 1900, PRO.
3. *Under the Union Jack*, 10 Feb 1900; WO 108/259; WO 108/260, PRO; W Nasson, 'Tommy Atkins in South Africa' in P. Warwick, *The South African War* (Longman, 1980) pp.128–29.
4. E Lee, *To The Bitter End* (Harmondsworth, 1986) pp.162–190; WO 108/260; WO 108/259 p.6; letter of 20 Dec 1901, 'Boer War' file, RMPA: Tyler, p.219.
5. Tyler, p.210, 215–16; WO 108/259; TG Fergusson, *British Military Intelligence 1870–1914* (Arms and Armour, 1984); letter, 12 Dec. 1900, 'Boer War' file, RMPA.
6. Tyler, p.211; WO 108/259; WO 108/260.

Part Two: The First World War, 1914–18

The 1914–18 War is covered in Lovell-Knight, *History* pp.66–88 and Crozier, pp.18–27. See also GD Sheffield, 'The Operational Role of British Military Police, 1914–18' in Paddy Griffth (ed) *British Fighting Methods in the First World War* (forthcoming).

Chapter 7: Mons to Neuve Chapelle, 1914–15

1. WO 154/114, WD, APM L of C, 6–10 Aug 1914, PRO; D Englander and J Osborne, 'Jack, Tommy and Henry Dubb: The Armed Forces and the Working Class', *HJ* 21, 3, (1978) pp.595; P Simkins, *Kitchener's Army* (Manchester, MUP, 1988) p.xiv.
2. WO 154/33 WD of APM 5th Div., 20, 25, 28 Aug, 3 Sept. 1914, PRO; J Charteris, *At GHQ* (Cassell, 1931) pp.19; JE Edmonds papers, III/9/12, LHCMA; Lovell-Knight, *History* pp.78–9 (Rogers' original report seems to have been destroyed in the 1960s).

3. *Training and Manoeuvre Regulations 1909* (HMSO, 1909) pp.74–5; *Field Service Regulations Part II* (HMSO, reprinted 1911) p.120; *Notes from the Front. Collated by the General Staff* (1914) pp.39–41; DH, 1914–19 p.3, RMPA.
4. WO 154/33, 26–7 Aug 1914. WO 95/25, WD, AG GHQ, Appx VII, Aug. 1914, PRO; J Terraine, *Mons: The Retreat to Victory* (Leo Cooper, 1991 edn.) pp.150–2.
5. WO 154/33, 4, 8 Sept 1914; A Babington, *For the Sake of Example* (Leo Cooper, 1983) p.5; J Putkowski and J Sykes, *Shot at Dawn* (Barnsley, Wharncliffe, 1989) pp.23–4.
6. 'Straggler Posts', FWW File, RMPA, [hereafter SP]. This is a short history compiled shortly after the war. It quotes at length from contemporary documents, most of which have since disappeared.
7. R Blake, (ed) *The Private Papers of Douglas Haig* (Eyre and Spottiswood, 1951) p.79; Anon, *The History of The Welch Regiment* (Cardiff, Western Mail, 1932) p.326.
8. WO 154/101, WD of APM 5th Aus. Div, 6 Feb 1918, PRO; SP p.2–4.
9. 'Provost Arrangements, VI Corps . . .' 4 Mar 1918, Acc. 300, RMPA; SP, pp4–5; P. Creek papers, p.48, 87/31/1, IWM.
10. R.G. Garrod papers, p.33, 79/44/1 IWM; SP pp.2,5.
11. SP p.5; WO 95/154, WD, First Army GS, Appx D, Mar. 1915, PRO; WO 95/721, WD, IV Corps A & Q, 10 Mar 1915, PRO; WO 95/181, WD of First Army, A & Q, Appx C to Mar 1915, PRO.

Chapter 8: Second Ypres and Loos, 1915

1. WO 154/6, WD, APM V Corps, 22 Apr 1915, PRO; JE Edmonds and GC Wynne, *Military Operations, France and Belgium, 1915*, (Macmillan, 1927) vol I, pp.176–84.
2. This account of traffic control at Loos is based on material in WO 106/390, PRO. See also T Travers, *The Killing Ground* (Unwin Hyman, 1987) pp.16–19.
3. HL Smyth diary, 25 Sept 1915, RMPA.
4. JE Edmonds, *Military Operations. France and Belgium, 1915*, (Macmillan, 1928) vol II, p.278.
5. Maj J Buckley, letter of 1 Jan 1927; Maj Gen BR Mitford, letter of 23 Jan 1926; Col JR Wethered, letter of 19 Jan 1926, all in CAB 45/120, PRO.
6. Lecture by Lt Col Wingfield in Misc 134 Item 2072, IWM (I owe this reference to Nigel Steel); OH 1915, II pp.294–5; Maj Gen Sir F Maurice, letter of 10 Jan 1920, CAB 45/120.
7. SP pp.5–6; Wingfield; Maj Gen Sir G Jeffreys, letter, nd, CAB 45/120, PRO.

Chapter 9: Battles of Attrition, 1916–17

1. SP pp.6–7.
2. WO 95/1631, WD, 7th Div GS, 'Notes on Attacks carried out by 7th Division in July 1916' PRO; WO 95/2316 WD, 30th Div GS 'Report on Operations July 1 till July 5' [1916] PRO; WO95/2315 WD, 30th Div A&Q, 'Report on Operations 1 July 1916' and 'Report on Operations 23 July 1916', PRO; SP p.6.
3. WO 95/2316, 'Operation Order 18' 16 June 1916 and Appendix G June 1916.
4. CAB 45/138, HB Wilkinson, letter of 6 May 1930, PRO; Sir I Maxse papers, file 23, 69/53/7, IWM.
5. M Middlebrook, *The First Day on the Somme* (Allen Lane, 1971) pp.94, 108, 221. See also Sheffield, 'Operational Role'.
6. *Regulations for Use of Provost Marshal's Branch, British Armies in France* [hereafter *Regulations 1917*] (2nd edn., Sept. 1917) p.25; *Military Operations: France and*

Belgium, 1916, II Maps and Appendices, (Macmillan, 1938) pp.99, 102. J Ellis, *Eye Deep in Hell* (Fontana edn, 1977) p.187; WO 154/78, WD of APM, 3rd Aus. Div, Appx 3 to Aug 1917, PRO.

7. W Childs, *Episodes and Reflections* (Cassell, 1930) pp.143–45; D Lamb, *Mutinies: 1917–21* (Solidarity, nd.) pp.3–4, drawing on FP Crozier, *A Brass Hat in No Man's Land* (Cape, 1930); Sir G Jeffreys, letter, nd (c.1935) CAB 45/114, PRO.
8. *Military Operations: France and Belgium, 1917* I, Appendices, (Macmillan, 1940) pp.31, 86; SP, pp.7–8.
9. WO 154/8, WD of APM IX Corps, 'Report on . . . action of 7 June 1917', PRO; WO 32/11355, PRO; *Preliminary Notes on Recent Operations on the Front of the Second Army* (HMSO, July 1917) p.6.
10. SP 8–9; GW Durham papers, letters of 3 & 4 May 1916, IWM.
11. WO 154/78, 14 Oct 1917, Appx 1 to Oct 1917, PRO.

Chapter 10: Retreat and Victory, 1918

1. SP p.25; MS 300 RMPA; 'Farewell Order . . . 30 Oct 1919', FWW File, RMPA.
2. WD, 2nd (G) Bn KOYLI, KOYLI Museum.
3. 'APM XIX Corps Provost Diary . . . 21 March to 5th April 1918'; 'APM XIX Corps Report(s)' SP.
4. AW Bradbury papers, p.55 IWM.
5. SP pp.10, 22, 25–7, 37; WO 154/8, 26 Mar 1918; F Grey, *The Confessions of a Private* (Oxford, Blackwells, 1920) p.163, W Shaw Sparrow, *The Fifth Army in March 1918* (Bodley Head, 1921) p.17; WO 95/2315, Appx F, Apr 1918. Earlier in the campaign the Guards Division had used straggler posts: see Ms. 284, RMPA.
6. Quoted in JFC Fuller, *Memoirs of an Unconventional Soldier* (Nicholson and Watson, 1936) p.204.
7. JE Edmonds, *Military Operations, France and Belgium, 1918*, IV, (Macmillan, 1947) pp.17, 570–71; EL Roberts, 'Dirty Work at the Crossroads in 1918', *Great War Adventures*, p.87 (undated copy in IWM).
8. Based on material in Ms 154, 155, 206–226, RMPA.
9. WO 154/104, WD, APM NZ Div. report month ending 31 Aug 1918; WO 154/78, Appx D, Sept 1918.
10. TH Westmacott papers, letter, 5 Nov 1918, IWM; Ms. 227–277 and 322–425, (especially 241 and 254), RMPA.
11. EA McKechnie, papers, pp.71–73, Acc 1369, RMPA. He appears to be describing the offensive of 8 August 1918.
12. JH Boraston, *Sir Douglas Haig's Despatches* (Dent, 1979) p.341.

Chapter 11: Behind the Lines, 1914–18

1. WO 154/114, 31 Dec 1914, 30 June 1916,; HS Rogers, 'Application . . .' FWW File, RMPA: AV Lovell-Knight (ed) *The Corps of Royal Military Police* (Morcambe Bay Printers, Morcambe, 1953) p.37.
2. [Sir F Fox] 'GSO' *GHQ* (Philip Allan, 1920) pp.43–5; WO 154/114, 26 Jan, 6 Feb, 4 and 5 Mar 1915.
3. S Peel, *O.C. Beds Yeomanry* (OUP, 1935) pp.2–3, 17; WO 154/8, 9–10 Jan 1917.
4. COB 16 Jan 1916, Acc.683, 24 Jul, 30 Aug 1918, Acc.684, RMPA; Englander and Osborne, p.595.
5. *Statistics of the Military Effort of the British Empire During the Great War* (HMSO, 1922) p.642; *Army List* (May 1915).

6. WO 154/8, 18 May 1917; WN Nicholson, *Behind The Lines* (Cape, 1939) p.104; Acc. 629, RMPA.

7. J Lees-Milne, *The Enigmatic Edwardian* (Sidgwick and Jackson, 1986) p.264; *The Provost Times* 1, (June 1920), p.V.

8. 'GSO', pp.87–8; WO 154/72, WD, APM 62 Div, 8 Feb 1918, PRO; WO 154/114, 22 Dec 1914; see lists in WO 154/8, PRO.

9. I am grateful to Mr MG Hibberd for providing a copy of Lt HE Kingston's papers.

10. *Regulations 1917* p.9; GS Chaplin papers, PP/MCR/63, IWM, RHJ Steuart, *March, Kind Comrade* (Sheed and Ward, 1931) pp.101–103.

11. JH Dible papers, pp.178, IWM; WO 154/114, 25, 29 May, 10, 15, 22 June, 27 Jul, 22, 30 Aug, 3 Oct 1916; WO 154/8 25 Dec 1917.

   For Etaples, see G Dallas and D Gill, *The Unknown Army* (Verso, 1985) pp.63–76; J Putkowski, 'Toplis, Etaples and the Monocled Mutineer', *Stand To!* Winter 1986, pp.6–11; WO 95/4027, PRO. For the role of provost in the demobilisation disturbances see J Putkowski, *The Kinmel Park Camp Riots, 1919* (Hawarden, Flintshire Historical Society, 1989).

12. See 'Captain Immals' in CE Montague's novel *Rough Justice* (Chatto and Windus, 1926). Montague had served as a camp policeman during the war.

13. J Brophy and E Partridge, *The Long Trail* (Deutsch, 1965) pp.82, 170; Englander and Osborne, p.599.

14. GS Chaplin papers, IWM; WO 95/4027, 9 Sep 1917; H Heeseman diary, IWM; WO 154/114 Appx II to July 1915.

15. AH Maude, (ed) *The 47th (London) Division 1914–1919* (Amalgamated Press, 1922) p.221.

16. WO 154/114 21 Aug, 29 Sept, 14 Nov 1914; N Macready, *Annals of an Active Life*, I, (Hutchinson, 1924) pp.231–4; pp.231–4; M Gilbert *The Challenge of War: Winston S. Churchill 1914–16* (Minerva, 1990) pp.694–7.

17. WO 154/177 WD of APM 2nd Can. Div, 8–10 Sept 1915; WO 154/6, 1 and 8 April 1915.

18. WO 154/114, Appx 1 to Mar 1915; AH Clayton, *Forearmed* (Brassey's (UK), 1993) pp.38–40; J Maclaren's notes in 'Intelligence 1914–18' file, RMPA.

19. OH 1918, IV, Appx VII, pp.571–3; 'Notes for Third Army IP', 12 April 1916, pp.1, 12, 'Intelligence 1914–18' file, RMPA.

20. WO 154/114, Appx XIII to June 1915, Appx III and Appx VI to July 1915, Appx IV to Sept 1915.

21. J Haswell, *British Military Intelligence* (Weidenfield and Nicolson, 1973) p.83; WO 154/114, 23, 31 May, 3 June 1916.

22. G Cornwallis-West, *Edwardian Heyday* (Putnam, 1930) pp.296–8; NCR, pp.29–30, RMPA.

23. WO 154/114 22 Jun, 12 Jul, 3, 15 Aug, 25, 28 Sept, 15, 29 Oct, 5 Nov 1916; WO 154/8, 24 Feb 1917; WO 154/73, WD of APM 63rd Div, 5 Jan 1917, PRO.

24. NCR p.29; AIR 1/552/16/15/39, 6 Oct 1918; AIR and 1/553/16/15/40, Nov 1918–19 Apr. 1919, both in PRO; SR Ward, 'Intelligence Surveillance of British Ex-Servicemen, 1918–20', *HJ*, XVI, I, (1973) pp.179–188.

Chapter 12: The Great War: Home Front

1. COB 4 Aug – 29 Sept 1914, Acc. 680, RMPA; WO 154/114, Appx 1 to Sept 1914.

2. CS Havers papers, Acc. 1667, RMPA.

3. RMPJ 3/1971 p.16.

4. EAR pp.1–2, 5 RMPA; NCR p.1, RMPA; FC Ransley papers p.9, 87/55/1, IWM; MCR pp.6–8, 19–20, RMPA.

5. Bullock, *History* p.68; NCR pp.2–3, 17–18, 31–3; COB 27 June 1916–21 Mar 1917, Acc. 681, RMPA; DH, 1914–19 pp.11–12. For the syllabus of a Provost course, see *Regulations 1917* pp.79–85.
6. EAR pp.2, 7–8; NCR pp.23–26, Appx IV; *New York Herald* 27 Jan 1918 p.7 (I owe this reference to Julian Putkowski) JB Priestly, *Margin Released* (Mercury, 1966) pp.119–20; Cornwallis-West pp.297, 301.
7. J Lock, *The British Policewoman* (Hale, 1979) pp.21–29, 77.

Chapter 13: The Great War: Secondary Theatres

1. WO 95/4266, WD A & Q, MEF, *passim*; Viscount Mersey, *A Picture of Life 1872–1940* (Murray, 1941) p.257–60; O Teichman, *The Diary of a Yeomanry MO* (Fisher Unwin, 1921) p.43; C Mackenzie, *Gallipoli Memories* (Cassells, 1929) pp.101, 120.
2. J Gillam, *Gallipoli Diary* (Stevenage, Strong Oak Press, 1989) p.52; Maj Gen G Egerton, diary, 22 Jul 1915, CAB 45/249, PRO; PC Fenwick diary, 1 June 1915, LULLC.
3. Material in 23 (=41)/3, [Campbell, PM], IWM. I owe this reference to Nigel Steel.
4. WO 154/239, WD of GHQ APM, Mesopotamia, 16, 20 Apr, 1 Oct–30 Nov, 2–10 Dec 1915, 14 Aug, 1916; S Blythman, letter to author, 8 July 1989.
5. WO 154/239, 2 July, 23 Sept, 4 Oct, 1 Dec 1916, 1 Jan, 28 Feb, 10 May, 11, 20 Mar 1917; Blythman.
6. B Canning diary, 3 Apr 1915, LULLC; CH Rastall papers, letters, 26 May 1915, 2 Feb 1916, IWM.
7. WO 54/129, WD, Aus. Provost Corps, Egypt, 6 Aug 1916, PRO. No British provost war diaries seem to have survived from this theatre.
8. C Falls, *Military Operations: Egypt and Palestine*, II (Longmans, 1930) pp.51–61; WO 154/129 29–31 Oct, Appx I, May, II, Oct, III, Nov, 1917, 22–24 May 1918; RMP Preston, *The Desert Mounted Corps* (Constable, 1921) pp.97–99; R Coldicott, *London Men in Palestine* (Arnold, 1919) pp.84–5.
9. Correspondence book of 1/1 Bucks Battalion, 21 Mar and 3 July 1918, LLC Reynolds papers, IWM (I owe this reference to Dr IFW Beckett); T.A. Heathcote, *The Indian Army* (Newton Abbot, David and Charles, 1974) pp.141–2.
10. See WO 154/296, WO 154/299, WO 154/300, PRO.
11. *The Times* 7 Dec 1916; 'Scheme of Defence' 8 Feb 1916, P Howell papers, III/B/1, LHCMA.

Part Three: The Second World War, 1939–45

Chapter 14: From War to War, 1919–1940

Generally, see Crozier pp.28–35, 152–3 and Lovell-Knight, *History* pp.89–135.
1. Cornwallis-West pp.303–5; notes of J Maclaren's interview with C Stilwell, 1988.
2. JH Moore papers (for an example of provost work in Baku, see H Gough, *Soldiering On* (Barker, 1954) p.1987); CAB 45/81; interview with JC MacLellan, 1989; J Cusack and I Herbert, *Scarlet Fever* (Cassell, 1972) pp.85–94.
3. L/MIL/7/5467, IOL (I owe this reference to Dr TA Heathcote); RJ Wyatt and DA Kyd, *A History of 163 (Ports) Provost Company RMP (V) and the AA's Involvement with the Military Police 1938–1988* (nd) pp.2–8; WO167/312, WD, 3rd Div. PC, Sept 1939, PRO.
4. WO168/91, WD, DAPM, Rupert Force, 15, 16, 30 Apr, 13 May 1940.

5. Anon, *The Diary of a Staff Officer* (Meuthen, 1941), 19 May 1940, p.26; G Blaxland, *Destination Dunkirk* (Kimber, 1973) p.115.
6. WO 167/215, WD, 2nd Div. PC, 11–16, 28–29 May 1940, PRO; VV Tozer, ts account, pp.36–7, RMPA.
7. A Bryant, *The Turn of the Tide* (Fontana, 1965) p.96; Montgomery of Alamein, *Memoirs* (Companion, 1958) p.54.
8. A Neave, *The Flames of Calais* (Grafton, 1989) p.52; WS Calvert papers, p.9, RMPA.
9. D Divine, *The Nine Days of Dunkirk* (Pan, 1964) p.276.
10. N Harman, *Dunkirk: The Necessary Myth* (Hodder and Stoughton, 1980) p.167; WO 167/288, WD, DAPM 46th Div., 1 June 1940, PRO.
11. LF Ellis, *The War in France and Flanders, 1939–40* (HMSO, 1953) p.154. I am grateful to Maj Tyler for his guidance on this point.
12. WO 167/215, 30 May 1940; Blaxland, pp.309–12, D Brownrigg, *Unexpected* (Hutchinson, nd) p.155.
13. Tozer, p.39; H Dibbens, 'Redcap at Dunkirk', *War Monthly*, Feb 1982, p.85; RMPJ 4, 1987, pp.30–1.

Chapter 15: The Middle East, 1940–43

1. S Ogden-Smith, *A Record of the Activities of the Corps of Military Police in the Middle East, 1939–1944* (Printing and Stationary Services, MEF, 1946) pp.6, 7, 9; R Ganapathi, *The White Belts* (New Dehli, Lancer Press, 1982) p.98, 100.
2. Brig LF Richards, 'Provost in India and the Indian Army Overseas from 1939–1947' pp.2–3 in 'LF Richards' file, RMPA.
3. WO 169/1335, WD, Crete PC, PRO; 1 May–1 June 1941.
4. WO 169/2559, WD, 204 PC, 18 and 27 June 1941, PRO; Ganapathi, p.104.
5. WO 169/2557, WD, 202 PC, PRO; *Saga*, 8 Aug. 1944, TH Eaton papers, 'Italy 1943–45' file, RMPA.
6. WO 169/2559, 24–25 Nov. 1941.
7. Ganapathi, pp.112–13.
8. WO 169/4143, WD, 44th Div. PC, 23, 30, 31 August 1942.
9. This account of provost at Alamein is based on WO 169/4209, WD, 1st Armd. Bde PC, Appx D, Oct. 1942; Irvine's report of operations in Ogden-Smith, pp.11–21; WO 169/6662, WD, 501 TC Unit, 23 Oct 1942.
10. CE Lucas Phillips, *Alamein* (Pan, 1965) p.79, 147–8; J Lucas, *War in the Desert* (Arms and Armour, 1982) p.144.
11. 'Notes on the Work of Provost . . .', APM 9th Corps, 20 May 1943 and 'Report on Campaign', APM 4th Div, 25 May 1943, Brigadier EJ Paton-Walsh papers, 4, LHCMA.
12. 'Report to O.C. 103 Coy CMP (TC)', 4 Apr. 1943, and attached comments; 'First Army Provost Instructions' Feb. 1943 and 16 Mar. 1943, Paton-Walsh papers, I/1/1/ and I/1/3; WO 169/8788, WD, 50 Div PC, 16, 17, Mar. 1943.
13. Author's interview with Capt JC Atkinson; WO 175/1228, WD, 77 Coy CMP (TC), Appx. and 16–21 Jan. 1943.
14. 'Lessons of the Tunisian Campaign', 22 May 1943, Paton-Walsh papers I/1/4. For SIB work in Algiers, see CV Hearn, *Foreign Assignment* (Hale, 1961).
15. 'Report on Campaign', APM 6th Armd Div, 18 May 1943, Paton-Walsh papers, I/1/4.
16. RP Ratcliffe papers, 'North Africa 1939–45' file, RMPA; 'Lessons of the Tunisian Campaign' and 'Report . . .', APM 9th Corps, Paton-Walsh papers, I/1/4.

Chapter 16: The Italian Campaign, 1943–45

1. RMPJ 2/53 p.245.
2. WO 169/8806, WD, 51st Div PC, 3, 11 July 1943, PRO.
3. WO 169/8675, WD, 1st AB Div PC, Appxs to July and Aug 1943, PRO; information provided by Maj Tyler.
4. WO 169/8726, WD, 5th Div PC 12 July 1943, PRO.
5. WO 169/8825, WD, 56th Div PC 14 Sept 1943, PRO.
6. D Graham and S Bidwell, *Tug of War* (Hodder and Stoughton, 1986) pp.92–3 and H Pond, *Salerno* (Kimber, 1961) p.208.
7. The preceding five paragraphs have been largely based on a report of late 1944, in the Archer-Burton papers.
8. WO 170/111, WD, Provost HQ, Admin. Order, 25 Sept 1944, PRO; WO 170/3603, WD, 26 Sec. SIB, 4 Mar 1944, PRO; Hearn, pp.37–9.
9. WO 269/8825, 8 Dec. 1943.
10. WO 170/396, WD, 1st Div PC, 22, 25 Jan, 9 Feb, 25 Apr 1944, PRO; 'Life in the Beach-Head', A Conn papers, RMPA. Bidwell and Graham, p.123; WO 170/494, WD, 56th Div PC 19, 27 Feb 1944, PRO.
11. JC Atkinson, ts account, 'Italy 1943–45' file, RMPA; WO 170/512, WD, 78th Div PC 22–26 Apr. 1944, PRO; F Majdaleny, *The Monastery* (Corgi, 1957) pp.50–1.
12. J Harris diary, 5 Feb, 21 May 1944 (entry by E Welch), RMPA; RMPJ 1/87 p.6.
13. WO 170/3585, WD, 'R' PC (Beach)' 1 Jun 1944, PRO.
14. CH Butt papers, Dept. of Printed Books, 523.1, IWM.
15. EL Collins, Ms account, 'Italy 1943–45' file, RMPA.
16. WO 170/111, Appx, Sept. 1944; WO 170/3547, WD, 101 PC, Appx, Jun and 4 Sept, 1944, PRO.
17. WO 170/4403, WD, 78th Div PC 19 Apr. 1945, PRO.
18. WO 170/7014, WD, 200 PC, 8 May 1945, PRO.

Chapter 17: Defeat in the Far East

1. WO 172/1872, WD, DPM Southern Army, Appx, Apr. 1943.
2. Richards, 'Provost', pp.1–3; Ganapathi, *passim*; P Mason, *A Matter of Honour* (Cape, 1974) pp.479, 495.
3. Brig AR Forbes, letter, 5 Feb 1989, in 'Far East, 1939–45' file, RMPA: Ganapathi, pp.60–9, 70–1; WO 172/6930, WD, 15 Ind. Corps PU, 10 Jan 1945.
4. WO 172/30, WD, L of C PU, Malaya, 10–29 Dec. 1941; R Holmes and A Kemp, *The Bitter End* (Chichester, Bird, 1982).
5. WO 172/84, WD, 18th Div. PC, 13–29 Jan. 1942.
6. AE Percival, *The War in Malaya* (Eyre and Spottiswood, 1949) pp.211–12, 270–1, 277; *Daily Telegraph* 12 Jan 1993.
7. Ganapathi, p.232; 'Lessons from Malaya', Conf. 1000/1, SCL.
8. RMPJ, 1/1960, pp.141–3; Crozier, pp.144–6; 'Changi' file, RMPA.
9. A Hartfield, *British and Indian Armies on the China Coast 1785–1985* (A and J Partnership, 1990) p.454; GW Pringle papers, IWM.
10. WO 172/481, WD, 17 Ind. Div. PU, 22–3 Feb., 13–14 Mar, 6 Apr 1942; Ganapathi, pp.242–3.
11. *Supplement to the London Gazette* 11 Mar 1948, pp.1681, 1694, 1708.

Chapter 18: Victory in Burma, 1943–45

1. M Gilbert, *Winston S. Churchill* IV, *Road to Victory 1941–45* (Heinemann, 1986) p.936.

2.   WO 172/1959, WD, 14th Ind. Div. PU, 11, 19 Jan, 12 Mar–10 Apr 1943, PRO.
3.   W Slim, *Defeat Into Victory* (Four Square, 1958) pp.119.
4.   WO 172/4289, WD, 5th Ind. Div. PU, 4–24 Feb 1945; A Brett-James, *Ball of Fire* (Aldershot: Gale and Polden, 1951) pp.280–1.
5.   Ganapathi, p.260; G. Evans and A Brett-James, *Imphal* (Macmillan, 1962) p.114.
6.   WO 172/4308 WD, 17th Ind. Div. PU, 30 Mar 1944; Slim, pp.249–50.
7.   AJF Doulton, *The Fighting Cock* (Aldershot: Gale and Polden, 1951) p.101.
8.   Brig LF Richards, 'Provost, Parachuting and Para-Provost, 1941 to 1971', pp.5–6, 'LF Richards' file, RMPA; Letter, Maj WH Stabback, 29 Nov 1985, in 'Assam' file, RMPA.
9.   Crozier, pp.147–8; 'Provost Service ALFSEA Short History to 1945', [hereafter ALFSEA] pp.16–17, 23, 31, 34–5, 67 in 'ALFSEA' file, RMPA.
10. 'XXXIII Corps Account of Operations . . . [1944]' p.144, RMSAL; '5 Indian Division . . .' pp.14, Conf 3674, SCL; Ganapathi pp.267–8, 283; WO 172/3695, WD, 61 Ind. L of C PU, 16, 21 Jan. 1943.
11. Ganapathi, p.271, 274, 301; 'XXXIII Corps Account of Operations . . . [1945]' RMASL.
12. 'IV Corps . . .' Part IX p.1–2, Conf. 3682, SCL; Slim, p.332; 'XXXIII Corps [1945] p.87; R Lewin, *Slim: The Standard Bearer* (Pan, 1978) p.221.
13. WO 172/6995, WD, 17th Ind. Div. PU, 4 Mar 1945, PRO.
14. WO 172/7006, WD, 19th Ind. Div. PU, Appx. A to Mar 1945, PRO.
15. 'IV Corps' Part IX p.2; 'XXXIII Corps Account of Operations . . . [1945] pp.87–8; WO 172/7006, 11–22 Mar 1945; Ganapathi, p.298.
16. 'IV Corps' Part IX pp.1–3; ALFSEA, p.43; WO 172/9203, WD, 95 Ind. BM PU 4–5 May 1945, PRO; WO 172/6995, 25 Apr. 1945; WO 172/7006, 3 May 1945; SW Kirby, *The War Against Japan* IV, (HMSO, 1965) p.387.
17. WO 172/7054, WD, 26th Ind. Div. PU, 6 May 1945, PRO; WO 172/9202, WD, 94 BM PU, 6, 13–15 May 1945, PRO.
18. WO 172/6995, 15 Feb 1945; ALFSEA p.43–4; 'IV Corps', Part IX p.3; Richards, 'Provost' p.8.

Chapter 19: The Home Front, 1939–45

Generally, see Crozier, pp.37–63, 172–75, 183–91.

1.   Captain LE Finch, 'History of the London District Provost Company RMP' nd, c. 1979, RMPA; AB McPherson, *The Second World War 1939–1945, Army: Discipline* (WO, 1950) p.90; FRS Higgins, personal account, 1988, in 'Home Service, 1939–45' file, RMPA.
2.   WO 305/454, memo. on history on SIB, 5 Apr. 1950; G. Ripley, personal account, 1989, in 'Home Service, 1939–45' file, RMPA.
3.   R Belben, personal account, 1989, in 'Home Service, 1939–45' file, RMPA.

Chapter 20: Normandy, 1944

1.   245 PC, ts history, RMPA.
2.   RMPJ 2/1951 pp.7–8.
3.   McPherson, p.95.
4.   WO 171/436, WD, 6th AB Div. PC, 5–6 Jun 1944, PRO.
5.   WO 171/423, WD, 3rd Div. PC, 6 Jun 1944, PRO; 3rd Div. PC ts history, RMPA.
6.   241, 242, 245 PCs, ts histories, RMPA; WO 171/3390, WD, 245 PC, 6 Jun 1944, PRO.

7. M Van Creveld, *Supplying War* (Cambridge, CUP, 1977) p.209.
8. RMPJ 3/1951 pp.59–61.
9. McPherson, p.103; RMPJ 1/1952 p.169, 171; 2/1952 p.5–6; 70 Sec. SIB, ts history, RMPA.
10. M Lindsay, *So Few Got Through* (Collins, 1946) p.36; RMPJ 2/1952 pp.8–9; 'Historical Monograph . . .', [hereafter ['21 AG'] p.1, in '21 Army Group' file, RMPA.
11. N Kirby, *1100 Miles with Monty* (Sutton, 1989) p.17; 'Provost Tactical Headquarters' [hereafter 'Tac HQ'], pp.1, 3, 21 Army Group File, RMPA.
12. 73 Coy CMP (TC), ys history, RMPA; D Hawkins (ed.) *War Report D-Day to VE Day* (BBC, 1985) p.133; 'Road Movement . . .', p.2, CAB 106/991, PRO.
13. RMPJ 1/1952 p.169–70; 2/1952 pp.5–7; 4/1952 p.118–121; *The Polar Bear News* 15 Feb 1946.
14. WO 171/423, 18 Jul 1944; LF Ellis, *Victory in the West* I, (HMSO, 1974) pp.340–43; C D'Este, *Decision in Normandy* (Pan, 1984 ed) pp.372, 376; A McKee, *Caen, Anvil of Victory* (Pan, 1972) pp.275–77.
15. *The Red Cap* May 1946, p.4, July 1946, p.4, Feb. 1947, p.8; WO 171/176, WD, PM 21 Army Group, Provost Instruction No.8; RMPJ 4/1952 pp.119, 121.

Chapter 21: The Battle for Germany, 1944–45

1. P Forbes, *6th Guards Tank Brigade* (Sampson, Low, Marston, nd) p.43.
2. WO 171/727, WD, Provost Branch, HQ L of C 21st AG, Appxs, Sept, Oct. 1944, PRO; WO 171/787, WD, Provost Branch, 12 L of C Sub Area, 10 Sept 1944, PRO; 'Functions of the CMP . . .' in '21 Army Group' file, RMPA.
3. Crozier, p.127; WO 171/3390, 3, 29 Sept, 3 Oct 1944.
4. WO 171/390, WD, Guards Armd. Div. PC, 4, 15 Sept. 1944, PRO; 3 Div. PC ts history, RMPA.
5. WO 171/407, WD. 1st AB Div. PC 17–26 Sept. 1944, PRO; RE Urquhart, *Arnhem* (Pan, 1972) pp.131–2; RMPJ 3/1967 pp.13–14; '1st Airborne Div. Pro Coy' file, RMPA.
6. WO 171/3378, WD, 113, PC, 18, 22, 28 Sept 1944; Ellis, *Victory* II, (HMSO, 1968) p.42; Crozier pp.127–9; WO 171/390, 20 Sept; 1944; '21 AG', p.4, RMPA.
7. *The Red Cap* II, No.2 (Feb. 1947) p.8.
8. '21 AG' pp.5–6, RMPA.
9. WO 171/4475, WD, Provost Branch HQ L of C, Appx. May 1945, PRO; WO 171/7796, WD, 73 Coy. CMP (TC) 17 Jan 1945, PRO; '21 AG' p.6, RMPA; 73 Coy CMP (TC), ts history, RMPA.
10. WO 171/787, 26 Dec. 1944; WO 171/3414, WD of 81 Sec. SIB, 25 Nov, 11 Dec 1944, PRO; WO 171/4545, WD, DAPM 16 L of C Sub Area, 18 Jan and 'handing over report', 1945, PRO; 120, ts history, RMPA.
11. 70 Section SIB, ts history, c. 1945, RMPA.
12. 'ATS Provost' in '21st Army Group' file, RMPA; ATS Provost, ts history, RMPA.
13. '21 AG' p.6, RMPA.
14. 'Report on Operation *Veritable*', p.18, 70, CAB 106/991, PRO; B Horrocks, *Corps Commander* (Sidgwick and Jackson, 1976) p.178, 187; 53rd Div. Op. Order 27 and Admin. Order 30, 4 Feb 1945, Conf. 4000, SCL; '21 AG' p.7–8, RMPA; Ellis, *Victory* II, pp.262–3.
15. 22, 101 Coy CMP (TC) and 15th Div. PC ts histories, RMPA.
16. Sgt H Mitchell, 'From the Beaches to the Baltic' RMPA.
17. WO 171/4192, WD, 11th Amd. Div. PC, 12 April 1945, PRO; 603 Coy. CMP (VP), ts history, nd, c. Aug 1945, RMPA.

18. WO 171/7840, WD, 601 Coy. CMP (VP), 4 May 1945, RMPA; Kirby, *1100 Miles*
     pp.130–2; 'Provost with Tactical HQ, 21st Army Group', ts history, in '21st Army
     Group' file, RMPA; WO 171/4475, Appx., June 1945.

Part Four: The Postwar Era – From 1945 to the Gulf War

Chapter 22: The RMP in Europe, 1945–91

Generally, see Lovell-Knight, *Story* pp.81–114, 309–32.

1. RMPJ 3/1965, pp.60–1.
2. WO 170/4403, 28–29 May 1945.
3. WO 263/96, PRO; Captain M Hawkins, *interview.*
4. M Cuthbert-Brown, 'A History of 247 (Berlin) Provost Company RMP' p.25,
    RMPA; RMPJ 3/1953 p.314.
5. RMPJ 2/1979 pp.10–12.
6. Brig LF Richards, ts account, 'BAOR' file, RMPA.
7. RMPJ 4/1989 p.29; RMPJ 2/1987 p.10.
8. H Stanhope, *The Soldiers* (Hamish Hamilton, 1979) p.233; R. Jones, ms account,
    'Malaya and Singapore 1945–75' file, RMPA.
9. MW Morris, ts account, 'BAOR' file, RMPA; FJB Smith, ts account, 'Middle East
    1945–1970' file, RMPA; T. Royle, *The Best Years of Their Lives* (Coronet, 1988)
    p.271.
10. RMPJ 2/1959 p.4.
11. WO 32/15069, PRO.
12. RMPJ 1/1990 pp.4–7.

Chapter 23: The Far East Since 1945

1. Doulton, pp.276, 289; Ganapathi, pp.345.
2. F Dean Ms p.2 (I am grateful to Mrs Dean for lending me this document); Richards,
    Provost pp.4–6.
3. RMPJ Spring 1950 pp.44–45.
4. AC Dart, ts account, p.1, 'Malaya and Singapore, 1945–75' file, RMPA.
5. RMPJ Spring 1950 pp.45–6; 3/1951 pp.92–3.
6. Capt RJR Whistler, RMPJ 2/1951 p.11–12.
7. Capt JA Fayter, RMPJ 2/1953 p.242.
8. Dart, p.3; RMPJ 3/1954 p.77–78; RMPJ 2/1954 p.31.
9. Capt AL Thompson, RMPJ 3/1965 pp.70–1.
10. Maj DW Eking, RMPJ 4/1970 pp.15–17.
11. RMPJ 1/1966 p.180.
12. Sgt R Hackett, RMPJ 2/1967 pp.11–12.

Chapter 24: Retreat from Empire: The Middle East, Cyprus and Kenya

Generally, see Lovell-Knight, *Story* pp.120–61, 287–90.

1. DA Ashley Hall papers, in 'Palestine 1945–8' file, RMPA.
2. Copy in Acc. 1760, RMPA.
3. D Dyson, unpublished ms, pp.46–7 (I am grateful to Mr Dyson for lending me a
    copy of this document); RMPJ 4/1963, p.126.

4. H Burden, 'With Provost in the Canal Zone, 1951–53', Burden Papers, RMPA; RMPJ 1/52 pp.171–5.
5. Quoted in Lovell-Knight, *Story* pp.135–7.
6. Brig LF Richards, RMPJ 1/1957 pp.132–5, 2/1957 pp.4–6, Communication to author.
7. RMPJ, 2/1955 p.28, 3/1955, p.66, 4/1955, pp.109–110.
8. Lt Col NE Huber, RMPJ 3/1956 pp.47–50; materials in 'Cyprus' file, RMPA: RMPJ 1/1957, p.132.
9. RMPJ 2/1952 p.34.
10. RMPJ 3/1954 p.74.
11. RMPJ 2/1954 p.34, 2/1953 p.270, 4/1955 p.106.
12. C Allen, *The Savage Wars of Peace* (Futura, 1991) p.134. See also A Clayton, *Counter-Insurgency in Kenya 1952–60* (Manhattan, KS, Sunflower University Press, 1984) pp.37–42.
13. RMPJ 2/1967 p.39–40, 4/67 p.156.
14. RMPJ 1/1968 p.180, 4/1967 p.156.

Chapter 25: The Korea War

NB: The main source for this chapter is the Corps War Diary. Only specific quotations from this source have been footnoted.

1. RMPJ 4/1951, p.139.
2. War Diary, Korea [WDK], account dated 31 Dec. 1951, RMPA; J Grey, *The Commonwealth Armies and the Korean War* (Manchester, MUP, 1988) p.75.
3. RMPJ W/1951 p.191.
4. Maj Gen BA Coad, 'The Land Campaign in Korea', *JRUSI*, XCVII, 585, (Feb. 1952) p.8; WDK, account dated 31 Dec 1951; Grey, p.76.
5. WDK, 2 Jan to 4 Jan 1951.
6. WDK, 249 GHQ Provost Company, 25 Apr 1951.
7. RMPJ 1/1954, pp.403–7; WDK 'Corps History – Commonwealth Provost Integration', notes dated 1 August 1952.
8. RMPJ 2/1953 p.243.
9. RMPJ 4/1951, p.146.
10. RMPJ 2/1953, p.247.

Chapter 26: Northern Ireland

Generally, see Lovell-Knight, *Story* pp.211–44.
1. Maj AH Le Tissier, RMPJ 1/1973 p.20.
2. Capt SG Edwards, account in 'Misc. Historical Narratives' file, RMPA. This account of the initial months of the 'Troubles' is largely drawn from this source, RMPJ 4/1969 p.2, and C Ryder, *The RUC – A Force Under Fire* (Methuen, 1989).
3. Cpl HR Sams, RMPJ 2/1970 pp.15–16.
4. M Dewar, *The British Army in Northern Ireland* (Arms and Armour, 1985) p.54.
5. RMPJ 4/1971 p.26, 1/1972 p.30.
6. D Barzilay, *The British Army in Ulster* [Vol. I] (Belfast, Century Services, 1973) p.34; RMPJ 2/1972 p.28.
7. RMPJ 4/1972 pp.28–32.
8. Brazilay, IV, pp.25–6, 34; Ryder p.124.
9. JD Turnbull, *The Ulster Watchdogs* (no publication details given) pp.28, 68, 76; RMPJ 1/84 p.26, 4/84 p.23.
10. RMPJ 3/1980 p.25, 3/1986 p.9.

11. M Arthur, *Northern Ireland Soldiers Talking* (Sidgwick and Jackson, 1987) p.121.
12. RMPJ 4/1989 pp.21–22.

Chapter 27: The Falklands War, 1982

1. Astiz File, RMPA.
2. Letter of 7 June 1982, in Falklands File, RMPA. In fact, on this date one Lear Jet was brought down by a Sea Dart fired by HMS *Exeter* (not *Ajax*); an interesting example of the 'Fog of War'.
3. RMPJ 2/1982, p.46.
4. Letter of 19 June 1982, in Falklands File, RMPA; RMPJ 2/1982, p.46.
5. RMPJ 4/1982, pp.21–23.
6. RMPJ 4/1982, p.9.

Chapter 28: The Gulf War

NB Background details have been drawn from J Pimlott and S Badsey (eds.) *The Gulf War Assessed* (Arms and Armour, 1992) and N. Pearce, *The Shield and the Sabre* (HMSO, 1992).

1. This and following paragraphs are largely based upon: unit notes in RMPJ 4/1990 p.29 and 1/1991 pp.19–22; Maj DJA Bergin's account in RMPJ, 4/1991 pp.7–12; Lt Col SC McLean's account in RMPJ 2/1991 pp.6–7. I am also indebted to Capt PC House for expanding upon his RMPJ unit notes.
2. P de la Billiere, *Storm Command* (HarperCollins, 1992) p.32.
3. J Witherow and A Sullivan, *War in the Gulf* (Sidgwick and Jackson, 1991) p.137; D Anderson, 'The Build-Up' in Pimlott and Badsey, p.102.
4. McLean, p.7.
5. RMPJ 2/1991 p.19.
6. Pearce, p.99.
7. RMPJ 2/1991 p.19.
8. RMPJ 2/1991 pp.18–19.
9. RMPJ 3/1991 p.5.

EPILOGUE: The Adjutant General's Corps

1. RMPJ, 3/1991 p.1.

Appendix 1

1. Turnbull, pp.48–53; T Geraghty, *The Bullet-Catchers* (London, Grafton, 1988) pp.209, 219.
2. Capt RJ Evans, 'Close Protection in the Royal Military Police', RMPJ 3/1982 p.6.
3. RMPJ 4/1984 p.6.
4. RMPJ 4/1987 p.7.
5. RMPJ 1/1989 p.6.
6. Geraghty, inside back cover.

Appendix 2

1. RMPJ 2/1980 pp.7–8 & 3/1980 pp.18–19.
2. RMPJ 3/1968 pp.70–1

Select Bibliography

Only books directly concerned with military discipline and justice, and some of the more useful general works, are listed here. The more specialised references that were consulted, including articles, biographies, memoirs and theses are cited in the footnotes.

All books are published in London unless otherwise stated.

C Allmand, *Society at War* (Oliver and Boyd, 1973)

MS Anderson, *War and Society in Europe of the Old Regime 1688–1789* (Fontana, 1988)

C Andrew, *Secret Service* (Guild edn., 1985)

C Barnett, *Britain and Her Army* (Harmondsworth, 1974)

R Boyes, *In Glass Houses* (Colchester, MPSC Association, 1988)

H Bullock, *A History of the Provost Marshal and the Provost Services* (Aberdeen, Milne and Hutchinson, 1929)

J Childs, *Armies and Warfare in Europe 1648–1789* (Manchester, MUP, 1982)

S Claver, *Under the Lash* (London, Torchstream, 1954)

P Contamine, *War in the Middle Ages* (Oxford, Blackwell, 1984)

A Corvisier, *Armies and Societies in Europe 1494–1789* (Bloomington, Indiana University Press, 1979)

SF Crozier, *The History of the Corps of Royal Military Police* (Aldershot, Gale and Polden, 1951)

H Essame, *The Battle for Germany* (Batsford, 1969)

J Fortescue, *A History of the British Army* (13 vols, Macmillan, 1879–1930)

R Ganapathi, *The White Belts* (New Delhi, Lancers Publishers, 1982)

D Graham and S Bidwell, *Tug of War* (Hodder and Stoughton, 1986)

JR Hale, *War and Society in Renaissance Europe, 1450–1620* (Fontana, 1985)

M Howard, *War in European History* (Oxford, OPUS, 1976)

J Keegan, *The Face of Battle* (Harmondsworth, 1978 edn)

AV Lovell-Knight, *The History of the Office of Provost Marshal and the Corps of Military Police* (Aldershot: Gale and Polden, 1945)

AV Lovell-Knight, *The Story of the Royal Military Police* (Leo Cooper, 1977)

AV Lovell-Knight, (ed) *The Corps of Royal Military Police* (Morecambe Bay Printers, Morecambe, 1953)

F McLynn, *Crime and Punishment in Eighteenth Century England* (Oxford, OUP, 1991)

AB McPherson, *The Second World War, 1939–1945, Army: Discipline* (War Office, 1950)

J Pimlott and S Badsey, (eds.) *The Gulf War Assessed* (Arms and Armour, 1992)

M Prestwich, *War, Politics and Finance under Edward I* (Faber, 1972)

JH Sparrow, *The Second World War, 1939–1945, Army: Morale* (War Office, 1949)

EM Spiers, *The Army and Society 1815–1914* (Longman, 1980)

H Stanhope, *The Soldiers* (Hamish Hamilton, 1980)

RAJ Tyler, *Bloody Provost* (Chichester, Phillimore, 1980)

C Walton, *History of the British Standing Army AD 1660 to 1700* (Harrison, 1894)

P Warwick, (ed.) *The South African War* (Longman, 1980)

List of Subscribers

The Corps of Royal Military Police is grateful to the following people who have subscribed to this history:

KWC Adams
NC Allen
EV Allen
JF Allen
SJ Ansell
RJ Archer
JR Archer-Burton
TJ Archer-Burton
KJ Askew
J Aspinall
JC Atkinson
JC Atkinson
PR Attridge
R Axup

JH Baber
SCB Bailey
SAK Bailey
P Ball
HQ BAOR (PRO)
WB Barlow
CB Barker
PE Barton
NMB Barnard
SA Barrett
KAS Barker
CNR Barker
D Bastow
CP Batey
JA Beard
K Beckley
CJ Beeforth
K Bennett
DP Bennett
DC Bentley
DJA Bergin
PF Berry
WG Best
AJ Betty

GB Bevis
JC Birch
Birmingham Branch
   RMPA
JR Blackford
W Blair
NM Blair
Blackpool RMPA
AR Bloom
JM Bolland
AA Bolland
JK Bonell
DK Bowden
RE Boyce
AD Bradshaw
KG Brazier
AC Bridges
C Brice
W Britton
JM Brooks
RW Browne
L Brooke
H Browning-Bayly
PR Buckle
JK Buchanan
JV Buckland
VW Buck
M Buckland
H Burden
RJ Bywaters

PJ Callinan
R Calder
I Cameron
J Campbell
A Candler
MJ Carr
I Carpenter
ML Carroll

GH Cartwright
MC Caseman
PIA Charvat
FW Chipperfield
AG Clark
AJ Cleaveley
JJ Cleary
DJ Clinton
JVG Colburn
AE Collins
KE Collins
SD Coles
GM Cook
JG Cooke
DM Cope
DS Corbishley
KWJ Corrigan
BJ Cox RACMP
G Crosthwaite
FB Crownshaw
DR Cross
M Cuthbert-Brown

DJM Dain
N Dangerfield
AC Dart
ET Dartnell
AH Davies
RJ Davie
DG Deacon
CJE Derrick
MR Dillon
RG Ding
C Dixon
MJ Dixon
S Dorset
MR Downie
GA Duncan
AB Durrand

DW Dyson

PW Edmunds
SG Edwards
GR Edwards
SD Elliott
DL Ellis
JD Emsley
WR Epps
SG Evans
R Evans
RJ Evans
KJ Ewens

PR Fahrenholz
RJ Fairman
GT Farr
A Faulkner
RA Field
MJ Field
SM Fielder
AJ Figg
MA Finister
GW Flint
RH Flitton
AR Forbes
EO Forster-Knight
FH Foster
FJ Fox
IW Fulton

JK Gable
RT Gant
EJ Geary
GJF Gibbons
AP Gifford
DCN Giles
Gloucestershire Branch
   RMPA
RW Godwin
ID Goldie
JF Goodchild
CA Goodall
LB Gooding
M Gowers
M Gowen
AR Gratton
A Graves
GW Grant
RJ Gratton
JT Green
BT Griffiths

DP Griffin
I Grieveson
AP Guilfoyle
L Gwilym

CRF Hackett
JA Hadfield
DA Ashley Hall
RM&E Hallett
G Hallett
DM Hall
DE Hammond
AJ Handyside
BJ Harries
WD Hare
D Harmon
RE Harrison
RJ Hardiman
DA Harris
SM Haskins
D Hatchard
P Hawkings
G Haywood
C Van Heerden
U Hellmuth
PGW Hemsley
IL Hensman
MH Hennessey
EP Hennessey
PB Hewlett-Smith
MJ Hewitt
EJ Hide
IJ Higgins
S Higgs
HJS Hillyard
SH Hill
JW Hill
CAS Hinks
GB Hodgins
JA Hodges
RGB Holroyd
TF Holmes
Home Counties (N)
   Branch RMPA
PG Honour
CD Hopewell
GL Hopwood
RG Hopkins
PC House
RM House
J Howarth
PC Hughes

AF Humphries
BA Humphries
GS Hunter
A Huson
R Hutson

MRI Inglis

EA Jackson
PM Jackson
DG James
NL Job
GAK John
JW Johnston
FR Jones
J Jones
AG Jones
WF Jones
CFA Judge
NJ Justice

A Kay
GR Keighley
R Kemp
JF Kempton
RG Kensett
FW Kerridge
DAJ Kidman
S Kidd
SA Kilbride
SJ Kimm
SF King
DAH King
TH Knight

RJ Lambert
GF Lambert
JW Lanham
DB Larnach
JL Lawson
DAL Lawson
KC Lax
Officers Mess LDPC
SA Leach
AL Lee
DM Leigh
RC Leigh
JM Lightowler
ID St G Lindsay
A Liver
JW Lloyd
BJ Lockett

PJG Long
JES London
RE Lovell-Knight
A Lukas
WGH Lurcock
JR Lynes

HA Maitland
SD Major
K Malin
RA Manderson
AC Maple
KC Marum
CCH Martin
M Matthews
AD Mawer
GN Maye
RA McBride
JP McCarthy
ET McCarthy
AJ McGowan
CR McGregor
KP McHugh
AC McIntosh
J McIntosh
JH McIntosh
GD McKie
DG McKenzie-Brown
S McLeod
SC McLean
BM McMahon
MK McNally
JA McVey
CGD Mead
PD Mendel
DP Mepham
M Metcalf
RR Millar
WBP Millard
JA Mills
K Miller
GM Millan
AWH Miller
RM Moore
HF Morris-Metcalf
AK Mudd
JC Mullinder
GJ Mullan
DM Murphy
L Murray
R Musgrave

PN Nalden
SG Nelson
JAJ Nelson
JP Newell
A Newman
PJ Nicholls
TE Nicholls
VRK Nicholls
JL Nolan
KE Norris
Northumbria Army
  Cadet Force
M Nugent

T O'Brien
SD O'Brien
J O'Connor
JP O'Driscoll
SM O'Hare
JH Oliver
SF O'Rourke
PR Overington CT Bank
Oxford & District Branch
  RMPA

DE Page
SD Pake
WW Palmer
JN Palmer
VL Parker
RK Pashley
C Patterson
JS Patterson
RK Patten
NW Payne
DR Paynter
JS Pearson
RA Pearson
T Pemberton
MT Penman
DJW Perkins
M Perkins
M Pierce-Jones
M Pitman
J Pitt
GL Powell
P Powell
DGF Pringuer
T Priest
JW Pritchard
MD Price

SD Pryor
AI Purton

RP Ratcliff
BA Rawlings
Reading Branch RMPA
AL Redmon
DB Rendell
NG Rhys-Brown
CR Richards
LF Richards
RR Richards
D Ridsdale
NJ Ridout
S Robbins
E Roberts
HA Roberts
R Roberts
G Ross
PN Ross
D Rowe
R Rowe

PD Saunders
K Sayle
K Scanlon
GCD Scott-Lowe
GF Scott
RP Scott
S Scott
TG Scriven
GW Seatter
AI Seal
M Shanks
BA Shaw
F Shaw
W Shaw
AP Shewring
RJ Sherville
TR Smith
JA Shea
S Shea
WS Sheridan
M Shepherd
T Shepherd
S Shore
GS Shone
MS Siddiq
D Sim
PJ Simpson
FWA Slater
T Slinger

JA Smith
FJB Smith
JW Smith
JEG Spencer
RA Spence
PHM Squier
RG Stallwood
JR Standring
FW Stanton
DD Steele
PJ Steele
JM Stenton
LAB Stephens
M Stevens
R Stevens
RIM Stevenson
S Stewart
BEW Stone
PJ Stubbs
DJ Sturgeon
DM Swaby
HG Swift

R Tallis
JD Tasker
R Taylor
GA Taylor
G Taylor
AR Taylor
B Thomas
GP Thomas
JF Thomas

LM Thomas
GAC Thompson
P Thompson
GW Thomson
J Thorburn
RJ Tilston
AH Le Tissier
FEJ Toomey
A Townley
PE Townsend
A Townley
AE Trumper
RAJ Tyler

CM Ullmann-Jones

JR Van Dyke
DJ Venn

D Wade
R Wall
FB Walters
SJ Walker
RG Ware
HAG Ward
W Wastell
R Watson
TP Watton
TE Watson
I Waters
CJ Waters
JB Watkins

WE Watkins
SS Watson
MP Waters
JW Watson
DA Waygood
A Wells
JD Westwood
RCA West
GN Wheeler
J Whitfield
DA Whitby
R Wilkins
S Wilson
S Wilson
JM Wilson
CJ Williams
AD Williams
D Wingate
DW Wonson
GA Woodall
W Wood
G Woodcock
WGD Woodiwiss
SM Wood
EJ Wooldridge
AH Wright
KD Wright
RJ Wyatt

MGA Young
TJ Young

Index